Theatre in Madrid and Barcelona, 1892–1936

RIVALS OR COLLABORATORS?

DAVID GEORGE

UNIVERSITY OF WALES PRESS
CARDIFF
2002

British Library Cataloguing-in-Publication Data.
A catalogue record for this book is available from the British Library.

ISBN 0–7083–1737–5

The right of David George to be identified as author of this work has been
asserted by him in accordance with the Copyright, Designs and Patents Act
1988.

Typeset at University of Wales Press
Printed in Great Britain by Dinefwr Press, Llandybïe

To María Antònia, Elisenda, Carys and Mair

Contents

List of Illustrations

Foreword

Both Barcelona and Madrid are increasingly popular international tourist destinations. Barcelona, in particular, has become fashionable following its hosting of the highly successful 1992 Olympic Games. It is doubtful, however, whether most tourists will look much beyond its striking buildings and elegant streets to discover what makes this city distinctive, and quite different from its deadly rival, Madrid, the capital of the Spanish state. How many people are aware, for instance, that Barcelona is the seat of the Catalan Parliament in what is arguably the most decentralized political system in Europe? As they admire the Gaudí buildings, how much do they know about the often explosive socio-cultural cocktail which was the background to their construction? How many people know that Barcelona is a bilingual city? It is the centre of the so-called 'Catalan Lands', and Catalan is a language spoken by more than six million people. On the other hand, more books in Spanish are published in Barcelona than in Madrid.

How do the Barcelona-Madrid rivalries fit into the picture? Probably for most people this does not extend beyond the level of the football derby. At the cultural level, perhaps the sort of competitiveness which exists between London and Manchester would come to mind. To an extent such a comparison would be helpful, but the combination of political history and language sets the Madrid-Barcelona rivalry on a different plane.[i] By the early twentieth century, the reassertion of historical languages, cultures and identities in the Iberian Peninsula was really gathering pace. In this context, Barcelona had something of a schizophrenic identity. It was Spain's second city, the capital of a resurgent Catalonia, and a city with international pretensions. It was frustrated with what it saw as its subservient role to Madrid within the Spanish state, and longed to break free from the restraint. On the other hand, Madrid saw itself as the centre of Spanish life, and often looked on its rival as something of an upstart which needed to be controlled.

In some ways, theatrical life in the two cities mirrored the general atmosphere of mutual suspicion. But art often crosses boundaries of all sorts, and so it was with theatre. Rivalries and suspicions existed, but all sorts of collaborative projects abounded. What is sadly the case is that for scholars and students based outside Spain, and to a lesser extent for those inside the country, the theatre has usually meant what is happening in Madrid, and the important role of Barcelona in particular and Catalonia in general has been largely ignored. This study aims to redress the balance, and to attempt to answer the question of whether, at least as the theatre is concerned, Madrid and Barcelona could be more accurately described as rivals or collaborators.

Acknowledgements

I have accumulated many debts of gratitude during the preparation of this book. My Arts and Humanities Research Board award under the Research Leave Scheme was crucial in enabling me to complete the project. The Beca de Investigación en España para Hispanistas Extranjeros, awarded by the Spanish Foreign Ministry allowed me to pursue research in Madrid and Zaragoza in February 2000. The award of a Comunidad de Madrid grant jointly to Pilar Nieva de la Paz of the Consejo Superior de Investigaciones Científicas and myself allowed me to complete work in Madrid on Margarita Xirgu. The Modern Humanities Research Association awarded me a grant to cover the cost of the illustrations included in the book.

Andrew Anderson, David Basker, Angela Cutler, Maria Delgado, Dru Dougherty, Derek Gagen, Enric Gallén, Paul Garner, David Gies, María Àngels Heras, Henry Little, John London, Jim McCarthy, Roger Maidment, Pilar Nieva, Jesús Rubio, Serge Salaün, Anna Vàzquez, María Francisca Vilches de Frutos, Fernando Villar and Rhys Williams have all contributed to the writing of this book. To them, and anyone else I have inadvertently omitted, my grateful thanks.

Finally, it should be noted that all translations of quotations are my own.

Setting the Scene

'In the twentieth century, drama is unquestionably the branch of the arts in which Spain has the least to offer to the common store of European culture.'[1] Not only does such a view seem to belittle the major contributions of Valle-Inclán and García Lorca, but it also typified the limitations of much of what was written on the theatre of early twentieth-century Spain until fairly recently, particularly by British and North American Hispanists. As Jesús Rubio puts it, 'El teatro ha ocupado durante mucho tiempo un lugar secundario en el estudio de la cultura del cambio de siglo'[2] (For a long time, the theatre has occupied a secondary place in the study of *fin-de-siècle* culture). Spanish critics were not immune from sweeping, limited generalizations about the subject. Even a highly respected critic like José-Carlos Mainer, for instance, who, when comparing Spain unfavourably to other European countries, refers to 'una riqueza escenográfica que en España tenía como *único* representante a Martínez Sierra'[3] (a scenographic richness whose *only* Spanish representative was Martínez Sierra; my italics).

Such statements were due, in part, to a lack of detailed knowledge about the subject. Mainer was writing in 1983, but it is true to say that even now we may in some respects know more about the Spanish theatre of the sixteenth and seventeenth centuries than we do about that of the early twentieth. Another cause of incorrect or over-generalized comments is the tendency to equate dramatic literature with theatre, and the resultant failure to take account of directors, actors and actresses, stage designers and technicians, and theatre critics. Yet another reason was a lack of knowledge about what was going on in turn-of-the-century Barcelona, where Adrià Gual's innovative Teatre Íntim matched other European ventures like Lugné-Poë's Théâtre de l'Œuvre or Stanislavski's Moscow Art Theatre and where stage design was thriving in a creatively dynamic artistic scene. Far too often,

Spanish theatre has been equated by commentators with Madrid, while, at the same time, studies on Catalan theatre have tended to consider it separately from what was happening in the rest of Spain.

Thankfully, at least within Spain, significant advances have been made in theatre criticism, and a number of areas which had previously been ignored have recently received detailed critical attention. First, much more is now known about exactly which plays were performed, especially in Madrid and to a lesser extent in the provinces, during the first thirty years of the twentieth century.[4] Second, critics have demonstrated that, although Spain may have lagged behind in terms of the condition of its theatres, there was no lack of knowledge about new trends outside Spain.[5] Third, a number of Spanish publications have been dedicated to the consideration of issues beyond the dramatic text, including acting, directing and stage design.[6] Fourth, the contribution of Catalan theatre practitioners has begun to be recognized within Spain.[7]

However, as far as the English-speaking world is concerned, the picture is much more patchy. Criticism still tends to be limited to texts, often to the work of individual authors. There are some studies of wider issues, such as performance and reception,[8] but the importance of Catalonia in general and of Barcelona in particular in the development of the theatre in Spain has been largely ignored.[9] Madrid-based theatre practitioners of the period were strongly aware of what was going on in Barcelona and, at certain periods, Barcelona was an important reference point for them. There is clear evidence of close links between the two cities, involving playwrights, directors and designers.

One of the two principal aims of this book is to examine these links and to question to what extent there was mutual respect between the two cities and how far they were rivals. Is political tension mirrored in the theatre, or do collaborative artistic instincts run counter to political trends? Running through the study will be evidence of tensions and contradictions which surround the sometimes problematic but often dynamic and fruitful interaction between theatre practitioners in the two cities and their place within the wider panorama of Madrid–Catalan relations in the period under discussion.

The book's other main purpose is to consider the theatre in a wider context than texts alone. In the prologue to the first edition of his ground-breaking history of twentieth-century Spanish theatre, Ruiz Ramón writes:

> es un libro incompleto, pues sólo nos hemos ocupado de los autores y sus obras, dejando afuera de él o en sombras otros aspectos o elementos teatrales de capital importancia, como son los relativos al público, las compañías teatrales, el montaje y la representación, o la dirección escénica.[10]

> (this is an incomplete book, in that we have been concerned only with authors and their works, leaving aside other aspects or elements of the theatre which are vitally important, including those to do with audiences, theatre companies, staging and performance, and directing.)

This is another area in which this study will differ from others. The text will be viewed as one element of the theatrical whole, which will allow us to undertake a more complete analysis of theatre. Playwrights were not writing in a void, but were working with directors, stage designers and others. This approach will permit us better to explore the real contacts between Madrid and Barcelona and to provide more valid answers to the question: were they rivals or collaborators? The study of the reception of their own, each other's and foreign plays will also aid an understanding of artistic tastes and awareness of theatre in the two cities, and the extent to which these were allied to political questions.

The starting date of 1892 has been chosen because in that year various events occurred which changed the course of theatre development in Spain and of Madrid's relationship with Catalan theatre. The year 1892 marks the beginning of the relationship between the leading Catalan playwright of the period, Àngel Guimerà, and three key figures in the evolution of the Spanish stage: the actress María Guerrero, her husband the actor Fernando Díaz de Mendoza, and José Echegaray, a prolific and popular playwright and winner of the Nobel Prize for Literature in 1904, who specialized in Romantic melodrama and who translated a number of Guimerà's plays into Spanish (see Chapters 2 and 5). The year 1892 also saw the beginning of the relationship between Guerrero and Benito Pérez Galdós, while the latter's *Realidad* (Reality),[11] which marked the commencement of an albeit tentative move in the direction of naturalism in the Spanish theatre, was premiered in that year.[12]

The same year also saw two events which were important in the development of symbolist theatre in Spain, a significant strand of the theatre in nineteenth-century Europe: the publication of Jacinto Benavente's *Teatro fantástico* (Fantastic Theatre) and, more significantly, the production of Maeterlinck's *L'Intruse* (*The Intruder*) at Santiago Rusiñol's *Festes Modernistes* in Sitges. This event is usually perceived as marking the penetration of symbolism not only into Catalan but more generally into Spanish theatre. The end date for the period covered by the present study is obvious. Normal theatrical activity in the two cities was interrupted at the end of the Spanish Civil War and with the subsequent advent of the Franco regime, during the early years of which productions in the Catalan language were banned.

The Economic and Political Background of the Two Cities

Before beginning our detailed analysis of the topic, we need to set theatre activity in a wider socio-political and economic framework and consider how theatre development interacts with this.[13] Tension between the centre and the periphery has been a constant feature of modern Spanish history, between the centralizing forces concentrated in Castile and the outlying regions or national entities. During the last 150 years, this conflict has centred on the Basque Country and Catalonia, and, in the case of the latter, has manifested itself in the rivalry between the two largest cities in the Spanish state, Madrid, its capital, and Barcelona, the capital of Catalonia. The emergence of Barcelona in the last decade of the twentieth century as a major European city came after the long period of the Franco dictatorship, when economic and, more specifically, political power was concentrated in Madrid and when manifestations of Catalan identity were repressed. Since the death of Franco, Catalonia has recovered and developed her political, linguistic and cultural institutions, re-establishing herself as the most important economic area of Spain.

Less than a century earlier, the culture, language and economy of Catalonia in general and Barcelona in particular had flourished in similar fashion. Following a long decline of Catalan power and culture since the 'unification' of Spain in 1492, and more particularly after the early eighteenth century, the long road to recovery began in the mid-nineteenth century. During this cultural renaissance, known as the *Renaixença*, Catalan re-emerged as a literary language after three centuries of confinement to virtual patois status. Writers of the *Renaixença* tended to look back nostalgically to an idealized Middle Ages (the period when Catalonia was a major European power), and their work is often characterized by an emphasis on localism and picturesque rural environments. Cultural competitions, known as Jocs Florals, were another localist characteristic of the movement. Nevertheless, the part it played in recreating a sense of Catalan nationhood was highly significant and, as in other European countries, this was bound up with the development of Romanticism.

By the late nineteenth century the values of the *Renaixença* seemed outdated as Catalan society – or at least the society of Greater Barcelona – had been transformed by industrial development. Textile manufacturing was the dominant industry, and Barcelona became known as the Manchester of the Mediterranean. A dynamic entrepreneurial spirit characterized Catalan economic life, and Catalan industrialists saw themselves as the economic powerhouse of Spain. This was accompanied by a growing frustration with the central Spanish state, which the Catalans felt was hampering rather than aiding the new capitalism. There was certainly a mutual suspicion and, on occasions, hatred between the two cities, as Barcelona's resentment at what was perceived as Madrid's hindrance of its development was mirrored by Madrid's view of Barcelona as self-interested and separatist.

The crisis caused by Spain's disastrous military defeat at the hands of the USA in 1898 and the corresponding loss of Cuba, Puerto Rico and the Philippines, her last major overseas colonies, served to enhance the frustration felt by the Catalans, for whom Cuba had been a major source of income and, above all, a protected market. Frustration with the Spanish political process, combined with a growing sense of self-confidence in their business ability and Catalan-language-based cultural life, led to the development of autonomy movements in Catalonia in the late nineteenth and early twentieth centuries. The most important of these was the Lliga Regionalista, a grouping of conservative Catalan business and other leaders who desired a political system more suited to the development of free-market economics.

Conservative Catalanism had its biggest success with the establishment in 1913 of a limited form of self-government in the form of the Mancomunitat, or 'commonwealth' of the four Catalan provinces. The first leader of the Mancomunitat was Enric Prat de la Riba, and, under him, it 'devoted much of its energy to "modernizing" Catalonia by technical education and an ambitious road and telephone system'.[14] Unlike other large centres of minority cultures in Spain, such as Bilbao or Valencia, where the economic elite have traditionally spoken Spanish, the mother tongue of many members of the Catalan bourgeoisie was Catalan.[15] However, although there is a divergence of critical opinion on whether it was essentially a bourgeois or a working-class phenomenon, Catalan nationalism was complex and constantly shifting, and crossed the social divide.[16]

The opportunistic nature of Catalan business was strongly in evidence as they took advantage of Spain's neutrality during the First World War to increase their trade. As their business activity grew, so did their feeling that what Spain needed was a 'fully fledged capitalist system. However, as their advice went unheeded and opportunities for consolidating upon the wartime situation slipped past, a rift opened up between the business community and the land-based political oligarchy in Madrid.'[17] The frustration with Madrid had the effect of pushing industrialists closer towards Catalan nationalism, although the result of serious social disturbance (as in the Tragic Week of 1909 or the wave of political killings between 1919 and 1923) was to drive them back to the law-and-order safety of the Spanish state, which accounts for their broad support of the Primo de Rivera dictatorship (1923–30).

A result of the unfettered growth of capitalism in Barcelona was exploitation of workers and low wages.[18] This was probably more marked in Barcelona than anywhere, and resulted in a corresponding increase in working-class militancy. Barcelona, like Madrid, suffered a rapid growth in population, as people flocked to the cities from the countryside in search of work. Migration from the countryside of the centre and the south of Spain was by far the largest source of the population growth.

Barcelona was more radical than Madrid as far as left-wing politics is concerned. It was possibly the principal European centre of Anarchism, and there were regular episodes of Anarchist direct action from the late 1880s onwards, accompanied by the corresponding police repression. Some of the violent actions were committed against theatres, including the bombing in 1893 of the Liceu, Europe's first privately built opera house, and a symbol for the Anarchists of the Barcelona bourgeoisie. The Anarchist trade union, the CNT, was founded in 1910. It was the more radical of the two main trade union groupings, the other being the UGT (also founded in Barcelona, in 1888), which was aligned with the Socialist Party. From 1919 to 1923, apart from numerous strikes, Barcelona was a city at war between Anarchist gunmen and the hired assassins of the so-called 'free trade unions' paid by the employers. The victims included the respected CNT leader, Salvador Seguí, assassinated in March 1923. The strikes and the murders were brought to a temporary end by the dictatorship of Primo de Rivera in the 1920s, supported by conservative Catalan businessmen who had earlier flirted with Catalan nationalism, but social conflict reached its apogee during the Second Republic (1931–6).[19]

It was also during the Second Republic that Catalonia acquired more autonomy than it had had for centuries. It obtained its statute of self-government in 1932 under the leadership of Francesc Macià.[20] The left was the main political force in Catalonia during the early 1930s and, although the Lliga made something of a comeback in 1933, the Catalan Republican Left, or Esquerra Republicana Catalana (ERC), remained in the ascendancy until the advent of the Civil War.[21] According to Salaün, it was the Barcelona lower middle class (represented by the Esquerra) rather than the upper bourgeosie or working class which was the driving force behind the social and cultural changes.[22]

Madrid, unlike Barcelona, did not become a genuinely industrial city until the twentieth century. In other ways, however, Madrid shared many of the qualities and problems of an urban centre with Barcelona. Ugarte sums up its particular characteristics:

With the rise in population, a little more than half a million by the end of the century (small in comparison to London and Paris yet sizeable for the Iberian Peninsula), the capital city acquired that air of sordid sophistication and differentiation from country life that large cities are known for. [. . .] Madrid was the center of the bureaucratic monster; as such it had to cater to visitors even though it was not particularly successful at doing so. Small industries arose – cabinetmaking, silversmith [*sic*] and print shops – and these industries grew as the twentieth century approached. But the most accurate indicator of Madrid's economic history is its role as capital: the presence of civil servants, parliamentarians, people associated with the court, sellers of services (such as rentals), theatrical companies with all the economic apparatus that goes with them, and commercial enterprises known for luxury and status. For these reasons there has always been something of an artificial flavor associated with Madrid, a city of outsiders whose children are as much natives of the neighborhood as of the city. Moreover, at the level of politics, Madrid was (and still is) the center for the parliamentary debate, the demonstration, the place where polemical opinions are published and controversial positions promulgated; one might say that politics itself has been Madrid's most pervasive commodity.[23]

Indeed, it should not be thought that Madrid was a peaceful backwater compared with Barcelona's turbulent dynamism. As a long-established centre of country and empire since 1561, Madrid was a political axis in a way Barcelona could not be. It was the capital of a nation in seemingly endless political and social turmoil, and as such was the hub of intrigue and turbulence. As the revolution which overthrew Queen Isabel II was succeeded by the often corrupt political system of the Restoration, Madrid was the centre of an unstable country. As mentioned earlier, Madrid was as much a destination for mass immigration from rural areas as Barcelona. The social conditions in which the booming population of the early twentieth century lived were often deplorable: 'In the outer suburbs, the post-war building boom left a population of a hundred thousand without sewers and as a consequence the "African death rate" of Madrid was twice that of London.'[24] Although Madrid lacked the extreme Anarchist radicalism of Barcelona, it did become the focal point of the socialist movement, and the headquarters of the UGT were transferred from Barcelona to Madrid in 1899.

Urban and Cultural Development in Madrid and Barcelona

The difference between Barcelona as the focal point of an important industrial area and Madrid as the bureaucratic and political centre of a major nation state is stark, and yet the urban and cultural development of the two cities in the late nineteenth and early twentieth centuries is not dissimilar. Raymond Carr sees the 1890s as the decade when both Barcelona and Madrid took on the appearance of modern cities.[25] They were also focal points for writers and artists. The likes of Pérez Galdós, Baroja and Valle-Inclán were at the heart of Madrid intellectual life, which often centred on the literary *tertulias*.

Although some of the stimuli for debate and thought – decline of Spain and loss of empire – were the same, the atmosphere of the two cities was quite different. The reaction to defeat and loss in Spanish intellectual circles was encapsulated in the Generation of 1898 group, who saw them as the culmination of centuries of decline. The regeneration had, they believed, to come from Castile, the heart of the country. They were generally highly critical of the modern city in general and of Madrid in particular:

> En las obras de los escritores españoles de la generación del 98 hay una preocupación general y un rechazo de la ciudad moderna. [. . .] Económicamente se veía como un monstruo, une *ville tentaculaire* que chupaba los recursos humanos del campo creando el proletariado de las chabolas. Culturalmente, la ciudad moderna, y especialmente Madrid, era considerada como algo deforme, sin lazos con el pasado y la tradición, algo construido de prisa y sin consideraciones estéticas de ninguna especie.[26]

> (In the works of the writers of the 1898 Generation, there is a general concern about and a rejection of the modern city. [. . .] In economic terms, it was seen as a monster, a *ville tentaculaire* which sucked human resources from the countryside, creating the slum proletariat. In cultural terms, the modern city, particularly Madrid, was considered to be a deformed creature, unconnected to the past and to tradition, constructed in haste and with no thought whatsoever for aesthetic considerations.)

However, they were also conscious of the need to 'Europeanize' Spain, and, likewise, Catalan writers and artists rejected the nostalgic ruralism of their predecessors, looking outwards towards the cultures of northern Europe rather than inwards at Spain. They found their inspiration not in medieval Catalan history but in the bohemian world of contemporary Paris or in

Wagnerian total theatre. According to one critic, this interest in European culture had political roots:

> El desastre de esta contienda dio lugar a que el incipiente catalanismo, que hasta aquellas fechas carecía de importancia política, se trocara en un movimiento de europeización de Cataluña, paralelo al que en el mismo sentido se produjo en el ámbito general de la nación.
>
> Por lo tanto, se aspiró desde este momento a la formación de una cultura catalana propia a base de las corrientes dominantes en los países más adelantados de Europa.[27]
>
> (The result of this disastrous conflict [i.e. the 1898 colonial wars] was that incipient Catalanism, which had hitherto lacked political importance, was converted into a movement intent on Europeanizing Catalonia, in parallel with what was happening within Spain as a whole.
>
> Therefore, the aspiration of this movement was the creation of a specifically Catalan culture based on the prevailing currents in the most advanced European countries.)

The new energy was encapsulated in Catalonia's particular version of art nouveau, known as *modernisme*.[28] This was the period when the exciting architecture which attracts today's tourists to Barcelona was created, and it was the money made from the new industries which financed the ambitious projects of the likes of Antoni Gaudí. *Modernisme* was essentially a middle-class movement, although, naturally enough, many of these products of economic stability – although not the conservative Catholic Gaudí – rejected commercialism and embraced bohemianism. The period saw the construction of some of Barcelona's great buildings, including Gaudí's La Pedrera and Sagrada Família Cathedral, as a combination of economic prosperity and artistic creativity transformed and beautified the city.

As respectable Catalanism and with it a civic pride developed in the 1910s, *modernisme* was replaced by *noucentisme*, which rejected northern European decadentism and favoured instead Mediterranean classicism. The nationalist agenda became more organized and the 1910s were the decade of the development of specifically Catalan political and cultural institutions, including the Mancomunitat, public libraries and the Institute of Catalan Studies. A civic pride characterizes this period, although, in general, the *noucentistes* were not sympathetic to theatre, seeing prose and poetry as superior genres.[29]

As well as *modernisme* and *noucentisme*, of course, Barcelona in the period after the First World War was a major centre for the avant-garde, particularly in painting. Picasso had lived in the city at the turn of the century, and the first exhibition of Cubist art outside Paris was held at the Gallery of Josep Dalmau in 1912, while Salvador Dalí held his first one-man show there in 1926. Both Dalí and Joan Miró were Catalans with strong roots in Barcelona, although, as Fanés puts it:

> Cultural life in Barcelona had been able to admit Cubism [. . .] since *Noucentisme*, with its classical direction, had accepted anything that could be seen as an extension of the pictorial world opened up by Cézanne. But there was no way that Surrealism, which implied disorder and a free rein given to instinct and offered a radical critique of artistic and social values, could be accepted by this world.[30]

Late nineteenth- and early twentieth-century Barcelona was, indeed, a series of sometimes violently incompatible worlds: bourgeoisie and proletariat, right and left, neo-classicism and the avant-garde. New theatres were built and old ones transformed, especially in the Eixample, the area of grid-patterned streets designed by Ildefons Cerdà, which was home to the growing middle classes. The Jardins del Tívoli were transformed into a covered theatre in 1875, and the Teatre Espanyol was built in the fashionable Passeig de Gràcia in 1870.[31] Catalonia had no equivalent to the Spanish Golden Age in drama, and, as in politics, the period from the mid-nineteenth to the early twentieth century was one of creating new structures, both metaphorically and literally.

Likewise, a number of Madrid's most famous theatre buildings date from the late nineteenth century, including the Fontalba (1871), Comedia (1875), the Español (1885), the Lara (early 1880s) and the Princesa (later the María Guerrero) (1895). In Madrid there was a longer theatrical tradition than in Barcelona. The Español was built on the site of the old Corral del Príncipe, the performance site of plays in the sixteenth and seventeenth centuries. Many of these theatres – in Madrid and Barcelona – were designed as comfortable entertainment palaces for the burgeoning middle classes. The following extract from a contemporary press account of the opening of the refurbished

Princesa Theatre in Madrid in 1909 captures perfectly the sense of luxury, elegance and comfort demanded by middle-class audiences:

> Al dar vista al teatro sorprende la intensa nota blanca que da su fachada, espléndidamente alumbrada.
>
> Para el coche debajo de una marquesina de cristales, y al ingresar en el transformado edificio, su antiguo porche, convertido hoy en un elegante vestíbulo cubierto de recia alfombra de coco y calentado por dos grandes irradiadores, nos da la sensación de un gran *confort* y de una deliciosa temperatura.
>
> [. . .] Las butacas y sillas de todos los palcos son de madera color blanco marfil, forradas de terciopelo rojo.
>
> [. . .] El color rojo obscuro del terciopelo de las cortinas, antepechos, butacas y la alfombra del patio corta y combina de manera tal con el blanco marfil de las paredes, columnas [. . .] que da al total de la sala una placidez de tonalidad exquisita y una distinción soberana.
>
> La base del proscenio la cierra una gran celosía de terciopelo rojo, detrás de la cual está el sitio destinado para la orquesta.
>
> [. . .] La instalación de la luz, tanto por la parte importantísima que toma este elemento en los espectáculos modernos cuanto por la trascendencia que tiene este servicio en los lugares destinados a espectáculos públicos es acreedora a mención especial.[32]

(One is surprised by the intense whiteness of the splendidly lit facade of the theatre.

The carriage stops beneath a glass canopy. When we enter the transformed building, its former porch, which has now been converted into an elegant hall covered with a sturdy coconut carpet and heated by two large radiators, gives us the feeling of great comfort and a delicious temperature.

[. . .] The seats and chairs in all the boxes are made of white ivory wood, lined with red velvet.

[. . .] The dark red of the velvet of the curtains, parapets, seats and the carpet in the stalls breaks up and blends so well with the white ivory of the walls, columns [. . .] that it lends an exquisitely toned tranquillity and supreme distinction to the theatre as a whole.

The proscenium base is closed off by a huge latticework in red velvet, behind which is the orchestra space.

[. . .] The lighting system is worthy of special mention, as much for the very important part it plays in modern spectacles as for the significance this service has in places where public spectacles are held.)

The article then describes a special two-storey building adjoining the theatre which offers residential facilities for the famous husband-and-wife acting team, María Guerrero and Fernando Díaz de Mendoza (the Princesa changed its name to Teatro María Guerrero in 1928). The first storey contains an English-style living room and a ladies' drawing room decorated in the style of Louis XIV, while on the second storey was a dining room, bathroom and two bedrooms for the couple. The article highlights the almost god-like status of the leading actor and actress in Spain and clearly no expense had been spared in this restoration project, whose size and splendour show just how important theatre-going had become in Madrid as a social as well as an artistic event.

Commercialism was also a major factor in theatre construction in Barcelona. However, like so many other aspects of civic and cultural life, it was linked to the attempt to develop a distinctive Catalan, as opposed to Spanish, culture. Writing in 1917, the theatre critic Francesc Curet relates the revival of Catalan theatre during the period directly to the growth of civic pride and Catalan nationalism:

Cuando todos nos dimos cuenta de que la situación triste y precaria del teatro catalán era un grave mal y nos avergonzaba a los ojos forasteros, al propio tiempo que quedaba interrumpida una gloriosa tradición y dejábamos a nuestro pueblo sin el levado cultural que necesita para nutrir su espíritu, comenzaron a sonar voces de alerta y los hasta entonces indiferentes se preocuparon de estudiar y proponer medios para que el Teatro Catalán se redimiera de su sopor y no fuese un elemento discordante con la prosperidad de gran número de instituciones culturales nacidas al calor del resurgimiento de Cataluña como pueblo consciente, reintegrado a su vida civil . . .

[. . .] El pueblo comienza a hacerse cargo de que también es acto de elevado patriotismo proteger una manifestación artística a la que tanto debe el nacionalismo . . . Si el arte dramático decae es que la patria está en un trance peligroso.[33]

(When we all realized that the pathetic, precarious situation of Catalan theatre was a serious problem which embarrassed us in the eyes of outsiders, and that at the same time a glorious tradition was broken and our people were left without the cultural yeast[34] to nourish its spirit, the alarm bells rang and people who had hitherto been indifferent began to study and to make suggestions as to how Catalan Theatre could redeem itself from its lethargy and cease being out of tune with the prosperous state of many of the cultural institutions which had been created in the glow of the revival of Catalonia as a conscious people, reintegrated into its civic life . . .

[. . .] The people are beginning to take on board the fact that to protect an artistic form to which nationalism owes so much is also an act of great patriotism . . . If dramatic art declines, it is the fatherland itself which is at risk.)

Here the word 'patria' (fatherland) quite clearly refers to Catalonia, and is a recurring feature of conservative Catalan nationalist discourse of the period.[35] Curet's concern is that the theatre should be developed as an integral part of the recovery of Catalan civic life within a Catalan nationalist agenda. He founded and directed the theatre journal *El Teatre Català* (1912–17), whose agenda, as we shall see in later chapters, was overtly nationalist. Curet's emphasis on the need to reconnect with a lost tradition is characteristic of the more conservative element of the Catalan cultural revival, while his preoccupation with the image Catalonia presents to the outside world is, on the other hand, indicative of its sense of internationalism which was a feature of both *modernisme* and *noucentisme*. Catalonia's sense of her own separate identity was reflected in her feeling of solidarity with other small European nations such as Greece, Ireland and Finland, which were likewise trying to assert their identity in the context of domination by a much larger and more powerful entity.[36] However, Curet was critical of the *noucentistes* for what he saw as their cultural snobbery, and felt that the theatre needed an injection of illiterate proletarian muscle if it were to develop fully.[37] Interestingly, one Madrid-based critic used the example of the Generalitat de Catalunya to urge the Spanish government to create a Spanish National Theatre in order to finance the theatre properly.[38]

However, the theatre in both Barcelona and Madrid was about more than nationalism or middle-class elegance. Its development was a reflection of a rapidly changing social and political landscape. Variety was the keynote of the theatre culture in both cities: 'Multiplicados y diversificados los locales de espectáculos ofrecían una variedad enorme de funciones en Madrid o Barcelona y también en las ciudades más notables de las provincias'[39] (The many and varied entertainment palaces offered multifarious performances in Madrid and Barcelona as well as in the main provincial towns). Alongside middle-class theatres were others which specialized in spectacles of a more popular nature, the *género chico*, or 'minor theatre', which really drew the crowds in Madrid and Barcelona. The early part of the century was a time when mass culture and spectacle as an industry, 'surtout dans la recherche du profit'[40] (above all in the search for profit), became widespread. Between the 1880s and 1920 over twenty theatres devoted to the *género chico* opened in Madrid.[41] Rather than theatre, one should say entertainment, as *género chico* consisted of musical comedies as well as full-length plays and short sketches. The genre contained a certain tradition of anti-establishment satire, but its ideology was overwhelmingly conservative. Its social content was often limited to the presence of stereotypes, especially those representing the different regions of Spain. It could be sentimental or folksy, as in some of the plays of the Álvarez Quintero brothers, although at its best it offered cynicism and even poetic quality.

The development of the so-called *café theatres* in Madrid during the last thirty years of the nineteenth century gave access to the theatre to ordinary lower middle- and working-class people, who could not afford to go to theatres like the Teatro Español or the Teatro de la Zarzuela.[42] According to Espín Templado, the mainstream theatres were jealous and fearful of the success of this type of theatre, and were in league with the press who attempted to discredit them.[43]

Barcelona too had its own version of *género chico*, with the tradition of the satirical *sainet* being especially potent.[44] The touring Madrid companies also brought their *zarzuelas* to Barcelona, and there was clearly an audience for such a quintessentially Madrid play as Carlos Arniches's *El santo de la Isidra* (Isidra's Saint's Day). This suggests that language and tradition were less important than entertainment as far as the great mass of the theatre-going public was concerned. The popularity of one particular season is illustrated in a contemporary review of the *zarzuela* season at the Teatro de Cataluña during the 1897–8 season:

Abrió sus puertas el 22 de setiembre con una compañía de zarzuela . . . Trabajó dicha compañía hasta el 10 de junio, y durante este tiempo reprodujo numerosas zarzuelas en un acto representadas en temporadas anteriores y estrenó otras, entre las cuales obtuvieron aceptación *La Viejecita*, del maestro Fernández Caballero, *La Guardia amarilla* y *La Casa de los escándalos*, del maestro Jiménez, *La Revoltosa* del maestro Chapí, y *El Santo de la Isidra*, del maestro Torregrosa.[45] Dichas obras alcanzaron estraordinario [sic] número de representaciones que produjeron muy buenas entradas.[46]

(It opened its doors on 22 September with a *zarzuela* company . . . , which played there until 10 June. During this time, many *zarzuelas* from previous seasons were performed again, as well as new ones. The following were well received: Fernández Caballero's *The Little Old Woman*, Jiménez's *The Yellow Guard* and *House of Scandal*, Chapí's *Rebellious Woman* and Torregrosa's *Isidra's Saint's Day*. These works received an extraordinary number of performances and made a lot of money at the box office.)

Zarzuelas were just one part of what was a much more varied kind of popular theatre in Barcelona than in Madrid. As well as *sainetes*, *sainets* and *zarzuelas*, there was an array of offerings from the area of the city known as the Paral.lel, which was the home of music-hall and cabaret, as well as prostitution and drug addiction, and general degeneracy. Salaün highlights some differences between *género chico* in Madrid and Barcelona: 'Lo que sí caracteriza al Paralelo de principio de siglo es su dedicación intensísima al cuplé y a las variedades en general, cuando Madrid tarda todavía en dejarse conquistar'[47] (What does characterize the Paral.lel at the beginning of the century is its intense dedication to variety theatre and its songs, whereas Madrid took much longer to be won over). Popular entertainment had thrived in theatres which were situated in the Passeig de Gràcia area of the Eixample, but the new middle-class theatres which were built there in the second half of the nineteenth century forced many of their lower class equivalents to relocate to the Paral.lel.[48] The most famous of these theatres was El Molino, a Barcelona version of the Parisian Moulin Rouge. The respectable middle classes avoided the area around the Paral.lel or the so-called 'Chinese' Quarter (the Barrio Chino, or Barri Xinès in Catalan) which are both situated to the right of the famous Ramblas thoroughfare as one travels from the Plaça de Catalunya to the port. Fàbregas sees this theatrical divide as symbolic of a wider cultural and social divide in early twentieth-century Barcelona:

Els habitants de Barcelona, entre 1900 i 1936 es divideixen en dues classes; els qui no passen la ratlla de la Rambla, posats de cara al mar a mà dreta; o sigui, els qui prescendeixen del Barri Xino i del Paral.lel, i els qui no se'n mouen. Hi ha tot un ramat de ciutadans conservadors, gent d'ordre, senyors esteves, partidaris d'un art domesticat i excels, que ignoren la part infernal de la ciutat.[49]

(Between 1900 and 1936, the inhabitants of Barcelona were divided into two classes: those who did not venture to the right of the Rambles as one faces the sea, that is those who never visited the Barri Xino and the Paral.lel, and those who never moved from the area. There was a whole raft of conservative, repectable citizens, Senyor Esteves,[50] defenders of domesticated, lofty art, who knew nothing about that hellish area of the city.)

Some Spanish and Catalan writers were drawn to *género chico* as popular art, while comic farce was the preferred genre of Carlos Arniches and Pedro Muñoz Seca. Arniches's highly acclaimed versions of the Madrid variety of the often satirical localist comedy known as the *sainete* and Pedro Muñoz Seca's *astracanes*[51] were extremely popular with audiences and raised the genre to a higher artistic level, although simultaneously Muñoz Seca's plays satirized high culture.[52] His *La venganza de don Mendo* (Don Mendo's Vengeance) (1918) is a hilarious verse parody of neo-Romantic historical plays. In Barcelona the *modernista* artists and writers associated with the bohemian café Els Quatre Gats – including Santiago Rusiñol – saw in the low-life establishments of the Paral.lel the other side of the bourgeois society they rejected.

However, not all playwrights who were concerned with social injustice were impressed with *género chico*. The Catalan dramatist Ignasi Iglésies, for instance, believed it devalued working-class culture, which, in its genuine form, was pure and dignified.[53] His outspoken views on the need for a moral, honest popular theatre are encapsulated in an article he wrote on the Italian actress Italia Vitaliani's season at the Apolo Theatre in the Paral.lel district in 1907. Iglésies praises her love of popular culture, 'un amor intensíssim per la cultura del poble y per la regeneració artística dels públics embrutits'[54] (an intense love for the culture of the people and for the artistic regeneration of sullied audiences). Iglésies contrasts what Vitaliana has to offer with the usual Paral.lel fare and praises the sacrifice she has made en pro d'aquelles multituds incultes, de paladar estragat, acostumades a les xavacaneries del *género chico* y a les torturadores pantomimes dels Onofri, que diariament se serveixen en els teatres d'aquella populosa vía de la nostra ciutat nomenada el Paralelo.

(in favour of those uncultured masses, with their deadened palates, accustomed to the vulgarities of the *género chico* and the excruciating pantomimes of the Onofri,[55] which are served up daily in the theatres of that densely populated avenue of our city known as the Paral.lel.)

Iglésies did not share the affection for the low life of the Paral.lel and its entertainment felt by such contemporaries as Rusiñol, nor, despite his use of the word 'regeneration', did he feel that the *género chico* possessed the artistic quality often absent from so-called cultivated literature. Iglésies lambasts the 'escenari infestat ab les bafarades del melodrama horripilant o ab les grolleries embrutidores del *género ínfimo*' (stage which is infested by the stench of horrendous melodrama or the sullying coarseness of the *género ínfimo*[56]). He admires the financial sacrifice which performing at the Apolo meant for Vitaliana. In her previous visits to Barcelona, writes Iglésies, she has always played at a top theatre. He laments the small size of the audience at the Apolo when she performed Gorki's 1905 play, *Children of the Sun*: there were the usual art lovers, some well-meaning artisans and small groups of cultured working-class people. Missing were the snobs and the dilettanti who went to the theatres of the Paral.lel merely to drool over sensual actresses dressed in the latest Parisian fashions. According to Iglésies, Vitaliana also put on Catalan plays which, were it not for her, the Barcelona public, indifferent as they were to their own theatre, would never have seen. For Iglésies, the Italian actress points the way to the future, in which the sort of filth habitually seen in the Paral.lel may be cleansed and a better future assured as far as the theatre was concerned. Using almost messianic language Iglésies refers to her 'campanya de sanejament' (cleansing campaign), and describes her art as 'altruista, regenerador de públics embrutits'[57] (altruistic, a force for the regeneration of sullied audiences).

In his own plays – *Els vells* (The Old Folk) is an excellent example – Iglésies aimed to heighten public awareness of the lot of the Barcelona working classes. Such a critical attitude to social injustice was not uncommon in Catalan *modernisme*, which was not all art-for-art's sake decadentism. The paintings of gypsies by Isidre Nonell, of social scenes by Ramon Casas and Picasso's rose period depictions of circus folk are indicative of how certain *modernistes* exposed the injustice and inequality of the brave new capitalist world. The plays of Iglésies, who was closely associated with the movement, are probably the best example in drama.[58]

Joaquín Dicenta's plays portrayed the Madrid working classes in much the same way as Iglésies did with their Barcelona counterparts.[59] Dicenta was a member of the Spanish Socialist Party, and his plays were a plea for social justice for the urban proletariat. His *Juan José* (1895) is a case in point, and yet it attained immense popularity among middle- as well as working-class audiences, becoming the second most-performed Spanish play ever. Although its theme – a worker taking revenge on his boss – and its portrayal of an urban proletarian environment were new in Spanish terms, its idiom remained that of Romanticism. It fell to Benito Pérez Galdós, in plays such as *Realidad* and Benavente, in his urbane satires of the developing middle class, to bring a more naturalistic dialogue to the Spanish stage. Naturalism in its Zolaesque sense, however, had only a limited impact in Spain, its most representative example being Dicenta's *Daniel* (1907).[60]

The presence of amateur working-class theatre groups, often connected with the Anarchists, gave an extra dimension to theatrical life in Barcelona. Indeed, the Catalan actress Margarita[61] Xirgu, such an important figure in the theatre of both cities in the first third of the twentieth century, played the leading role in *Thérèse Raquin* in the Círculo de Propietarios de Gracia in 1906. Catalonia also had the principal proponent of naturalism in the Iberian Peninsula in the theatre critic Josep Yxart.[62]

However, not all dramatic literature written in this period deals with the problems of the city. In Catalonia the new industries were heavily concentrated in the Barcelona area, and a gulf developed between urban and rural Catalonia. The contrast between the city and countryside or country town is a recurring theme of both Catalan and Spanish literature of the period, including the theatre. This is sometimes a nostalgic view of the countryside, reminiscent of the Horatian Golden Age vision of the superiority of the countryside over the court, but more often a critical view of its narrow-mindedness, as for example in Guimerà's *Terra baixa*

(*Marta of the Lowlands*) and Rusiñol's *El místic* (The Mystic).[63] It was an era in which the perceived decadence of traditional Spain was an important literary theme, as writers sought to break away from what they considered to be stultifying localism and looked both to new European movements in art and literature and to capitalism as ways of modernizing the cultural and social life of their country. It was a time of taking stock in Spain and Catalonia, not only in the light of demographic and social changes but also in the context of the crisis provoked by the loss of Spain's overseas colonies. The town-country question was part of the wider revaluation of socio-political and cultural issues associated with regenerationism in Catalonia and Spain as a whole.

Both *Terra baixa* and *El místic* were, as Chapter 5 will illustrate, popular with audiences and critics in Barcelona and Madrid. However, the average theatrical fare in Spain during the late nineteenth and early twentieth centuries neither shared the social and cultural concerns nor possessed the quality of these two plays. As much as in any other European city at the time, the theatre in Madrid and Barcelona was essentially a commercial enterprise aimed at entertaining a middle-class audience:

> Por lo que a la situación en España se refiere, la escena finesecular estaba dominada, al igual que en el resto de Europa, por un teatro hecho primordialmente a la medida del consumo burgués.[64]

> (As far as the situation in Spain is concerned, the stage at the turn of the century was dominated, just as in the rest of Europe, by a theatre aimed principally at bourgeois consumption.)

Abellán points to a growing class gap amongst theatre-goers in Barcelona in the early twentieth century, which he links to the increasing diversity of types of entertainment and to commercial interests:

> Debieron de ser muchas las causas que contribuyeron a deshinchar aquel pequeño imperio teatral que había conseguido la implantación del teatro, de sus autores, en una afirmación verdaderamente interclasista. La popularización del cine, la prioridad de los intereses comerciales sobre los artísticos que al primer síntoma de infidelidad, llevaban una y otra vez al repertorio de boulevard a las estrellas que

atraían el público. El vodevil y la alta comedia de importación fueron ganando terreno en el ambiente cada vez más urbano de una ciudad, por otra parte conflictiva, que separaba a pasos agigantados trabajadores y burgueses incluso en los hábitos de diversión.[65]

(There must have been many reasons which contributed to the deflation of that small theatrical empire which had achieved the implantation of a theatre and its playwrights in a way that truly cut across the classes. The popularization of cinema, the priority of commercial over artistic interests which, at the first sign of infidelity, continually brought to the boulevard repertoire the stars who pulled in the audiences. Vaudeville and drawing-room drama from outside Spain were gaining ground in the increasingly urban but at the same time troubled environment of a city which created an ever widening gap between the working and the middle classes, even in their entertainment habits.)

In short, the theatrical scene was rich and varied, and shared what Allegra describes as the 'muchas aparentes contradicciones del mundo literario europeo finesecular, anarquista y reaccionario, aristócrata y "popular" al mismo tiempo'[66] (many apparent contradictions in the European literary scene at the end of the century, which was Anarchist and reactionary, aristocratic and 'popular' at the same time). Salaün's view is that contradiction and dichotomy are an integral part of drama, performance and theatre-going of turn-of-the-century Spain:

Son los mismos profesionales, adictos a los sectores diferentes, cada vez más identificados con la derecha, los que introducen y propagan unas mercancías que perjudican al teatro 'nacional'. La paradoja es que los que se benefician intensamente del sistema (consumidores o productores) y los que lo van a condenar por razones morales pertenecen a las mismas clases sociales. Lo que caracteriza la primera década del siglo es precisamente esta dicotomía cultural y moral, perceptible en la producción teatral misma y en la sociabilidad que la acompaña.[67]

(It was the same professionals, supporters of different sectors, more and more identified with the right, who introduced and disseminated products which harmed 'national' theatre. The paradox is that those who benefited from the system (whether as consumers or producers) and those who condemned it on moral grounds belonged to the same social classes. What characterizes the first decade of the century is precisely this cultural and moral dichotomy, visible in theatre production and in the sociability which accompanied it.)

Above all, despite the popular successes of such Spanish playwrights as Benavente and Dicenta, and their Catalan contemporaries like Guimerà and Rusiñol, the gap between commercial and art theatre was growing.[68] The development of poetic theatre in Spain in the early twentieth century as a Spanish version of European symbolism widened this gap. A well-informed elite was as knowledgeable and sophisticated as their counterparts in other European countries, and there was a much greater awareness of foreign theatre in Spain than is sometimes supposed, as Chapter 4 will make clear. The presence of intelligent theatre criticism in Spanish newspapers by the likes of Alejandro Miquis,[69] Enrique Díez-Canedo, Ramón Pérez de Ayala and Manuel Machado meant that readers were exposed to new ideas, while frequent tours by Spanish and French companies provided a certain degree of exposure to theatre from outside the Iberian Peninsula.[70] The existence of small, experimental groups, such as Miquis's Teatro de Arte (Art Theatre, 1908–11) and the Teatro de los Niños (Children's Theatre, 1909–10), in which the playwright Jacinto Benavente was a prime figure, is an indication of the development of an alternative theatre culture in Madrid.[71] Later came the playwright and director Gregorio Martínez Sierra's art theatre at the Teatro Eslava in Madrid (1917–20), in which various young stage designers who had spent formative periods in Barcelona participated. These included the Catalan Manuel Fontanals, the German Sigfrido Burmann and the avant-garde Uruguayan painter Rafael Barradas, whose work will be considered in Chapter 2.[72] This said, however, the facilities available to informed and creative theatre practitioners were not of the level experienced by their peers in other countries.[73]

It is Pérez de Ayala, writing in 1915, who perhaps best sums up what the proponents of poetic theatre were aiming to achieve, encapsulating it in the word *reteatralización*. For Pérez de Ayala, the term signified the union into one single whole of various disparate elements, including the text, the staging, the acting, the decorative element, music and the spectator.[74] He considered naturalism to be an aberration, a temporary blip in the history of theatre. The links with symbolist or Wagnerian total theatre are evident, and the return to the primitive roots of the theatre was a pan-European phenomenon.[75] One must not exaggerate what was achieved by the attempts to develop an alternative to the commercial theatre in early twentieth-century Spain. Writing on French theatre performed in Madrid between 1918 and 1936, Martín Rodríguez considers that the tastes of critics were out of sync with the realities of the theatre.[76] The critics and playwrights like Jacinto Grau, Ramón del Valle-Inclán and García Lorca who lamented the shortcomings of the commercial system were undoubtedly right. But neither should the efforts of certain critics, directors, stage designers and playwrights be dismissed, and nor should it be supposed that Valle-Inclán and García Lorca were alone in attempting to modernize Spanish theatre.

It was in Barcelona that the first and most significant manifestations of art theatre occurred, with Adrià Gual the key figure. He worked as dramatist, director and teacher at the Teatre Íntim in Barcelona, which he founded in 1898. Gual, an early mentor of Xirgu, collaborated with stage designers like Salvador Alarma and Oleguer Junyent and the composer Enric Morera, and put on many foreign works as well as plays by himself and other Catalan and Spanish contemporaries. He later founded the Catalan School of Dramatic Art in 1913, which was an attempt to form the basis of a Catalan National Theatre. Gual was well-known and highly respected in Madrid, and as late as 1923 Rivas Cherif tried to persuade him to mount a version of the Teatre Íntim there.[77] He introduced technical innovations into the theatre, including the dimming of the lights during actual performances, which did not happen in Madrid until a few years later. In European terms, Spain was backward in technical questions. Gas lighting had been used in Paris since the 1820s, but did not reach Barcelona until 1847 and Madrid until the 1850s.[78] Electric light had been introduced into the theatre only in 1880, and even then in a rudimentary fashion which was considered dangerous by some practitioners.[79] With Gual, the theatre entered into the modern age in more senses than one.

Gual himself was not immune from the radicalization of Spanish society in general and Catalan nationalism in particular that took place in the late 1920s and 1930s. He continued as head of the Catalan School of Dramatic Art during the Primo de Rivera dictatorship, but agreed to its name being changed to Instituto del

Teatro Nacional – the 'Nacional' referred to Spain – and to the exclusion of the Catalan language from the school. At the end of the dictatorship Gual was accused of collaboration with the regime and dismissed from his post. Gual's perception of the theatre as both popular and elitist was clearly not possible in the Spain of the 1930s.[80] The new direction was that of those such as Rivas Cherif and Xirgu who combined artistic experimentation with a radical social agenda. It was Rivas Cherif who was the prime mover behind some not entirely successful ventures into experimental theatre during the 1920s. Following the failure of his New School Theatre in the early part of the decade, he developed El Mirlo Blanco (The White Blackbird), El Cántaro Roto (The Broken Pitcher) and El Caracol (The Snail) as small experimental theatre groups which began with literary gatherings, readings and performances at the Madrid home of Ricardo Baroja and his wife Carmen Monné.[81] Early performances of Valle-Inclán, the great Spanish dramatist whose relationship with the commercial theatre was mutually hostile, were undertaken by small groups such as these. It was in the 1930s that Rivas developed a more radical social agenda, and became closely associated with the Second Spanish Republic.[82]

The Teatre Íntim, on the other hand was, quite intentionally on Gual's part, minority-interest theatre, although he aimed to reach as wide an audience as possible without compromising his aim to add dignity to Catalan theatre.[83] As an observer put it in 1899:

> La misma impresión que produjo en la temporada anterior, en la que se dieron algunas representaciones de este género, produjo esta vez. Las personas más inclinadas a la literatura llamada simbolista, escucharon con deleite y aplaudieron con fe; los que van a buscar en el teatro unas horas de solaz, y la masa del público, no se dieron por convencidos.[84]

> (They produced the same impression as last year, when they gave several performances in this genre. Those who like so-called symbolist literature listened with delight and applauded with belief; those who go to the theatre in search of a few hours' solace, and the public in general, were not convinced.)

This hard-headed assessment could be applied to most art theatre of the period, in Madrid as well as Barcelona: it was not really until García Lorca's folk tragedies of the 1930s that this situation changed. Rubio considers art theatres like Alejandro's Miquis's Teatro de Arte (1908–11) to be 'ante todo de literatos y para literatos innovadores' (above all of the literati and for the innovative literati),[85] but feels that the Catalan public was more open to new ideas:

> En Cataluña esta aceptación fue mayor y más temprana haciendo posible que una tentativa de producción teatral como el *Teatre Íntim* de Adriá Gual se mantuviera durante años y conviviera con otras muchas de teatro aficionado que solía alcanzar una relativa calidad sobre todo en los círculos obreros anarquistas.[86]

> (In Catalonia there was greater and earlier acceptance, which made it possible for a theatrical production venture like Adrià Gual's Teatre Íntim to run for years and to coexist with many other amateur ventures which often reached quite a high standard especially in Anarchist workers' circles.)

Hormigón's view, too, is that Barcelona was more radical than Madrid in the development of theatre outside the commercial circuits.[87] The most important Spanish theatre director during the 1920s and 1930s, Cipriano de Rivas Cherif, expressed this view clearly and forcefully:

> No tiene Madrid en su historia teatral el haber con que Barcelona ha contribuido al movimiento artístico y moderno por obra y gracia de Adrián Gual.[88]

> (In the history of its theatre Madrid never had the assets with which Barcelona has contributed to the artistic and modern movement by grace of Adrià Gual.)

This may be generally true, but the mass of the Barcelona theatre-going public was no more receptive to radical new ideas and forms than their Madrid counterparts. Nevertheless, as Chapter 4 will demonstrate, Barcelona was quicker off the mark in actually putting on plays that reflected developments in the theatre which were occurring outside Spain, whereas, as Chapter 3 will show, there was a feeling in Madrid that they were more adept at spotting 'home-grown' talent, including that based in Barcelona.

In an exploration of the interaction between Barcelona and Madrid theatre groups and individuals, I shall consider a number of areas of collaboration. Chapter 2 is concerned with the various ways in which Barcelona and Madrid acquired knowledge of each other's theatrical activity and looks at collaborative ventures between Barcelona- and Madrid-based theatre practitioners. Among these are actor/directors, playwrights, stage designers and critics. Chapter 3 concentrates on the acting profession, and considers the case of a famous Catalan actor and actress – Enric Borràs and Margarita Xirgu – who began working in Barcelona but who acquired greater fame once they had moved to Madrid. Reactions to the actor and the actress in their native and their adopted cities are gauged using contemporary press reviews of their theatrical activity. Contemporary press reviews also form the basis of the conclusions drawn in Chapters 4, 5 and 6, on the reception in the two cities of foreign, Catalan and Spanish plays respectively. Extensive use is made of such reviews and of articles on the theatre as a major source of information and as a barometer of contemporary taste.

My study of mainly first-night reviews of selected productions in the two cities enables me to draw conclusions on comparative critical tastes, and to glean from contemporary critics how the theatre-going public reacted to Spanish and Catalan plays. The texts chosen represent a cross-section of different theatrical styles across the period covered, although the Catalan plays belong, for reasons which will become apparent, to the years around the turn of the century. Another criterion which has been used is the involvement of Catalan actors/actresses and stage designers in productions of individual plays; this will allow detailed and specific illustration in the later chapters of observations which will have been made about them in Chapters 2 and 3. Through study of the reception of individual plays in these last two chapters, I hope also to determine the extent to which social and political changes – such as the development of Catalan nationalism and class conflict – are reflected in theatre criticism, and how far artistic considerations were able to survive in the turbulent societies of Madrid and Barcelona.

Building Bridges between Madrid and Barcelona: Mutual Awareness and Joint Ventures

As has been seen, although Madrid and Barcelona were in many ways quite different as theatre centres, they were hardly two worlds apart. They were to an extent united by one common language, although bilingual Barcelona enjoyed the advantage over Madrid of being receptive to two native languages. In the present chapter we will see how, despite the differences, in the period from the 1890s to the 1930s there were a number of collaborative ventures between Madrid- and Barcelona-based theatrical practitioners. There was also quite a high degree of awareness in each city of theatrical activities in the other. Madrid-based theatre companies included Barcelona in their spring provincial tours, while regular reviews from Barcelona in certain Madrid newspapers kept the readership of the Spanish capital informed about what was going on in Barcelona.

An early source of information for the Madrid public on the theatre in Barcelona was *El Diario del Teatro*, a Madrid-based daily newspaper owned by the Catalan theatre impresario Salvador Canals, who was based in Madrid. It ran from 1894 to 1895, at a time when the work of Guimerà was beginning to make an impact in Madrid, and reported on the theatre in Madrid and Barcelona, in the Spanish provinces and abroad, and contained photographs of performances. In the language used to praise the most famous Catalan playwright of the nineteenth century, Serafí Pitarra (pseudonym of Frederic Soler), an article published in the paper seems to anticipate the Catalan nationalism of such publications of the 1910s as *El Teatre Català* (see Chapter 3). Its evocation of Barcelona and Catalonia is sentimental in its chauvinism: 'En Barcelona, en esa hermosa región catalana, donde parece que los sentimientos son más hondos, las ideas más nobles y más varonil el lenguaje' (In Barcelona, in that beautiful Catalan region, where feelings are deeper, ideas nobler and language more virile).[1]

In January 1894 Canals wrote a long piece on Catalan theatre and on Santiago Rusiñol's role as innovator within it. He makes some strong assertions about Rusiñol, for example:

Desproporcionado parecerále seguramente al lector el emparejar con el nombre de Sitjes [*sic*], poco resobado por la fama, el modernismo en España: pero es así en realidad.[2]

(It may appear disproportionate to the reader to link the name of Sitges, which is hardly brimming over with fame, with *modernismo* in Spain, but that is the truth of the matter).

According to Canals, ideas which have taken root in Catalonia have yet to do so in 'nuestra Madrid orgullosa de su metropolitanismo' (our Madrid, which is so proud of its metropolitanism). As Chapter 5 will illustrate, Rusiñol was one of the Catalan playwrights who, in early twentieth-century Madrid, were considered to be modern and to point the way forward for Spanish theatre. The early date of the Canals article is significant, suggesting that he was ahead of his time in spotting a trend. However, he does not write approvingly of the new direction which is being taken by Catalan theatre, and resorts to racial stereotypes in his description of the penetration of northern European culture into Catalonia via the *modernistes*:

sorprendente es, en efecto, que en España haya entrado y tomado hospedaje precisamente por Cataluña, cuya fama legendaria y cuya vida real acusan como característica una perfecta ecuanimidad a flor de tierra y una positivista concepción de la existencia, nunca la bulliciosa y turbulenta excitación meridional más propicia a la importación de semejantes exóticos rumbos.

(in effect it is surprising that it should have entered and taken root via Catalonia, whose legendary fame and everyday life demonstrate a perfect equanimity just below the surface and a positivist concept of existence, and never the noisy, turbulent southern excitability more typical of such exotic directions.)

Canals seems to be suggesting that the *modernista* interest in northern Europe is not typical of Catalonia, whose reputation for exclusiveness makes foreign importations surprising. He emphasizes the conservative side of Catalan nationalism, which often saw as its enemy liberal, anticlerical Madrid.[3]

In Madrid, interest in Catalan theatre – and in Rusiñol in particular – grew at the start of the new century. In Martori's words, 'des de 1904 el referent de modernitat per a la crítica i els autors del teatre espanyol es trobava a l'escena de Barcelona'[4] (ever since 1904, the reference point for critics and authors within Spanish theatre was the Barcelona stage). *El Liberal* and *La Lectura* contained accounts of plays performed in Barcelona, while volume 2 of the 1901 *La Lectura* has a long article on Rusiñol (pp. 727–42). It quotes sections of his work in Catalan, and takes the view that, when Rusiñol abandoned Spanish for Catalan, his writing acquired a freedom it had hitherto lacked (p. 739). The author of the *La Lectura* articles was Ramon D. Perés, who, according to Casacuberta, tried to form a bridge between Madrid and Catalan intellectual circles.[5]

La Lectura was an important source of information on Catalan (as well as foreign) theatre in the first few years of the twentieth century. For example, its 'Teatro Catalán' section in volume 1 of 1903 devoted six pages to Catalan theatre.[6] Of these three are dedicated to *Els vells*, a play by another influential young Catalan playwright who became fashionable in Madrid in the early part of the century, Ignasi Iglésies (pp. 436–9).[7] At the turn of the century, Gual, Rusiñol, Iglésies and Crehuet from Barcelona were seen as modernizers by Madrid, as opposed to Guimerà, who was considered to be rural and out of date. Writing of the late nineteenth century, Albert Bensoussan expresses a similar view:

> s'exerce à Barcelone, bien avant Madrid, cette fascination pour un autre théâtre dépassant les limites du naturalisme et s'inscrivant dans les préocupations du groupe moderniste.[8]

> (this fascination for another type of theatre beyond naturalism was found in Barcelona long before it was in Madrid, in the context of the *modernista* group.)

Although it is in the early part of the century that Catalan theatre seems to have most to offer the Madrid theatrical circles who desired renovation, it is not until the 1920s and 1930s that more regular columns appear in the Madrid press on the theatre in Barcelona, for example in *ABC, El Heraldo de Madrid, El Sol* and *La Voz*. As was observed in Chapter 1, Gual and his Teatre Íntim were much admired in Madrid up until the 1920s. Over a long time span he was regarded as an example to be followed.[9] Chapter 5 will examine press reviews of his *El geni de la comèdia* (The Genius of Comedy) in Madrid in 1912 (which was organized by Díaz de Mendoza), while a 1917 *ABC* article by Joaquín Montaner presents the Íntim as a model for Martínez Sierra in his newly established venture at the Eslava. Montaner explains how the Íntim developed from a minority theatre at the outset into an enterprise involving close collaboration between impresarios, actors and audiences.[10] For this critic, Gual's efforts meant that foreign plays were performed in Barcelona well before they were in Madrid.[11] Montaner says that nothing he writes about the Íntim will be news to Martínez Sierra, who knows Catalonia well and will undoubtedly have the Íntim in his thoughts. However, Montaner recalls other attempts at art theatre in Madrid which seem to have disappeared from view, so what is needed now, he writes, is 'el reposo, la serenidad, la competencia, la voluntad que tuvieron los organizadores del Teatro Íntimo' (the tranquillity, the serenity, the competence and the determination which the organizers of the Teatre Íntim had).

Gual himself was the Barcelona correspondent for a 1925 *El Heraldo de Madrid* review of Valle-Inclán's version of the Salomé legend, *La cabeza del Bautista* (The Baptist's Head). In it he praises the author and the famous actress Mimí Aguglia, and describes Rivas Cherif as 'el heraldo heroico de la escena nueva'[12] (the heroic herald of the new stage). *El Heraldo* had a regular high-quality theatre/arts page at this period, which included occasional reviews from Barcelona.[13]

The Madrid press demonstrated particular interest in quality theatre in Barcelona, but rather less in what was termed regionalism, or 'Catalanness'. Barcelona as viewed from Madrid was Spain's second city rather than the capital of a distinct linguistic and cultural entity. The coolness towards and occasional contempt for regionalist theatre which was present in some circles of the Madrid press had been analysed as early as 1896 by Salvador Canals, in his review of the previous year's theatre programme in Madrid. Writing apropos of Guimerà, he makes a plea for a more open attitude in Madrid towards regional cultures:

Todavía llevamos el odio al regionalismo hasta el punto de pedir a los catalanes que no escriban en catalán, so pena de que los menospreciemos eternamente. No importa que tengan una historia propia y un estro literario característico: en castellano han de escribir. No importa que su sociedad, sus costumbres y su carácter sean muy distintos de los nuestros. No importa que sean de temperamento esencialmente sobrio en su arte: deben sucumbir a una lengua en ocasiones harto estrecha y en ocasiones asaz amplia para ellos.[14]

(We still bear such hatred towards regionalism that we ask the Catalans not to write in Catalan, on pain of our eternal contempt. It matters not that they have their own history and a characteristic literary inspiration: they must write in Castilian Spanish. It matters not that their society, their customs and their character are very different from ours. It matters not that they are of an essentially sober temperament in their art: they must succumb to a language which is on some occasions too narrow and on others rather broad for them.)

An appeal for tolerance of so-called regional theatres is made in an obituary in the mouthpiece of the Lliga Regionalista, *La Veu de Catalunya*, for the Catalan dramatist Josep Feliu i Codina, who died in 1897.[15] Having begun the obituary by declaring that the theatre is one of the most splendid illustrations of the literary renaissance in Catalonia, the article uses Feliu i Codina's move to Madrid not to complain about Catalans abandoning their homeland or about the poor conditions in the theatres which caused the exodus, but rather to appeal for tolerance towards the different regional theatres in Spain.[16] Its view is that Feliu i Codina proved the theatre can act as a civilizing influence as far as tolerance of regional variety in Spain is concerned:

> ¡Llástima gran, que la mort inconsiderada no li haja dexat continuar tant hermosa tasca, com era la de demostrar en lo teatre, aquest element civilisador que tant pot influir en la propaganda de les idees, la existencia real de la varietat en la unitat política que no deu tenir altre fí sinó lo d'agermanar, sens pretensons ridícules d'assimilació, tots aquestos pobles als qui Déu volgué enclóurer en la península ibérica.

> (What a pity that inconsiderate death did not allow him to continue that wonderful task of demonstrating in the theatre that civilizing element which can have so much influence in the propagation of ideas, the real existence of variety within political unity whose only purpose must be to bring together, without any ridiculous pretensions of assimilation, all those peoples whom God wished to include within the Iberian Peninsula.)

Despite the reservations on the part of some conservative sections of the Madrid press, a constant theme to emerge from their reviews of the theatre in Barcelona during the whole of the period that interests us is that it was more advanced than the theatre of their own city. José Alsina, for instance, writing in *La Voz* in 1924, was fulsome in his praise of the way audiences in Barcelona were more open to new ideas than their Madrid counterparts. He felt that they were more capable of creating a hard core of spectators who were open to and supportive of bold experimentation.[17] His picture of an intellectual elite capable of appreciating experimental theatre parallels what was happening with Gual and his Teatre Íntim at the turn of the century, and suggests that, in the 1920s, Barcelona was still viewed as a city where artistic experimentation in the theatre was prevalent. Through his columns in *El Sol*, Alsina was a strong supporter of such experimental, non-commercial theatre groups as Ricardo Baeza's Atenea.[18]

Another of the most outward-looking Spanish theatre critics of the 1920s, Estévez-Ortega, was fulsome in his praise of Barcelona, which he saw as more advanced than that of Madrid and more open to foreign influences:

Si en Madrid se consideran [sic] a Martínez Sierra, a la Xirgu, a Artigas, etc., como elementos de la vanguardia teatral hispana, Barcelona cuenta con otros tantos o más, posiblemente mejor capacitados, y desde luego en inmediato contacto con las orientaciones nuevas de fuera.

Supone Cataluña, y más concretamente Barcelona, el punto vulnerable por donde suelen colarse en nuestro país las bellas expresiones artísticas de fuera, [. . .] y sus experimentaciones más características. Es, además, la región española donde la actividad artística general tiene más y mejor acogida y desarrollo y donde han sido posibles ensayos, actuaciones y representaciones que son aún imposibles e inéditos en la capitalidad española.[19]

(If Martínez Sierra, Xirgu, Artigas, etc. are considered in Madrid to be part of the Hispanic theatrical vanguard, then Barcelona can count on as many if not more, possibly more qualified, and certainly in more immediate contact with new trends outside Spain.

Catalonia – and more specifically Barcelona – is the weak point through which the most beautiful artistic expressions from other countries, [. . .] and their most characteristic experimentation normally enter Spain. Furthermore, it is the Spanish region where artistic activity in general is best received and developed and where it is possible to see rehearsals, performances and productions that are still impossible and unprecedented in the Spanish capital.)

A more detailed but very different analysis is offered by José Escofet in 1926, also in *La Voz*, which sheds interesting light on how the theatre and indeed entertainment more generally in Madrid and Barcelona seem to have developed in quite different ways.[20] According to Escofet, the crisis in the theatre is more acute in Barcelona than Madrid since the Barcelona public is more sensitive to changes in fashion and more susceptible to economic pressures than its Madrid counterpart, which in turn conditions their respective theatrical tastes.[21] There are more theatres in Madrid than in Barcelona, says Escofet, which he considers surprising as the cities are roughly equal in size. Escofet then declares that Barcelona citizens are looking for a more frivolous and superficial kind of entertainment than their Madrid counterparts:

Aquí se ha entronizado la frivolidad cosmopolita; no tenemos teatros, pero abundan en Barcelona los *cabarets* de lujo, los *music-halls* y los *cines* de todas clases, desde el caro y fastuoso para los ricos, que ningún teatro iguala en *comfort* y elegancia, a la sencilla y espaciosa nave que permite los precios populares. [. . .] Por otra parte, de los pocos teatros que funcionan, la mayoría vive de la revista, a base de una suntuosa presentación escénica y de un impresionante desfile de mujeres guapas.

(Cosmopolitan frivolity has become entrenched here; we don't have theatres, but in Barcelona there are plenty of luxury cabarets, and all kinds of music halls and cinemas, from the expensive and opulent for the rich, which no theatre can equal in comfort and elegance, to the simple, spacious premises charging prices which ordinary people can pay. [. . .] On the other hand, the majority of the few functioning theatres live from revues, based on sumptuous staging and an impressive parade of beautiful women.)

The Barcelona businessman prefers the immortal grace of a beautiful ballerina to the well-worn dramatic formulae of Spanish authors like Martínez Sierra, the Álvarez Quintero brothers or Benavente, and he finds a Chaplin film much funnier than a Muñoz Seca *astracán*.[22]

Escofet denies that he is condemning Spanish theatre, adding that he has not mentioned Catalan theatre since, in his view, it is even less important. The inescapable fact for Escofet is that what the theatre-going public wants is frivolous spectacle, something to take their minds off serious thought. Not that the intellectuals are any better, according to Escofet, as they rarely go to the theatre. The overall picture he paints is gloomy: actors who do not know how to declaim, poor, shabby presentation, uncomfortable, cold, deserted theatres – everything, in short, indicates decadence. Escofet's view is that the cinema will finish off the theatre.[23] It is a young art form, uncontaminated by the commercialism which infects the theatre.[24]

Adolfo Marsillach, writing in 1933 in one of his regular monthly *ABC* columns on the theatre in Barcelona, also believes that the cinema is now dwarfing the theatre there:

> Los *cines* se lo llevan todo. Contra siete u ocho teatros que están vacíos la mayor parte de los días, tenemos más de cincuenta *cines* que en su mayoría hacen buenos negocios.[25]

> (The cinemas carry all before them. As against seven or eight theatres which are empty most days, we have more than fifty cinemas, the majority of which do good business).

Marsillach is one of the regular sources of information on the state of Barcelona theatre during this later period. It must be remembered, of course, that his perspective is conservative, and that he is not favourably disposed towards Catalan nationalism. A case in point is his February 1933 article, which reveals his social snobbery as well as his aversion to Catalan nationalism and left-wing politics:

> Todo se aplebeya, vulgariza y baja de tono. El Liceo de Barcelona, un tiempo relativamente aristocrático, desde que por primera vez lo frecuentan los amos y caciques de Cataluña, parece una ampliación del Romea. Aparte algunos representantes del viejo régimen, que le dan tono, es de una cursilería abrumadora. [. . .]
> Con decir que con el actual régimen, mejor dicho, con el advenimiento de la *esquerra* al Poder, el Liceo, como no podía ocurrir de otra manera, se ha aplebeyado, basta. El Sr. Maciá con su presencia no logra darle jerarquía. Aunque yo no creo que vaya a eso casi todas las noches, sino a que le toquen los *Segadors*. [. . .]
> [. . .] va al Liceo, donde se satisface su vanidad haciéndose tocar los *Segadors*, que ni una sola vez perdona. ¡*Los Segadors*! La canción del odio y matanza de castellanos. ¿Pero no quedamos, al discutir el Estatuto, en que éste haría a Cataluña más española que una Agustina de Aragón? ¿Pues a qué viene ahora este canto fúnebre y rencoroso? Si los catalanistas fueron (sic) leales, si sus propósitos no fuesen los mismos de

antes del Estatuto, no nos molestarían los oídos con su canto de guerra [. . .], con enchufes de España. Maciá, lejos de procribirlo [*sic*], como sería su deber si jugara limpio, va al Liceo sin otro objeto, tal vez, que el de que se toque en su honor el himno separatista.

Hasta la saciedad se tocó en la función que se organizara en el propio Liceo para honrar al gran catalán Amadeo Vives, cuya inspiración y ciencia musical ofrendó, casi enteras, al teatro castellano.[26]

(Everything becomes plebeian, vulgar and the tone is lowered. Barcelona's Liceu Theatre, which was once relatively aristocratic, looks more like an enlarged version of the Romea since the Catalan business and political bosses have begun to frequent it. Apart from some representatives of the old regime, who lend it class, it is now numbingly affected. [. . .]

With the current regime, or rather with the coming to power of Esquerra Republicana, everything has become plebeian, as was bound to happen. Nothing further needs to be said. Señor Maciá just cannot lend it any class. Although I think he goes there every night just to hear *Els Segadors* played for him. [. . .]

[. . .] he goes to the Liceu, where he satisfies his vanity by having *Els Segadors* played, which he does every single time. *Els Segadors*! The song of hatred and slaughter of the Castilians. But didn't we say, when we were discussing the Statute of Autonomy, that this would make Catalonia more Spanish than Agustina of Aragon? So why is this funereal and resentful song being played now? If the Catalanists were loyal, if their aims were not the same as they were before the Statute was granted, they would not offend our ears with their song of war . . . , with connections from Spain. Maciá, far from banning it, as he would consider it his duty to do if he were playing the game, goes to the Liceu just so that the separatist hymn can be played in his honour.

It was played ad nauseam in the function that was organized in the Liceu in honour of the great Catalan Amadeu Vives,[27] whose inspiration and musical science it offered, almost in its entirety, to Castilian theatre.)

Marsillach's point is that, contrary to what was said in Catalonia, the granting of the Statute of Autonomy has increased rather then lessened their desire for independence. He also complains about the leftward movement of Catalan nationalism ('esquerra' means 'left' in Catalan and refers specifically to the the Catalan Republican Left Party, or Esquerra Republicana Catalana (ERC)),[28] exemplified here by the proletarianization of the elite opera house, the Liceu Theatre, which had been bombed by the Anarchists in 1893 as a symbol of bourgeois culture. The Romea, founded in 1863, has traditionally been the home of Catalan theatre.[29] Marsillach finds the intrusion of nationalist symbolism into the theatre, in the form of the Catalan national anthem, *Els Segadors* (*The Reapers*), repulsive. He is commenting on the politicization of the theatre, while at the same time using it to make political comments himself. It is an illustration of what happened in the Spanish theatre of the 1930s, the best-known example of which is García Lorca's *Yerma* (see Chapter 6). It also typifies the increasing polarization of Spanish society in the years leading up to the Civil War: in the eyes of this conservative theatre critic, Catalanism, linked as it is to separatism and republicanism, is unacceptable.

This brief survey of reports on the theatre of Barcelona in the Madrid press has given us a sense of how it was perceived in the Spanish capital. Barcelona's knowledge of what was happening in Madrid came from their press and from the tours undertaken by Madrid-based companies of the provinces, which included Barcelona. Articles in Barcelona newspapers from theatre correspondents in Madrid were comparatively rare. One such exception concerned the distinguished critic E. Estévez-Ortega's section 'La actualidad teatral en Madrid' in *El Noticiero Universal*.[30] In the Madrid press, the early twentieth century is marked by a constant interest in what was happening in Barcelona, and by the desire in more advanced circles to expose Madrid audiences to the best of Catalan theatre. It contributed to an exodus of some theatre practitioners from Barcelona to Madrid (to be analysed in Chapter 3), but it also resulted in joint ventures between playwrights, actors/actresses and stage designers.

The first of these that interests us involves Angel Guimerà, considered to be a major playwright in Madrid theatrical circles in the last decade of the nineteenth century. As was seen in Chapter 1, 1892 marks the beginning of his relationship with three key figures: the actress María Guerrero, her husband, the actor Fernando Díaz de Mendoza, and José Echegaray, a prolific and popular playwright and winner of the Nobel Prize for Literature in 1904, who specialized in Romantic melodrama and who translated a number of Guimerà's plays into Spanish (see Chapter 5). The year 1892 also saw the beginning of the relationship between Guerrero and Pérez Galdós and the premiere of the latter's *Realidad*, which marked the commencement of an albeit tentative move in the direction of naturalism in the Spanish theatre. Guimerà's plays may also be seen in the same light, although some of them contain an Echegarayesque element of melodrama.

The Spanish theatre historian Manuel Bueno, writing in 1909, a year in which Barcelona saw the violent upheavals of the Tragic Week, sums up attitudes to Guimerà: 'Admiro mucho a este autor y le juzgo, no por una obra sino por la totalidad de su Teatro'[31] (I admire this author a lot and I judge him not on one play but on the whole of his theatre). According to Martori, the relationship of Guimerà with Guerrero and Díaz de Mendoza was a case of self-interest all round: 'Els interessos de María Guerrero i d'Echegaray de captar nous actors coincidien amb l'afany de Guimerà de projectar la seva obra en el teatre espanyol'[32] (María Guerrero and Echegaray's concern to find new actors coincided with Guimerà's desire to project his own work into the Spanish theatre). However, the relationship was not always smooth. Guerrero's strong-willed character asserted itself when she insisted that *Maria Rosa*, one of Guimerà's best-known plays, which had been promised to her, should not be performed in Catalan before she did it in Spanish translation. Much to her annoyance, it was premiered simultaneously in both cities on 24 November 1894. When it came to the premiere of another Guimerà play, *La filla del mar* (The Daughter of the Sea), it was Díaz de Mendoza who tried to be assertive, insisting that Guimerà change its harsh, pessimistic ending and make it more acceptable to audiences:

¿Qué escrúpulos tiene V? ¿La crítica de Barcelona? ¿El público de Barcelona? ¿Sus amigos de Barcelona? El público ya tiene juzgada la obra. El público se alegrará mucho de que cambie usted el final, sus amigos, ¿qué importan? Esos no encuentran nada bueno en usted, más que catalán. No creen en usted más que cuando le ven en barretina y sobre todo tiene usted la disculpa, si la necesitase (que no la necesita) de que se lo hemos pedido nosotros para nuestro uso particular y que nos ha querido V hacer este favor.[33]

(What qualms do you have? Barcelona critics? Barcelona audiences? Your Barcelona friends? The public has already judged your work. The public will be very happy if you change the ending, and as for your friends, what do they matter? They find nothing good in you, apart from the fact that you are Catalan. They believe in you only when they see you wearing the Catalan peasant's cap. Above all, you have the excuse – if you needed it, which you don't – that we have asked you for it for our own private use, and that you have wished to do us this favour.)

Díaz de Mendoza is here suggesting that Guimerà's Catalan friends appreciate him only for his Catalanness, symbolized by the wearing of the distinctive Catalan peasant's cap known as the *barretina*. This is another example of an individual Catalan figure being appreciated in Madrid while his cultural background is not and is also an attempt to pressurize Guimerà to give in to demands in part by cynically using a notion of Catalanism which suggests that Díaz de Mendoza's love for Catalan, expressed in the same letter,[34] was only skin deep. According to Martori, Guimerà did not agree to change the ending, but Díaz de Mendoza changed it anyway. In the new version the lovers were saved.[35] However, it is clear that the ending in the Madrid performance was the original one.[36]

Guimerà was born in Santa Cruz de Tenerife to a mother from the Canaries and a Catalan father. When he was eight years old, the family moved to Catalonia, where the dramatist spent the rest of his life. His first language was Spanish and he did not learn Catalan until after the family's move. As a result, he felt himself to be an outsider during his first years in Catalonia. He was deeply marked by this experience, and many characters in his plays are outsiders in closed communities or are of mixed racial origin. In his adoption of the Catalanist cause, both political and cultural, Guimerà displayed the fervour often associated with converts. He became actively involved in Catalan nationalist politics, and in 1895 he was elected President of the Ateneu Barcelonès (Barcelona Athenaeum), 'which from then on was to become a centre of Catalanist action'.[37]

The whole question of Spanishness or Catalanness is an important ingredient of the reception of Guimerà in Madrid, which is also closely bound up with his politics. According to Martori, the Madrid press tried to depict him as a Spanish writer (for example, by claiming that he translated his own plays) just as they tried to present Borràs as a Spanish actor in their reviews of his 1904–5 season in Madrid.[38]

Francos Rodríguez was one of the contemporary critics who strongly defended the view that Guimerà belonged to the whole of Spain and was appreciated all over the country. According to Francos, when Guimerà's plays were performed at home or abroad, they were considered to be Spanish:

> Cuando los dramas de Angel Guimerá se representan en Madrid, en Sevilla o en Zaragoza, se sabe que aquellas obras son de un esclarecido

compatriota. Cuando se representan en un teatro de Francia, de Italia o de Alemania, se anuncian como de un hijo de España.[39]

(When Guimerà's plays were performed in Madrid, Seville or Zaragoza, one knows that they are by an illustrious compatriot. When they are performed in a theatre in France, Italy or Germany, they are announced as being by a son of Spain.)

For Francos, Guimerà was one of the greatest playwrights in Spain.[40] The Catalans claim him as one of their own, writes Francos, because he writes in Catalan despite being born in the Canaries. However, says the critic, Guimerà's renown is a source of pride for the whole of Spain.[41] Francos shows his respect for Catalan by giving the titles of Guimerà's plays in their original language, but his attitude is basically that being (an adopted) Catalan does not exclude Guimerà from being Spanish as well: 'este amor [a la tierra catalana] no excluye, no puede ni debe excluir el otro, el santo amor a la Patria española.'[42] (this love [for the Catalan soil] does not exclude, nor can it or must it exclude, the holy love for the Spanish fatherland). Interestingly, Francos does not mention Guimerà's strongly pro-Catalan views, nor his involvement in political Catalanism.[43] González Blanco, writing in 1917, took a very different view from that of Francos:

Guimerà había surgido como un maestro nuevo, pero Guimerà era al fin catalán, y en Cataluña había delimitado su zona de acción . . . Iba siendo conocida en el resto de España su obra; pero aún se le aclamaba a él como un maestro remoto, cuya fama llega a nosotros confusamente, sin que sepamos descifrar bien de qué se compone el humo de aquel incienso.[44]

(Guimerà had emerged as a new master, but, when all said and done, Guimerà was Catalan, and in Catalonia he had limited his field of action . . . His work was becoming known in the rest of Spain; but he was still being acclaimed as a remote master, whose fame reaches us in a confused fashion, without our being able to work out what the smoke of that incense is made of.)

With time, the question of Catalan nationalism affected the relationship between Guimerà and Guerrero–Díaz de Mendoza, which worsened over the years, to a large extent for political reasons.

It culminated in their withdrawing *El alma es mía* (the Spanish translation of *L'ànima és meva*, The Soul is Mine) from the Princesa programme in 1920 as a result of a scandal caused by a militantly pro-Catalan speech by the author at the Jocs Florals cultural competition of 1920, and Díaz de Mendoza's patriotic speech to the Seville public in order to justify the change of programme. The results of the decision are analysed by Martori:

> La prensa de Barcelona reaccionó desfavorablemente hacia la decisión de los actores del Teatro de la Princesa. Las consecuencias para la compañía se alargaron en el tiempo: 1) se enfrió la relación de Guimerà con sus amigos María y Fernando, 2) los famosos actores perdieron su público catalán y 3) encontraron obstáculos a lo largo de sus frecuentes giras por América, motivados por la oposición de los grupos de emigrados catalanes allí instalados.[45]

> (The Barcelona press reacted unfavourably to the decision of the actors of the Teatro de la Princesa. The company felt the consequences over a long period of time: (1) relations cooled between Guimerà and his friends María and Fernando, (2) the famous actors lost their Catalan public, (3) they met obstacles during their frequent Latin American tours caused by opposition from groups of Catalan émigrés living there.)

In the end, the political differences between the couple and the dramatist became stronger than the mutual theatrical interests which had bound them together.[46] Politics, in the form of developing Catalan nationalism and its rejection in Madrid, sometimes became more important than artistic concerns and presented a barrier to collaborative theatrical ventures.

One man who normally managed to overcome such obstacles was Santiago Rusiñol. An accomplished prose writer and painter as well as a dramatist, Rusiñol was perhaps the key figure in the development of theatrical – and more generally artistic – contacts between Catalonia and the rest of Spain. His diplomacy and charm were obvious assets, and according to one of his contemporaries, he was a smooth operator.[47]

Rusiñol is associated with early *modernisme*. He was the moving force behind the *Festes Modernistes* (Art Nouveau Festivals) which took place between 1892 and 1899 in the town of Sitges to the south of Barcelona. The production of Maeterlinck's *L'Intruse* in the 1892 Festival is often considered to mark the beginnings of the penetration of symbolism into Catalan – and more widely Spanish – theatre. Rusiñol's own work is characterized by his depiction of a conflict between the artist and bourgeois society, but, although he is associated with art-for-art's sake decadentism, he was, as recent criticism has demonstrated, far from apolitical or uninterested in social concerns.[48] The social criticism in his plays is sometimes acid, and often laced with ironic humour. One of his most critical plays is *L'hèroe* (The Hero) (1903), which is a harsh exposé of Spain's military disaster in the Philippines.

Rusiñol was involved in several collaborative theatrical ventures with his Spanish counterparts. These involved joint authorship and translation of plays, while he used his contacts and diplomatic skills to open doors for others. In Rubio's words, he was 'un verdadero puente entre Barcelona y Madrid dentro de sus actividades de gran animador cultural, que lo era'[49] (a real bridge between Barcelona and Madrid within his activities as a great cultural *animateur*, which he was).

One of the most interesting of his collaborative ventures was his joint bilingual authorship with Gregorio Martínez Sierra who, as we have seen, did more than anyone to develop an alternative art theatre in Madrid.[50] María Martínez Sierra (who sometimes wrote under her maiden name of María O. Lejárraga), Gregorio's wife and the real moving spirit behind her husband's own plays – if not their actual author – tells us much about Rusiñol the man and the joint ventures between him and her husband in her 1953 account of the latter's life and works.[51] Her view is that she and her husband owed their initial success as playwrights to their friendship with Rusiñol.[52] What she had in mind was Rusiñol's offer to write a play jointly with the Martínez Sierras: María sheds interesting light on exactly how the bilingual play in question came to be written. Having praised Rusiñol's generosity towards herself and her husband (Rusiñol was already a major figure while they were still relatively unknown), María describes the process of what she found to be a very rewarding process of bilingual writing:

Instalámonos en nuestra casa, en tres habitaciones contiguas, después de habernos repartido la tarea, planeado la comedia y decidido el orden de las escenas. Rusiñol escribía en catalán; nosotros en castellano. Comunicábamos el respectivo 'fruto', discutíamos, aprobábamos, desaprobábamos, cortábamos, suprimíamos, añadíamos con absoluta imparcialidad, con buen humor, con rapidez, en perfecta armonía. Terminada la bilingüe comedia, Rusiñol puso en catalán nuestro castellano, yo puse en castellano su catalán, y así aquella hija feliz de tres ingenios se lanzó al mundo hablando en dos lenguas y tuvo, en cada una, nombre distinto: Llamóse en castellano *Vida y dulzura*, y en catalán, *Els savis de Vilatrista* (Los sabios de Villatriste). Rusiñol dibujó con fino trazo caricaturesco las figuras de los sabios. El primer acto es casi exclusivamente suyo. Estrenóse la comedia al mismo tiempo en Madrid y en Barcelona, y en ambas ciudades logró excelente fortuna. La incomparable actriz Rosario Pino, tal vez la mejor actriz española del siglo XX, alcanzó en el papel de Julia uno de los triunfos supremos de su arte seductor.[53]

(We settled down in our house, using three adjoining rooms, having divvied out the tasks, planned the play and decided the scene order. Rusiñol wrote in Catalan, and we wrote in Spanish. We shared our respective 'fruit', we discussed, approved, rejected, cut, suppressed, added with absolute impartiality, with good humour, quickly, in perfect harmony. Once the bilingual play was finished, Rusiñol put our Spanish into Catalan, I put his Catalan into Spanish, and thus the felicitous daughter of three inventive minds was launched into the world speaking two languages and had a different name in each one. It was called 'Life and Sweetness' in Spanish and 'The Wise Men of Sad Town' in Catalan. Rusiñol drew the figures of the wise men with the fine stroke of a caricaturist. The first act is almost exclusively his. The play was premiered simultaneously in Madrid and Barcelona, and was very favourably received in both cities. The incomparable actress Rosario Pino,[54] arguably the best Spanish actress of the twentieth century, achieved in the role of Julia one of the supreme triumphs of her seductive art.)

Vida y dulzura/Els savis de Vilatrista (first performed in 1907) seems, then, to have been a genuinely collaborative composition, while Rusiñol's typically *modernista* all-round artistic skills as well as his sharp, satirical sense of humour are demonstrated by his illustrations for the play. This was one of two plays Rusiñol wrote in collaboration with Martínez Sierra, the other being *Ocells de pas* (Migrant Birds), which was performed at the Teatre Novetats in Barcelona in 1908, directed by Gual.

Rusiñol's single-authored plays became known in Madrid in their Spanish translations. We have already seen how, in the early twentieth century, the theatrical scene in Barcelona was of great interest to Madrid, and its young authors were much in demand in the Spanish capital, none more so than Rusiñol. As Chapter 5 will demonstrate, his *El místic* drew an enthusiastic response from Madrid audiences and critics when it was performed by Borràs in Catalan in Madrid in 1904, and the demand was clearly there for it to be translated into Spanish.[55] The translation was done by Joaquín Dicenta, one of the bright new Spanish dramatists, whose own *Juan José* had created a stir among audiences and critics alike when it was first performed in 1895 and who was an admirer of Rusiñol.[56] It is significant that Dicenta, a committed socialist and leading figure in the limited introduction of Zolaesque naturalism to the Spanish stage, should translate *El místic*, whose social and moral content gives the lie to any notion of Rusiñol as nothing more than an art-for-art's sake decadent.[57]

This impression is confirmed in another of Rusiñol's plays from the early twentieth century which was translated into Spanish by a leading contemporary playwright, *Llibertat!* (Liberty), translated by Jacinto Benavente. A recent bilingual Catalan/Spanish edition of the play highlights several interesting features of the Benavente translation, or adaptation which is what Jaume Melendres, who revised the translation, calls it. Melendres stresses the changes Benavente made to the original Catalan, most of which, he claims, were aimed at making the play as politically correct as possible.[58] Melendres also observes that some of the difficulties faced by any translator of the play stem from the intrusion of Spanish into the Catalan texts, which in turn derives from the fact that Barcelona was (and still is) a bilingual city. This lends a richness and a complexity to theatrical discourse, while Melendres's comments on Benavente's translation of *Llibertat!* are also applicable to translation more generally and warn us to beware of the reception of plays in their translated form. One further point of interest about *Llibertat!* is that Rusiñol actually wrote it for the company of the Italian actress Italia Vitaliani, who premiered it – in an Italian translation by Alfredo Sainati – at the Novetats Theatre in Barcelona on 21 August 1901. This underlines once more that language in Barcelona is more of an opportunity than a barrier.

Rusiñol was probably the best-known Catalan writer and artist of his period outside Catalonia. His desire to promote and spread his own culture and to absorb others led to the collaborative ventures discussed above. However, other figures in the Barcelona theatre world at the turn of the century were both in demand in Madrid and themselves keen on collaborative ventures. A case in point is Adrià Gual who, as Chapter 1 demonstrated, was the leading protagonist in the development of a non-naturalistic, non-commercial theatre in Catalonia and, indeed, in the whole of Spain.

One of the earliest attempts to attract Gual to Madrid was made by Jacinto Benavente, who, as we have already seen, was one of Rusiñol's translators. In an undated letter, Benavente encouraged Gual to bring the Teatre Íntim to Madrid:

> No he asistido a las representaciones del teatro catalán en Madrid, porque no voy al teatro de la Comedia, desde que reñí con su empresario. Es lástima que no haya representado El Misterio del Dolor, que me parece la mejor obra de V que de seguro hubiera tenido un gran éxito. Para el año próximo debe V animarse y venir con su teatro Intimo, ya ve V que en Madrid no hay prejuicios contra nada y el teatro de V que también tiene carácter más amplio, más cosmopolita, y más abierto sería muy bien recibido.[59]

> (I haven't attended any of the Catalan theatre productions in Madrid,[60] since I haven't been to the Comedia since I quarrelled with the owner.[61] It's a shame they didn't perform 'The Mystery of Grief', your best play, I think, and one which would have been a major hit. You should pluck up the courage to bring your Teatre Íntim here next year. You can see that Madrid is not prejudiced against anything, and your theatre, which is broader, more cosmopolitan and open, would be very well received.)

Interestingly, Benavente feels that it is Gual's cosmopolitanism rather than his Catalanness which would be appreciated in Madrid. Benavente clearly has in mind the sort of elite audiences which, as Chapter 5 will show, would attend Gual's successful series of lecture-performances to illustrate the history of Western theatre at the Princesa Theatre in 1912.

In another undated letter, however, Benavente says that Madrid is not open to new ideas, and that conditions in Barcelona are much more favourable for experimental theatre. He declares that the time is not right for Gual's plays to be performed in Madrid:

> [Admiro en V] el exquisito sentimiento del arte, el buen gusto y la cultura que revela V en sus dos obras. Si el teatro estuviera en otras condiciones, tendría mucho gusto en traducir cualquiera de las dos, pero

los directores de escena y los actores son imposibles y en teatro libre no se puede pensar por ahora. En Madrid en cuanto se intenta algo que salga de la rutina, todo es broma y llamado [??] es/en [??][62] y modernista y otras cosas peores. Por lo que se advierte, en Barcelona hay mejor ambiente para el Arte.[63]

([I admire your] exquisite artistic sense, your good taste and the culture you show in your plays. If things were different in the theatre, I would be delighted to translate either of the two plays, but directors and actors are impossible and it's not feasible to think of a *théâtre livre* for the time being. When you try and do something out of the ordinary in Madrid, everybody makes fun of it, and they call you [??] a modernist and worse. From what they tell me, there is a better climate for Art in Barcelona.)

Whether these views are genuine or an excuse is unclear, but they do contrast sharply with what was said in the other letter.[64] The failure of Benavente to bring Gual to Madrid would be remembered with bitterness in the Barcelona press years later (see Chapter 6).

It was not Benavente but the actor and impresario Fernando Díaz de Mendoza who eventually achieved what Benavente had failed to do. In his memoirs Gual explains how he met him in Barcelona in 1911 during one of the regular summer season tours undertaken by the Díaz de Mendoza–Guerrero company and how the Madrid-based actor reacted positively to Gual's proposal for a short Madrid season. The venture came to fruition in the spring of the following year when Gual mounted a successful series of performance/lectures at the Princesa Theatre (for further details see Chapter 5).[65] The fluidity of Barcelona–Madrid contacts is demonstrated by this episode: the Barcelona theatre-going public was regularly exposed to Madrid-based theatre in the shape of summer tours, while the more far-sighted theatre practitioners in the Spanish capital were alive to the artistic and possibly commercial possibilities offered by the more highly evolved scene in Barcelona. Indeed, the contact between Gual and Madrid-based theatre practitioners was a two-way process. Gual himself was receptive to Spanish authors, and wished to break down any barriers where quality material was involved. He viewed performances of their plays as a special feature of the Íntim's programmes:

La presència d'autors castellans en aquells programes va constituir un punt d'especial interès per a nosaltres, interès que s'explicava clarament

el meu criteri de temps sostingut, condüit a escurçar distàncies incon-
sentibles, i a prescindir de certs aïllaments contraris a tot propòsit
verament artístic i per tant generós. Amb aquest objecte, jo mateix
donava l'exemple en traduir l'obra de Benavente, escrita expressament
per a aquelles sessions, i el meu company Pujol i Brull es feia traductor i
adaptor de la que ens concedia don Benito Pérez Galdós, sempre disposat
a secundar-nos en els meus intents.[66]

(The presence of Castilian authors in those programmes represented a
point of special interest for us, an interest which was clearly explained by
my long-held view that we had to bridge unacceptable gaps, and to
ignore certain cases of isolation which go against any truly artistic – and
thereby generous – project. With this aim in mind, I translated the
Benavente play which was written specifically for those sessions, and my
colleague Pujol i Brull translated and adapted the play given to us by
Benito Pérez Galdós, who was always ready to support my efforts.)

In Carles Batlle's words,

sorprenentment, pel que suposem que podia ser la perspectiva de l'època,
les obres espanyoles que representa l'Íntim es tradueixen al català com
qualsevol de les altres peces estrangeres.[67]

(Surprisingly, given what we assume was the view of things then, the
Spanish plays performed at the Íntim were translated into Catalan like
any of the other foreign plays.)

Translated versions of Spanish plays performed by the Íntim include
Benavente's *La casa de la dicha* (The House of Happiness) and
Torquemada en la hoguera (Torquemada at the Stake), by Pérez
Galdós. Far more numerous than translations from Spanish,
however, were plays by Gual and his Catalan contemporaries, and
foreign works by playwrights as varied as Shakespeare, Molière,
Beaumarchais, Ibsen, Hauptmann and Sudermann.

Gual continued to be respected in Madrid and solicited for joint
ventures into the 1920s. As was observed in Chapter 1, the director
Cipriano de Rivas Cherif, a major figure in the development of a new,
dynamic type of theatre in Spain in the 1920s and 1930s, had long
recognized his contribution towards the evolution of a non-naturalistic
theatrical alternative, and in 1923 invited him to mount a Madrid
version of the Teatre Íntim. Rivas's high opinion of Gual's work at the

Íntim is encapsulated in a 1923 article, written under a pseudonym, in which Rivas declares that Gual's work is, in many respects, of a higher quality that that of his more famous European counterparts:

> lleva veinticinco años trabajando en su *Teatro Íntimo* de Barcelona, donde su labor semejante y superior en muchos aspectos a la de un Lugné-Poë, a la de un Copeau, a la de Gordon Craig, a la de los rusos célebres ya, no ha tenido en España y América el influjo que debiera.[68]

> (he has been working for twenty-five years at his Teatre Íntim in Barcelona, where his achievements are the equal of, and superior in many ways to, those of a Lugné-Poë, a Copeau, a Gordon Craig, and the famous Russians, and yet have not had the influence they should have in Spain and Spanish America.)

According to Aguilera and Aznar, Gual was the

> ejemplo de que se sirve Rivas Cherif para reivindicar la necesidad de que se consolide en España la figura del director de escena, cuya función juzga absolutamente decisiva para la renovación escénica.[69]

> (the example which Rivas Cherif used to defend the role of the director in Spain, which Rivas considered absolutely vital for the renewal of the theatre.)

Rivas was perhaps the first person in Spain to pursue the idea of directing as a craft. The rise of the director in Russia, Germany and France saw the emergence of some remarkable individuals who developed a directorial aesthetic, and Rivas was an equivalent figure in Spain. What is interesting here, however, is the extent to which Rivas himself recognizes the influence on his own work of the directorial aesthetic of Gual who, perhaps because he was working mainly in a 'minority' language, has, until recently, been less well-known than Rivas. Rivas was not known for overstatement, so it is remarkable that such an important figure should place Gual as at least the equal of the likes of Craig, Copeau and the Russians. In the end, the Teatro Íntimo venture came to nothing,[70] but there were appreciative articles in the Madrid press about Gual.

So far we have seen examples of interest from Madrid in theatre activity in Barcelona and of collaborative ventures involving play-wrights, directors and actors and actresses. These tended to be concentrated in the early part of the century around modernizers like Gual and Rusiñol and from Madrid involved such leading playwrights as Dicenta and Benavente. We have considered Rusiñol's bilingual authorship with Martínez Sierra, and Gual's Teatre Íntim as a possible model for the latter's development of the principal alternative to the commercial circuit in Madrid at the Eslava. Gual and Martínez Sierra are, according to Aguilera and Aznar, two of only three exceptions (the other being Rivas Cherif) to the general rule that in Spain the director's role was usually performed by the leading actor.[71] As such, they are the only figures who come near to ideas on directing that the likes of Gordon Craig and Jacques Copeau were propagating in other European countries.[72]

As has already been stated, Martínez Sierra had close connections with Barcelona and more widely with Catalonia. His collaborative authorship with Rusiñol was followed by tours to Catalonia. In 1915 he formed a company with his mistress, the famous Spanish actress Catalina Bárcena, and Enric Borràs, and together they played a season at the Novetats in Barcelona. Checa's view is that the venture was of mutual interest to Martínez Sierra and Borràs.[73] Checa's book contains the text of letters written by Martínez Sierra, in which he makes some revealing comments about Borràs and their working relationship. The general impression he gives of Borràs is similar to that held in most of Spain, that is, that he is a magnificent and an ever-improving actor.[74] However, writes Martínez Sierra, during their production of *Terra baixa* in Lleida, the audience hardly applauded at all, despite the fact that Borràs was better than ever. This last comment links with other instances of alleged lack of appreciation of the actor by his fellow Catalans which will be examined in Chapter 3. In another letter, Martínez Sierra claims that many people in Catalonia are unaware even of Borràs's existence. He asserts that the actor is virtually unknown outside Catalonia. However, not everything about Borràs pleases Martínez Sierra: he does not like his stage designs or certain perceived personal deficiencies of character. The picture painted by Martínez Sierra is of a capricious, domineering man.

His letters also shed interesting light on the relationship between Barcelona and the Catalan provincial cities. In a 1915 letter he tells his wife:

> Y los mismos, Borrás entre ellos, que en Barcelona nos decían que en estos pueblos da lo mismo una cosa que otra, son los que ahora andan asustados, afirmando que estos públicos son terribles.[75]

(And the same people – Borràs included – who were telling us in Barcelona that it doesn't matter what you give the people in these towns are now scared, and saying that these audiences are terrible.)

In another, he gives the other side of the coin, as seen by the provincials:

Me dijo el empresario de Reus que Borrás siempre ha hecho estas excursiones con compañías de bandidos y por eso el público se retrae mucho. (p. 411)

(The impresario in Reus told me that Borràs has always made these excursions with companies of bandits, which is why the public is so reticent.)

Finally, Martínez Sierra has some interesting things to say about the state of theatre in Catalonia and Spain in general. Despite his complaints about general living conditions in Reus, he admits that its theatre is superb. However, he finds the general state of theatre in Catalonia to be deplorable: 'Aquí también hay coupletistas por todas partes. Y además no tienen afición al teatro: sin duda por eso ha muerto el teatro catalán' (p. 422) (There are variety artists everywhere here. And they don't have any interest in the theatre: that's why, no doubt, Catalan theatre is dead). Having said this, he asserts that Barcelona audiences are more intelligent and sensitive than their Madrid counterparts. Curiously, in the light of his collaborative ventures with Rusiñol and the esteem in which the latter's *El místic* was held in Madrid, Martínez Sierra does not seem to have a high opinion of the play (pp. 416–17).

Martínez Sierra's Catalan experience was to help him in the Eslava enterprise. Much of the relative success of the venture was owed to the presence of designers, one of whom, Manuel Fontanals, was from Barcelona and the others, the German Sigfrido Burmann, and the Uruguayan avant-garde artist Rafael Barradas, spent formative years there. Barcelona was clearly a favourable environment for a stage designer to work in, which was reflected in the fact that, since the late nineteenth century, stage design had been in a more advanced and innovative state in Barcelona than in Madrid.[76] Part of the reason for this was that Catalan stage designers had contact with theatres in northern Europe and were influenced by the technical advances they saw there.[77] Modern stage design was established early in Barcelona, and is firmly linked with the creativity associated with *modernisme*. Such stage designers as Salvador Alarma were able to practise at such ventures as Gual's Teatre Íntim, while Gual himself was an integral part of the movement away from the naturalistic stage set as representational.

Another point that should not be overlooked is the fact that arguably the three greatest painters of the twentieth century – Picasso, Miró and Dalí – were either Catalans or spent formative years in Barcelona. All three made important contributions to developing stage design as an integral part of the international avant-garde. Picasso's designs for the Ballets Russes in such groundbreaking pieces as *Parade* and *Pulcinella* are well-known.[78] Miró's interest in theatrical themes was also inspired by the Ballets Russes and by Picasso's designs for *Pulcinella*.[79] Dalí did the designs for a number of plays, including Gual's *La família d'Arlequí* (Harlequin's Family) and García Lorca's *Mariana Pineda* (both 1927). As far as the three stage designers who were vital to the success of the Eslava are concerned, they are not, of course, so well-known internationally as Picasso, Miró or Dalí. Nevertheless, their role not only at the Eslava but also, in the case of Fontanals and Burmann, in the success of plays by the likes of Valle-Inclán, García Lorca and Alberti was vital.

Fontanals (1893–1972) was described by a contemporary commentator, Manuel Abril, as 'barcelonés por nacimiento, cosmopolita por inclinación'[80] (a Barcelonan by birth, a cosmopolitan by inclination). Abril also points out that Fontanals was well-read, a precondition in his view, for a successful stage designer. He had learned his trade in Barcelona in the workshops of the famous *modernista* architect who became President of the Mancomunitat on Prat de la Riba's death in 1917, Puig i Cadafalch. Fontanals had also been a designer in his father's furniture and interior-decorating business. So it was *modernista* Barcelona, with its arts-and-crafts emphasis, which gave Fontanals the practical experience which Martínez Sierra valued, but it was at the Eslava that he became a respected stage designer.[81] As well as stage design, Fontanals did book illustrations for Martínez Sierra's Estrella collection and one critic considers them to be plastic commentaries on the literary spirit of each work.[82] Fontanals continued to work in exile in Mexico – on occasions with Rivas Cherif and Xirgu – after the

Spanish Civil War, and was responsible for the designs for a Spanish translation of Tennessee Williams's *The Glass Menagerie* in 1957.

Sigfrido Burmann was the most technically able of the three stage designers: 'en Burmann tiene el Eslava el verdadero especialista'[83] (in Burmann the Eslava has the real specialist). Born in Germany in 1890, he was very familiar with the work of the avant-garde director Max Reinhardt. His first contact with Spain came when he arrived in Cadiz in 1914. He quickly learned Spanish, and developed a deep affection for Andalusia, in particular Granada. He subsequently went to Madrid and Zaragoza, and then on to Barcelona and Cadaqués. In Figueres he learned Catalan, established a friendship with Dalí's father and met Eduardo Marquina. Apparently the young Dalí loved watching Burmann paint, while the German was the first to notice Dalí's passion for painting, and actually bought him his first paintbox.[84] Following his work with Martínez Sierra at the Eslava, Burmann continued to live in Madrid, and subsequently married a Spanish national. He was known for his sumptuous productions and, according to the writer of one of his obituaries, introduced 'physical' sets into Spain.[85] He was the first to use glass in windows on the Spanish stage. He continued to live and work in Spain until his death in 1980, and, after the Spanish Civil War, was involved in various films, including Franco's *Raza* (Race).[86]

One of the dramatists whose work was performed at the Eslava was Eduardo Marquina, a Barcelona-born dramatist who wrote exclusively in Spanish.[87] Not only did Marquina not write in Catalan, but he was hostile to Catalanism, which was for him 'una doctrina socialmente inmoral, políticamente corrosiva y artísticamente [. . .] malsana y decadente'[88] (a socially immoral doctrine, politically and artistically corrosive [. . .] unhealthy and decadent'). In contrast to Grau who, politically, was a radical, Marquina was a conservative and became associated with Spanish nationalism, particularly in his most famous play, *En Flandes se ha puesto el sol* (The Sun has Set on Flanders). Some of his patriotic comments on Spanish drama border on the ridiculous. In an interview given to *España* in 1915, Marquina opined that it was one of the most thriving, if not the most thriving, in Europe, what with authors of the quality of the Álvarez Quintero brothers, López Pinillos, Martínez Sierra, Linares Rivas, plus Pérez Galdós and Guimerà from the previous generation.[89] Despite all this, he actively promoted Catalan authors in Madrid and was one of a number of

Catalans involved in getting García Lorca's *Mariana Pineda* premiered in Barcelona.[90] Although his views on Catalonia and his plays were quite different from Rusiñol's, both men were facilitators as far as contacts between Spanish and Catalan theatre practitioners were concerned, a quality they shared with the artistic director of the Eslava, Martínez Sierra. Furthermore, the production of Marquina's *Una noche en Venecia* (A Night in Venice) at the Eslava brought together a Catalan dramatist who wrote in Spanish, a Madrid-based director and playwright who had learned much from the theatre scene in Catalonia, and a German stage designer who had settled in Spain and had important connections with Catalonia. This illustrates both the importance of links between Barcelona and Madrid and also the growing internationalism of the Spanish theatre of the 1920s.

Una noche en Venecia was premiered at the Eslava in 1923. Alejandro Miquis's view is that Marquina had reached his peak with his nationalistic *En Flandes se ha puesto el sol*, and that subsequently he has been

> más lírico que dramático. Su inspiración, nacida para la epopeya, no se avienen [*sic*] bien con los niveles un poco más bajos y menos encrespados de la literatura teatral.[91]

> (more lyrical than dramatic. His inspiration, which is made for epics, does not go well with the slightly lower and less inflamed levels of theatrical literature.)

None the less, says Miquis, a pleasant evening was had by all at the Eslava. The audience enjoyed the poetry, although the characters were not sufficiently interesting. He comments on the brilliance of the acting, but makes no mention of the fact that Burmann and Fontanals were the stage designers. However, he praises the costumes and the stage design:

> Tal como en Eslava la han puesto en escena, merece, además, ser vista; la indumentaria es magnífica, apropiada y de exquisita gusto, y las decoraciones lo serían aún más si fueran más reales.

> (The way they have performed it at the Eslava makes it worth seeing; the costumes are magnificent, appropriate and of exquisite taste, and the sets would be more so if they were more real.)

In contrast to Miquis, the writer of the brief *El Mundo* review considers *Una noche en Venecia* to be one of Marquina's best plays, fully appreciated by the large, select audience.[92] He thought Bárcena was wonderful but is another who does not mention Burmann or Fontanals. At least José Mayoral in *La Voz* does refer to them by name, and considers that they 'decoraron la obra con el mayor gusto, dentro de las modernas tendencias de la escenografía'[93] (decorated the play with the greatest taste, within the modern trends in stage design), although without specifying what these trends were.

Díez-Canedo believes that, rather than a sequential plot, Marquina has provided suggestive poetry.[94] In contrast to Miquis, Díez-Canedo is of the view that the play has gained from being freed from a historical theme, and praises its poetic qualities and Burmann's stage designs. Like nearly all the first-night reviewers, Díez-Canedo praises Bárcena, although he was less happy with some of the rest of the cast.

L.B. in *El Liberal* also emphasizes the poetic aspects of the play, adding that it would be a mistake to assume that audience taste is so poor that they cannot appreciate this sort of play, which is so traditionally Spanish.[95] L.B. then develops this point, using it as an excuse to launch an anti-foreign theatre diatribe:

> La ovación tributada al poeta fue como un clamor que debiera servir de norte a cómicos a seguir si en verdad queremos que la escena española salga de su avillanamiento y se libre de la servidumbre de copia de los autores extranjeros, inferiores, sin duda, a los nuestros en inspiración y en recursos.

> (The ovation which the poet received was like a cry which should guide playwrights if we really want the Spanish stage to get out of its lamentable state and free itself from the servitude of imitating foreign authors who are undoubtedly inferior to our own in inspiration and resources.)

This kind of ill-informed, cheap patriotism is something the likes of Miquis, Manuel Machado or Díez-Canedo would never have indulged in. L.B. says very little about the play as theatre. He does say that Bárcena was splendid, and, almost as an afterthought, adds 'para que nada falte en el elogio, ha de consignarse también que el decorado, por el color y por la estilización, merece todo linaje de aprobaciones' (so that nothing be missed out in our praise, it must be placed on record that, for its colour and stylization, the set merits all kinds of praise), without mentioning Burmann or Fontanals.

Floridor devotes rather more attention to stage design, and does mention Burmann, although he is another critic who calls him 'modern', without defining what this means:

> Por su parte, Martínez Sierra dedicó a la comedia los debidos honores, confiando a un artista de tan moderna orientación como Bürman, cultivador de la actual estética escenográfica, la reproducción estilizada de los fondos de la comedia, sobre los que destacaban vivamente armonizadas las ricas y elegantes telas del vestuario.[96]

> (For his part, Martínez Sierra gave the play its due honours by entrusting to a truly modern artist like Burmann, who cultivates the contemporary aesthetic in stage design, the stylized reproduction of backgrounds against which the rich and elegant materials of the costumes stand out vividly.)

Although lacking in detail, most of the contemporary reviews make it clear that Burmann was for them a 'modern' stage designer.

As we have seen, then, some of the major innovators in early twentieth-century Spanish theatre were from the Barcelona area, but were forced to move to Madrid to develop their talents and to earn a wider acceptance. Some of these, like Guimerà and Rusiñol, were associated with Catalanism, while, at the opposite end of the scale, Marquina was an anti-Catalanist and the author of plays which encapsulate the growth of Spanish nationalist sentiment in the theatre during the late nineteenth and early twentieth centuries. Whatever their views on political and cultural matters, it is undeniable that such theatre practitioners enriched the Madrid stage in a wide variety of ways. However, this particular collaborative venture was of mutual benefit, as in the case of Fontanals, whose period spent designing at the Eslava was as decisive in his career as it was in Burmann's. Like their acting compatriots Enric Borràs and Margarita Xirgu, they had to move from Barcelona to Madrid to find fame and fortune, or to find theatres that would make full use of their abilities.

From Barcelona to Madrid and Back Again: Enric Borràs and Margarita Xirgu

As Chapter 2 has demonstrated, by the end of the nineteenth century the movers and shakers of Madrid's theatre scene were well aware of what was going on in Barcelona, an interest which continued well into the twentieth century. The interest was not limited to the theatre, but covered all branches of arts and letters. The Catalans were also keen to perform in Madrid and to 'conquer' the state capital. A brief article in *Quatre Gats*, the organ of the café and cultural centre of the same name, reports the favourable reception accorded the Catalan composer Amadeu Vives in Madrid in 1899 in the following terms:

LA CONQUISTA DE MADRID

Fem alusió á l'exit verdaderament gros qu'ha obtingut á Madrid nostre benvolgut amic l'Amadeo Vives, ab la particip-ació del *D. Lúcas del Cigarral* qu'es *Entre bobos anda el juego*,[1] arreglat segons las corrents actuals. Nos alegrém moltíssim de que tot Madrid hagi trobat magnífica l'obra d'en Vives, sobre tot sabent com sabíam, qu'es proposava cautivar el *público de la Corte*. Y sempre es un consol veurer qu'un home de talent, logra'l que 's proposa y ab facilitat relativa. Igual éxit l'hi desitjem, quant l'hi estrenin l'ópera en el Reyal.[2]

(THE CONQUEST OF MADRID

We are referring to the really major success that our beloved Amadeu Vives has had in Madrid, with his participation in 'The Revenge of Don Lucas', given a modern arrangement. We are delighted that the whole of Madrid considers Vives's work to be magnificent, especially knowing as we did that Vives set out to captivate the public of the capital. And it is always pleasing to see a man of talent achieve his aims, with relative ease. We wish him similar success when they premiere the opera at the Teatro Real.)

There is no suggestion of resentment that Vives has gone to Madrid, but a sense of satisfaction that he has conquered the capital. Another art-for-art's sake *modernista* journal, *Pel i Ploma*, also makes reference later the same year to Vives's success in Madrid, but seems pleased that he is to return to Catalonia. They use a cooking image to convey the fact that he needed to go to Madrid to find success and, having found it, can now return home:

> s'en aná a Madrid a buscar la fulla de llorer segura, que faltava pera fer bullir l'olla. Ara que la té tornará a fer escudella catalana.[3]

> (he went to Madrid in search of the assured bayleaf [= 'laurel leaf' in Catalan], which he needed to make Catalan stew; now that he has found it, he will return to make Catalan stew.)

The mild, almost gentle tone of these reviews contrasts, as we shall see, with a far more aggressive attitude in later years towards the departure of two Catalan actors/actresses, Enric Borràs and Margarita Xirgu.

By the 1920s Borràs and Xirgu were the leading figures in the Madrid acting world. They both began their careers in Barcelona, but fairly early on moved to Madrid, where they headed their own companies, which merged in 1919 to form the single most powerful group in Spain. Both Borràs and Xirgu were, in their different ways, central figures in the development of the second Golden Age of Spanish drama in the 1920s and 1930s.

Born in Badalona in 1863, Borràs made his name performing Guimerà in the 1890s. He was the leading actor at the Romea Theatre from 1901 to 1903, where he obtained great success in two of the plays which will concern us in Chapter 5: Rusiñol's *El místic* (which was specifically written for Borràs) and Iglésies's *Els vells* (both 1903). He performed to great acclaim a short season of plays in Catalan in the spring of 1904 in Madrid whose theatre-going public, according to Conteras y Camargo, hardly knew him because his career had been dedicated to 'regional' theatre.[4] Conteras interviews Borràs, who pays tribute to Antonio Vico, one of the leading Spanish actors of the nineteenth century, for rescuing him from playing melodramas in the suburbs of Barcelona. Borràs says he worked with Vico, playing the *galán* in a short season in Lleida, and studied madly, remaining for two years at the Romea, the home of Catalan theatre. However, he found its atmosphere highly traditional and old-fashioned, and went subsequently to the Novetats, where young-spirited writers were finding their way. Borràs feels that he is at the beginning of the road, and that Madrid will be his first stopping post. Conteras then concludes by underlining that Madrid high society would attend the Catalan season:

El abono abierto en el teatro de la Comedia para las veinte funciones en que se darán a conocer las obras más notables del teatro catalán, ha dado excelentes resultados, y especialmente en los días de moda será aquella sala el punto de reunión de la alta sociedad madrileña.[5]

(The open subscription at the Comedia Theatre for the twenty shows in which the best Catalan plays will be unveiled has produced excellent results, and that venue will be a meeting point for Madrid high society, especially on fashionable days.)

As a result of the favourable reception in 1904, Borràs was persuaded by the impresario Tirso Escudero to move permanently to Madrid, where he began with Pérez Galdós's *La loca de la casa* (The Mad Woman of the House) in October 1905. Borràs quickly became a star there, and had major successes in such plays as Calderón's *El alcalde de Zalamea* (*The Mayor of Zalamea*), Pérez Galdós's *El abuelo* (*The Grandfather*) and Dicenta's *Juan José*, as well as works by contemporary Catalan dramatists, including *Terra baixa, El místic* and *Els vells*. Borràs was considered by Rusiñol to be the most complete of all the contemporary Spanish actors,[6] while Eduardo Zamacois, writing in 1907, described him as a genius.[7] Borràs toured South America several times from 1907 onwards, even performing in Catalan there. After 1917, although he continued to be based in Madrid, he played regular seasons in Barcelona in both Catalan and Spanish. He maintained his early repertoire throughout most of his career, returning time and again to such favourites as *Terra baixa* and *El alcalde de Zalamea*. During the Civil War he put on Catalan plays at the Poliorama Theatre in Barcelona but, following the victory of General Franco in 1939, became firmly linked with the right and performed works by playwrights who were associated with the Franco regime, such as Marquina and Pemán.

Although there was a certain amount of overlap between Borràs and Xirgu, and, indeed, they both acted together in a number of

plays, their careers followed quite distinct paths and their acting
styles and political beliefs were also quite different. Xirgu was born
in Molins de Rei in 1888 and, as with the great majority of Catalan
actors and actresses, began her career in the amateur theatres of
Barcelona.[8] Her first triumph as a professional actress came in
Zola's *Thérèse Raquin* in 1906.[9] Xirgu tells her own story to Carmen
de Burgos:

> Pertenezco a una familia muy modesta que carecía de medios para
> educarme . . . En Barcelona no tenemos conservatorio . . . Me he ido
> formando yo sola . . . sola . . . de afición . . . movida por un impuslo
> interno.[10]

> (I come from a very modest family which did not have the means to
> educate me . . . In Barcelona we do not have a conservatoire . . . I have
> educated myself . . . because I wanted to . . . moved by an inner drive.)

She emphasized her wide reading, particularly in French and Italian.
She had a special love for Italian literature and greatly admired
contemporary Italian actresses. When asked what her ideal was in
art, her reply seems to anticipate García Lorca's views, particularly
in her attitude to audiences:

> Llegar a la naturalidad más absoluta – me dice como una paradoja – .
> Abomino de los efectos teatrales y de los latiguillos; yo hago siempre un
> trabajo honrado, sin pensar en el público, sin cuidarme de arrancar el
> aplauso.[11]

> (To achieve the most absolute naturalness – she tells me paradoxically – I
> hate theatrical effects and platitudes; I always do an honest job, without
> thinking of the public, without worrying about provoking applause.)

She worked at the Íntim with Adrià Gual, whose insistence on
actors and actresses learning their lines and being professional was
clearly beneficial to the young Xirgu. In Siguan's words, 'si esto le
trajo quizás a la larga problemas con los actores, él fue sin embargo
el maestro y "creador" de actrices como Margarita Xirgu'[12] (if this
perhaps brought him problems with actors in the long run, it was he
who was the teacher and 'creator' of actresses like Margarita Xirgu).
Gual also gave her an early experience of performing contemporary

European drama when she acted in Hauptmann's *The Sunken Bell* in 1908.

Xirgu really made her name with Oscar Wilde's *Salomé*, which she performed in Catalan in Barcelona and in Spanish in Madrid, Malaga, Santa Cruz de Tenerife and in various South American cities between 1910 and 1914 (see Chapter 4). Xirgu's *Salomé* illustrates how she was never afraid to take on difficult and challenging parts, particularly tragedies, such as Unamuno's version of Seneca's *Medea*. Her most famous roles were by established and new Spanish dramatists, including Pérez Galdós, Benavente, the Álvarez Quintero brothers, Alberti, García Lorca, and Valle-Inclán. Once she left Barcelona for Madrid in 1913, Xirgu's repertoire was essentially Spanish, and she rarely put on Catalan plays. She did occasionally return to perform in Barcelona, but almost always in Spanish, and with less frequency than Borràs.

Xirgu never shied away from controversy, most famously in García Lorca's *Yerma*. She angered conservative sections of society with her choice of plays, and, in one case at least, this was translated into anti-Catalanism. Following her performance of Alberti's *Fermín Galán* at the Teatro Español in Madrid in 1930, she was attacked and hit by a right-wing lady, who called her a 'Catalan shit'. She identified strongly with the Spanish Republic, and lived in exile in South America following Franco's victory in the Spanish Civil War until her death in 1969. There she continued to perform works by Golden Age and contemporary Spanish playwrights and to train South American actors. The *Diario de Barcelona* was able to write in her obituary that 'llegó a ser la primera actriz de la América Latina'[13] (she became the leading actress in Latin America).

Why did Borràs and Xirgu leave Barcelona for Madrid? They were not the only actors/actresses to do so, and Xavier Fàbregas suggests two reasons for their emigration: the early development of the cinema in Barcelona in comparison with Madrid, which badly affected theatre attendance,[14] and the fact that they had a much bigger potential audience in Madrid and, more particularly, in South America. However, Fàbregas notes that this process was reversed once the cinema really took hold in Madrid in the mid-1920s.[15] I shall be concerned in this chapter to examine briefly the reception of Borràs and Xirgu in Madrid (this will considered more fully in Chapters 4, 5 and 6 with analysis of the reception of individual plays in which they acted or which they directed). I shall also comment on the reception afforded them by the Spanish- and Catalan-language press on their periodic return to Barcelona.

One of Borràs's biographers, Vila San-Juan, recalls the stir caused by the news that Tirso Escudero, the owner of the Teatro de la Comedia, had invited the Borràs company to perform a Catalan season in Madrid:

> Se armó tal algarabía en Madrid, y especialmente en el mundillo teatral, al saber que don Tirso Escudero, empresario del Teatro de la Comedia, llevaba a su escenario una compañía de Barcelona y que, además – ¿cuándo, en aquellos tiempos, una compañía provinciana iba a la Corte en ese plan? – , trabajaría en catalán, que el gran Santiago Rusiñol quiso dar su nota de humorismo y se compró un fenomenal sombrero de copa con una hermosa y amplia cinta que decía, en grandes caracteres: 'COMPAÑÍA ENRIQUE BORRÁS, INTÉRPRETE'. Porque Rusiñol salió de Barcelona con la compañía del Romea, para conquistar Madrid, al lado de Borrás, y en catalán.
>
> Realmente, el caso era extraordinario. Estamos hablando de 1904, cuando los grandes teatros madrileños tenían compañías magníficas y propias, que, terminada la temporada oficial, iban a provincias para enseñar sus obras y sus actores; nunca se había dado el caso contrario, o sea, que una compañía de provincia fuese a Madrid a exhibir en la Corte su Arte y sus cómicos.
>
> Si a esto se añade que no había llegado el momento de la comprensión regional, y que el idioma catalán ni era entendido, ni contaba con excesivas simpatías en los medios madrileños, se comprenderá el asombro y, casi, casi, la antipatía con que la noticia, primero, y el hecho, después, fueron acogidos por una parte del público, y muy concretamente por la gente del mundo teatral.[16]

(There was such a fuss in Madrid, especially in the theatre world, when it became known that Tirso Escudero, the impresario of the Comedia, was bringing a company from Barcelona to his theatre and that, furthermore (when did a provincial company ever go to the Capital at that time with similar aims?) it would perform in Catalan, that the great Santiago Rusiñol decided to add a humorous touch and bought himself a huge top hat with a splendid wide band which announced in big letters: 'The Enric Borràs Company, Interpreter'. For Rusiñol left Barcelona with the Romea Company to conquer Madrid with Borràs, and in Catalan.

It was a really extraordinary event. We are talking of 1904, when the great Madrid theatres had their own magnificent companies which would do the provincial tour at the end of the season to show off their plays and their actors; the reverse had never happened, that is, a provincial company had never gone to Madrid to exhibit its art and their performers in the Capital.

If to this we add the fact that regionalism was still not comprehended, and that the Catalan language was not understood and had few sympathizers in Madrid, then one can understand the amazement and one might also say the resentment with which first the news and then the reality was received by a section of the public, and, in particular, by the theatre world).

Vila San-Juan is emphasizing that the strength of the established theatres in Madrid and the perception of so-called regional theatre from the capital made the Borràs Catalan season an extraordinary venture. While it was common for Madrid-based groups to take in Barcelona as part of their spring tours of Spain, it was virtually unheard of for Catalan groups to play in Madrid. One should also note the role played by Rusiñol as a link man in the promotion of Catalan theatre in Madrid, evoked by Rusiñol himself with characteristically ironic humour. Despite these initial reservations, the reaction to the season in the Madrid press was generally favourable and, to judge from these theatre critics, the Madrid public too welcomed the venture (for details see Chapter 5).

Borràs's popularity in Madrid continued to grow over the years. As was observed earlier, he retained his early hits in his repertoire, particularly *Terra baixa*, which he continued to perform into the 1930s, although his was not the only company to put on the play.[17] According to one newspaper, he received a rapturous reception from Madrid audiences when he presented a special benefit performance of the play in early 1926. The following review in *El Sol* describes the continuing popularity of a turn-of-the-century Catalan classic after nearly thirty years, and also the pulling power of the leading actor in Spain:

> El teatro estaba ocupado totalmente de un público que iba, no sólo a rendir un homenaje de cariño al beneficiado – a la persona – , sino de admiración al actor – al artista – , que en esta obra, más que en otras, por la robusta naturaleza del protagonista, halla ocasión de mostrarse en la plenitud de sus arrestos físicos y en la de sus dominios artísticos. Así fue, en efecto. Parecía – tal era el ímpetu de la creación – que el Manelic de anoche alentaba con un corazón de veinte años.
>
> El público tributó al ilustre Borràs espontáneos y férvidos aplausos en distintos momentos de la presentación, y con mayor entusiasmo al final de los actos de la obra.[18]

(The theatre was filled totally by an audience which went there not only to render affectionate homage to the object of the benefit performance – the person – but also out of admiration for the actor – the artist – , who, in this play more than in others, due to the sturdy character of the protagonist, gets the chance to show the full power of his physical energy and his complete artistic control. And so it turned out. Last night it seemed – such was the force of the creation – that Manelic[19] breathed with the heart of a twenty year old.

There was spontaneous and fervent applause for Borràs at various points of the performance, and this increased in intensity at the end of each act.)

It appears that not only was Borràs extremely popular in Madrid, but that he took the city to his heart. Vila San-Juan, claims that, while the Español was inextricably linked with Borràs's name,[20] Borràs himself also felt that the Español was like a home to him. In an undated interview quoted by Vila San-Juan, he extends his comments to include Madrid as a whole, and then goes on to describe his relationship with Madrid, Barcelona and Spain in general:

– El Español era ya como mi casa. Aquel sombrío miedo en mis primeros pasos había ido desapareciendo a fuerza de la bondad por parte del público y de mi propia estimación en estudiar y mejorarme para corresponderle. [. . .] El público de Madrid nunca me defraudó. Sabía que tenía en mí un entusiasta y cuando, en mi camerino, se enfrascaban en discusiones sobre ello y sobre mi procedencia catalana, los madrileños me oían estupefactos decir que me sentía tan catalán en Madrid como madrileño en Barcelona. Y que ambos sentimientos los tenía en el fondo del corazón arraigadísimos, con mi gran fervor e idolatría por España.[21]

(I was already perfectly at home in the Español. That sombre fear of my first steps had been gradually disappearing because of the audiences' kindness and my own respect in wanting to study and improve myself in order to repay them. [. . .] Madrid audiences have never let me down. They knew I was a great enthusiast and, when they engaged in discussions with me in my dressing room on that and on my Catalan origins, the Madrid people listened to me in amazement when I said that I felt as Catalan in Madrid as I did a *madrileño* [inhabitant of Madrid] in Barcelona. And that both sentiments ran very deep in me, as part of my great passion and idolatry for Spain.)

Borràs's sense of belonging equally to the two cities suggests that, as far as he was concerned, the term 'collaborator' would apply more than 'rival'. It is interesting that his love for the two cities is part of a general fondness for Spain rather than for Catalonia. However, this comment was almost certainly coloured by the time, place and circumstances of the interview. Although Vila San-Juan is generally a reliable critic, one has to bear in mind that his biography belongs to the middle of the Franco period, when the regime was engaged in a systematic attempt to de-Catalanize Catalonia, viewing it as just another Spanish region, whose language and culture were to be those of the rest of Spain. The sentiments which are attributed to Borràs in the above quotation – namely that a Catalan identity is subsumed into a broader Spanish one – fit perfectly into Francoist ideology. [22]

One must be similarly wary of another publication, namely Salvador Bonavía Panyella's biographical notes on Borràs, which are undated, but were almost certainly published during the early Franco period. According to Bonavía Panyella, the actor was much loved in both Barcelona and Madrid, and in May 1943 the Mayor of Barcelona awarded him the Gold Medal of the City. Bonavía ends his piece by calling Borràs 'uno de los más preclaros genios del Teatro Español' (one of the most eminent geniuses of the Español).

Another account of the earlier period published during the Franco regime, Martínez Olmedilla's history of the Madrid theatres, displays an entirely hostile attitude towards the arrival of Borràs and his fellow Catalans in Madrid:

> Desdichada idea fue la de contratar a Enrique Borrás para actuar con Rosario Pino. El gran actor se había presentado poco antes en la Comedia al frente de su compañía catalana, y obtuvo un gran éxito, con asombro de sus paisanos, para los cuales no pasaba de ser un actor discreto. Por entonces intentó don Antonio Maura una política de atracción catalanista, y era frecuente en las ramblas atribuir a manejos del gran gobernante el triunfo de Borrás para captar adeptos con barretina. Aquello era absurdo, porque los aplausos tributados en Madrid al creador de *Terra baixa* fueron desinteresados en absoluto. Siempre se ha dicho que nadie es profeta en su tierra.
>
> Borrás, junto a Rosario Pino, hizo la triste figura. Negóse ella, con razón, a interpretar las obras de alpargata a todo trapo, que constituían el repertorio del actor catalán. Alegó éste que 'no le iban' las comedias que encantaban a Rosario. Se quiso hacer la prueba de verlos juntos . . .

Con Borràs vinieron los autores catalanes, todos desdeñosos con la odiada 'meseta central', pero ávidos, no obstante, de triunfar en Madrid. Santiago Rusiñol, Ignacio Iglesias, Pompeyo Crehuet y algún otro. Eran las suyas obras amargas, tenebrosas e irremisiblemente 'de alpargata'. Desentonaban en el ambiente de aquel teatro, hasta entonces aristo-crático. Hubo que traducir apresuradamente las obras catalanas. [. . .] Martínez Sierra hizo sus primeras armas teatrales agarrado a los faldones catalanistas de Rusiñol. *Tierra baja* ya estaba traducida por Echegaray. *La fiesta del trigo*,[23] también de Guimerá y 'de alpargata', no se pudo representar porque fue prohibida gubernativamente a causa de sus tendencias demoledoras. Al terminar aquella temporada, Borrás quedó consagrado y el abono de la Comedia respiró tranquilo.[24]

(It was a most unfortunate idea to contract Enric Borràs to act with Rosario Pino. The great actor had been at the Comedia just previously with his Catalan company, to the amazement of his fellow Catalans, for whom he was no more than a modest actor. At around that time, Antonio Maura was adopting policies to try to attract the Catalans, and it was common to hear in the Ramblas people attribute Borràs's triumph to the great politician's scheming attempts to get the Catalans on his side.[25] That was absurd, because the applause the creator of *Marta of the Lowlands* received in Madrid was completely disinterested. It has always been said that no one is a prophet in his own land.

Borràs, next to Rosario Pino, looked pathetic. She quite rightly refused to perform hick Catalan plays, which formed the repertoire of the Catalan actor. He said that the plays that Rosario loved did not suit him. People were keen to see them act together . . .

Borràs was accompanied by the Catalan playwrights, all of them scornful of the reviled 'centre of Spain', but desperate, none the less, to triumph in Madrid. Santiago Rusiñol, Ignasi Iglésies, Pompeu Crehuet, and one or two others. Their plays were all bitter, sombre and irredeemably hick. They were out of tune with the ambience of that theatre, which had been aristocratic until then. The Catalan plays had to be translated quickly. [. . .] Martínez Sierra cut his teeth hanging on to Rusiñol's Catalanist coat tails. *Marta of the Lowlands* was translated by Echegaray. 'The Wheat Festival', also by Guimerà, and hick, could not be performed because it was banned for its destructive tendencies.[26] At the end of the season, Borràs was acclaimed and the Comedia management breathed easily.)

One may contrast these sentiments with María Martínez Sierra's account of their bilingual creativity cited in Chapter 2. The above philippic also illustrates just what Catalonia lost during the Franco regime, as Catalans and Spaniards in general had to endure bland generalities of the 'una, grande y libre' variety. The question of whether Borràs belonged to Catalonia, to Madrid or to Spain had been genuinely polemical earlier in the century. The issue was raised by the author of another biography of the Catalan actor, Josep Maria Poblet, who writes: 'A Catalunya es considerava Borràs com una cosa nostra, lligada íntimament amb el nostre esperit'[27] (In Catalonia Borràs was considered to be ours, intimately connected with our spirit). Poblet quotes a contemporary Barcelona critic, Bernat i Duran who, when Borràs left Barcelona to establish his company in Madrid, claimed that the actor was a part of Catalonia, had always been appreciated in Barcelona and would always belong there and not in Madrid or anywhere else:

Borrás es sangre de nuestra sangre, vida de nuestra vida. Le profesamos querer tan grande, que, por mucho que le mimen y agasajen los madrileños, jamás nos igualarán. No es cierto que Borrás se ausente de Cataluña por no haber correspondido los catalanes a sus méritos ni haberle reconocido sus talentos. En Barcelona ha sido Borrás aplaudido infinidad de veces. Le hemos aclamado y llevado en triunfo, obsequiado con valiosísimos regalos y serenatas en las fiestas mayores. [. . .] Borrás es y será siempre nuestro. Su gloria no nos la arrebatará Madrid ni el mundo entero que se lo propusiera.[28]

(Borràs is our flesh and blood. We love him so much that, no matter how much the *madrileños* may spoil and pamper him, they will never equal us. It is not true that Borràs absents himself from Catalonia because the Catalans do not repay his merits or recognize his talents. Borràs has been applauded countless times in Barcelona. We have acclaimed him and carried him in triumph, given him expensive gifts and serenaded him at local festivals. [. . .] Borràs is and always will be ours. Madrid and the whole world could not snatch him from us even if they wanted to.)

As Poblet himself pointedly puts it:

Crítics i públic semblaven oblidar que Borràs ja n'havia fet molt, de teatre castellà, si bé esporàdicament, en temporades curtes. Però, és clar, gairebé sempre l'havia representat a Barcelona. Ara no, es deia la gent. Ara se'n va a Madrid.[29]

(Critics and audiences seem to forget that Borràs had done a lot of Spanish theatre, even if only occasionally and for short seasons. But of course, he had always performed it in Barcelona. Not now, people would say. Now he is going to Madrid.)

The question of whether the actor was Spanish or Catalan was raised by the author of his obituary in *ABC*. He quotes the writer and critic Felipe Sassone, who underlines his dual identity:

> Catalán y español de corazón y de raza, estas dos condiciones y cualidades, que no pueden excluirse una a otra, se juntaban en él hacia adentro y hacia afuera en el tierno amor al campanario de su rincón nativo y a la lengua de sus primeros balbuceos.[30]

> (Catalan and Spanish by birth and by inclination, these two conditions and qualities cannot be mutually exclusive and were combined in him inwardly and outwardly in his tender love for the church bell of his home town and the language of his first mutterings.)

It is hard to think of another European country in which the arrival of a 'provincial' actor in the nation's capital could cause such a polemic. That it should do in Spain is testimony both to the political sensitivity of the 'Catalan question', and also to the fact that such often acrimonious sensitivity was reflected in theatre reception.

As far as Borràs himself was concerned, in a long interview with *El Teatre Català* given during his 1913 season in Barcelona, he explained his attitude to the Catalan and Spanish theatre traditions. He described how, when Tirso Escudero contracted him to play a season in Madrid, he (Borràs) insisted it should be in the Catalan language:

> Ja veu, doncs, com els meus primers passos cap a Madrid foren per a honorar el Teatre Català, que és el teatre del qual sóc fill, el que mai he oblidaré.[31]

> (You can see, then, how my first steps towards Madrid were taken in order to honour Catalan theatre, of which I am a son and which I have never forgotten nor will I forget.)

Some people, says Borràs, viewed his decision to accept Escudero's offer to become the leading actor with Rosario Pino's company in 1905–6 to be an unpatriotic act. Borràs denies the accusation, and sees himself as a kind of ambassador for Catalonia and a representative of its theatre throughout Spain and in South America:

a tot arreu m'han rebut molt bé; a tot arreu, al brindar amb mi i al donar
visques a Espanya no s'han descuidat de cridar també *visca Catalunya!* I
jo els he representat, encara que traduides – perquè en el nostre idioma
no m'haurien entès – obres catalanes en demasia, i en festes a mi
dedicades els he recitat versos dels nostres poetes, i Catalunya,
representada per la meva humil paraula, s'ha sentit victorejada i jo he
experimentat una sensació, que, cregui, no pot imaginar-se-la qui no s'hi
hagi trobat. Que quan jo vaig per Espanya i per Amèrica fent comedia,
no hi va en Borràs sol sinó que amb ell hi van en Guimerà, en Rusiñol,
l'Iglesias, hi va tot Catalunya travessant fronteres i veient-se aclamada
per tots el públics.[32]

(I have been well received everywhere; and everywhere, when people have
toasted me and Spain, they have always remembered to toast Catalonia
too. And I have performed for them, albeit in translation – for they
would not have understood me in our language – very many Catalan
plays, and in festivals held in my honour I have recited our poets for
them, and Catalonia, represented by my humble speech, has been
acclaimed, and I have felt something which, believe me, cannot be
imagined by someone who has not felt it. When I tour in Spain and
Spanish America, Borràs does not go alone, but along with him go
Guimerà, Rusiñol, Iglésies, and the whole of Catalonia, crossing
frontiers and being acclaimed by audiences everywhere.)

He says he finds it impossible to present one repertoire in Castilian
and another in Catalan as only two of his company speak Catalan
even though some of them were born in Catalonia. In another piece
in the same number of *El Teatre Català*, Josep Artís considers that,
even if Borràs and Xirgu were to return to Catalonia, they could not
on their own solve the crisis in the Catalan theatre. Artís does not
think that Borràs's exile prejudices Catalan theatre, since his greatest
triumphs have been in plays written in Catalan and not in Spanish.[33]
    A much more hostile attitude towards Borràs is expressed in an
open letter to him by Vilaró i Guillemí, again in the 17 May 1913
number of *El Teatre Català*. In a polemical piece which is full of
nationalist rhetoric, Vilaró i Guillemí urges Borràs to become the
ambassador for Catalonia by taking Catalan plays to Europe. The
following extracts give a good idea of the sentiments and extremely
rhetorical tone of the open letter:

Cal pas sortir de Catalunya per saber-la estimar, però sí que cal trobar-
se'n fòra per anyorar-la i saber com és amarg obrir els ulls, de bon matí,

en una terra ont res us parla de la patria que deixàreu allà al lluny i que qui sab si tornareu a veure! [. . .] Sols vos podreu portar gloriosament pel món els nostres autors i fer ressonar en terres, de la nostra sols apartades per la distància, la llengua catalana [. . .] Digueu-me ara vos com seria triomfal la vostra caminada a travers de l'Europa portant el nostre teatre i les nostres obres en braços, com una garba de flors! [. . .] Un cop això haureu fet, un cop siga Catalunya prou coneguda a l'estranger, els catalans beneiràn el vostre nom a totes hores i la Patria besarà vostre front com el d'un fill predilecte.[34]

(You do not have to leave Catalonia to learn to love her, but you do have to go away to miss her and to learn how bitter it is to open your eyes, one fine day, in a country where nothing speaks to you of the fatherland which you left far behind and which you may never see again! [. . .] Only you can bear our authors gloriously around the world and make the Catalan language resound in far-distant lands [. . .] Tell me now how triumphant your journey across Europe would be if you were bearing our theatre and our plays in your arms, like a bouquet of flowers! [. . .] Once you have done it, once Catalonia is sufficiently well-known abroad, the Catalans will continually bless your name and the Fatherland will kiss your brow as a prodigal son.)

The sentimental tone here is exaggerated and the critic seems to lack any awareness of his uncritical stance. 'Patria' refers specifically to Catalonia, while the use of the capital letter merely highlights the nationalist sentiments of the piece, which must be set in the political context of developments within Catalonia. The date of its publication – 1913 – came at the end of a two-year campaign for the Mancomunitat, which was finally set up in 1914. The language question – intimately bound up with nationalism in Catalonia – had been the subject of an earlier piece by another critic of the early twentieth century, Prudencio Iglesias, in which he compares Borràs with the Sicilian actor Giovanni Grasso, seeing their regional/ national situations as similar, but pointing out that, unlike Borràs, Grasso continues to use his own 'dialect':

Nacido el uno en Sicilia, la fiera región de Italia; el otro en Cataluña, en España; ambos dejaron estallar las pasiones de la juventud, en ambos bravías, en el cálido verbo de aquellos dialectos de sus lenguas patrias. El caballero Grasso persiste en aquel hábito de la juventud, y pasea triunfante por los escenarios del mundo la lengua de Sicilia. Borrás ha escogido ya definitivamente como lenguaje, el que es suyo también, el castellano.[35]

(One of them was born in Sicily, that wild region of Italy; the other in Catalonia, in Spain; they both let the brave passions of youth explode in the emotional language of the dialects of their native lands. The gentleman Grasso persists in that youthful custom, and triumphantly shows off the language of Sicily in the theatres of the world. Borràs has made a permanent choice of language, which is his too: Spanish.)

The views of Vilaró i Guillemí in his 1913 article echoed similar sentiments in *La Renaixensa* when the news broke that Borràs was to move to Madrid. The paper comments sarcastically on the news that so-called high-ranking elements from the Catalan theatre world will go to Madrid, when the common view in Barcelona was that such elements were non-existent:

ROMEA A MADRID – Hem rigut molt ab una gazetilla. – Diu la gazetilla que'l senyor Borràs anirá a Madrid ab una companyía catalana constituhida per *elements d'altura.* – Ja feya be la vella. – Elements d'altura! – No havíam quedat en que no teníam cap barba, ni cap ingénua, ni cap galán jove, ni cap primera dama, ni cap primer actor, ni cap comparsa, ni cap apuntador? Afortunadament aqueixos ignots *elements d'altura* estaven amagats a l'obra, arraulits els uns contra els altres, esperant l'hora de la llum. Y l'hora de la llum ha vingut.[36]

(THE ROMEA IN MADRID – We have had a good laugh at a gossip column. – The gossip coulmn says that Mr Borràs will go to Madrid with a Catalan company made up of *important elements.* – That's a good one! – Important elements! – I thought we didn't have an older male character, or an ingénue, or a young gallant, or a leading lady, or a leading actor, or an extra, or a prompter. Fortunately, these unknown *important elements* were hidden away, huddled against each other, waiting for the day to dawn. And now the dawn has arrived.)

Nevertheless, such questions did not seem to bother the Barcelona theatre-going public. In its review of Borràs's season at the Romea in February 1924, in which, unlike Xirgu, he performed his normal repertoire (*Terra baixa, El místic*, plus *Edipus Rex*), *El Liberal* wrote of the public appreciation of and affection for him. According to the paper, there was wildly enthusiastic applause, and Guimerà (not long before his death) was led onto the stage by the company's actresses, also to great acclaim. Borràs seems to have been associated with a Catalan repertoire in a way Xirgu was not.[37] He played the old favourites, and his audiences lapped them up.

The dual identity of Borràs as Catalan and Spanish actor received a typically ironic treatment from one of the leading Catalan-language publications, *L'Esquella de la Torratxa*.[38] In a slightly barbed, tongue-in-cheek, even ambiguous opening to its review of the Borràs season, the reviewer writes

> Tenim en aquest teatre [the Romea] a l'Enric Borràs. Avui com avui, el més gran actor espanyol. I el més gran actor català, naturalment.[39]

> (We have Enric Borràs in this theatre [the Romea]. For the time being, he is the greatest Spanish actor. And the greatest Catalan actor, naturally.)

Although she played in joint functions with Borràs and indeed their two companies merged in 1919, Xirgu was in many ways diametrically opposed to her fellow Catalan. She was constantly pushing back frontiers, and trying new, often difficult plays. She was widely acclaimed, not only by critics, but also by those Spanish dramatists whose reputation she was in no small way responsible for making. García Lorca called her an 'actriz de inmaculada historia artística, lumbrera del teatro español'[40] (an actress with immaculate artistic record, genius of the Spanish theatre). Many other contemporary Spanish and European playwrights – including Benavente, Alberti, Casona, Unamuno, Lenormand and Pirandello – expressed their admiration for Xirgu's qualities as an actress.[41]

When when she left the Catalan stage for Madrid, she took longer to settle there than Borràs had done. This seems to have been, at least in part, because of her imperfect mastery of the Spanish language:

> Xirgu llegó de Barcelona a Madrid, como quien llega con una 'compañía extranjera'. Era ya una estrella en Cataluña. Y en catalán. 'Yo siempre hablé el catalán y mi teatro fue catalán. El castellano lo aprendía en poco tiempo, en menos de un año; pero figúrese usted ¡con qué miedo trabajaría las primeras veces! [. . .] ¡Horroroso!' (A *El Caballero Audaz*, en 1914). En Cataluña había crecido teatralmente de la mano de Adrià Gual, en el célebre 'Teatre Íntim'.[42]

(Xirgu went to Madrid from Barcelona, as if she were arriving with a foreign company. She was already a star in Catalonia. And in Catalan. 'I always spoke Catalan and my theatre was Catalan. I learned Spanish quickly, in less than a year; but just imagine how fearful I was in my early performances! [. . .] Dreadful!' (Interview with El Caballero Audaz in 1914). In Catalonia, she had cut her teeth in the theatre with Adrià Gual, in his famous Teatre Íntim.)

In general, however, the reception was warm, something which, according to Guansé, she had not expected.[43] Guansé describes how great efforts were made to help Xirgu acquire confidence in spoken Spanish when she first took up residence in Madrid, while at the same time she was always keen to be a good ambassador for Catalonia, no matter in which language she performed (pp. 42–3).

By the time she returned to play in Barcelona in the spring of 1914 she had acquired the status of a leading Spanish actress. Her season there gave rise to a more polemical response than had been provoked by Borràs's return a year earlier. However, as in Madrid, the reception was generally favourable, in both the Catalan-language press and the conservative Spanish-language press. *El Diario de Barcelona* writes proudly of her success in one of the plays she performed during the season, Dario Niccodemi's *L'Aigrette* :

Los días 28 y 29 [de mayo] dio dos funciones, por vez primera en Barcelona, la compañía dramática española de la primera actriz Margarita Xirgu. Había una gran expectación por ver a la eminente actriz catalana actuando al frente de una compañía castellana, con la cual había ya obtenido éxitos ruidosos en diversas provincias españolas, en las naciones sudamericanas y últimamente en Madrid. Y la señora Xirgu confirmó la fama que entre nosotros había alcanzado en la escena catalana y la de que venía precedida en el teatro castellano.
En *L'Aigrette*, sobre todo, se manifestó a la altura de las grandes actrices, miniaturizando la psicología femenil, en las principales situaciones, con toques admirables de observación y de arte.[44]

(On 28 and 29 May, the company of the leading actress Margarita Xirgu gave its first two performances in Barcelona. People were really looking forward to seeing the great Catalan actress performing at the head of a Spanish company, with which she had already obtained tumultuous hits in various Spanish provinces, in South America, and finally in Madrid.

And Señora Xirgu confirmed the reputation she had acquired here on the Catalan stage and which went before her in the Spanish theatre.

In *L'Aigrette*, above all, she showed that she is at the same level as the great actresses, portraying female psychology in great detail in the main situations, with admirable touches of observation and art.)

Times seem to have changed for the *Diario*. Despite their reservations about the play's moral content, they are fulsome in their praise of Xirgu. One may contrast this with their dismissive review of Wilde's *Salomé*, which Xirgu performed in Barcelona in 1910:

> En la primera decena de febrero se estrenó, vertida al catalán, *Salomé*, de Oscar Wilde, obra detestable por más de un concepto.[45]

> (During the first ten days of February she premiered, in Catalan translation, Oscar Wilde's *Salomé*, a detestable play in more than one respect.)

They do not even mention Xirgu by name in their *Salomé* review: perhaps the fact that by 1914 she had acquired fame outside Catalonia, and in particular in Madrid, has made them take notice of one of their own. This parallels the general impression in Madrid of Borràs: that he remained unrecognized by the Barcelona public and press until he had made his name in Madrid.

La Vanguardia, too, is complimentary about *L'Aigrette* : 'La actriz catalana, que representó en castellano, estuvo acertadísima. Diría que ha ganado en delicadeza su trabajo, en homgeneidad'[46] (The Catalan actress, performing in Spanish, was really sharp. I would say that her work is now more delicate and more even). *La Publicidad* is similarly impressed by Xirgu's acting. Following an exhaustive summary of the plot, the reviewer makes the following thoughtful and detailed comments on Xirgu's acting:

> Pose, gesto, vestidos y detalles los cuidó con tal cariño, que bien merece plácemes sinceros. La impresión que me produjo la señora Xirgu – sin asomos de adulación – fue la de una actriz que sin haber alcanzado aún la plenitud de su talento, ha mejorado en tercio y quinto desde que la aplaudiéramos en anteriores fechas. Se preocupa de llevar al teatro un reflejo natural de la vida sin acudir a los desplantes y necios recursos que suelen ofrecérsenos.

Y de que esto sea así y por serlo recoja aplausos y ovaciones, es cosa
que debe satisfacernos doblemente, que a fin de cuentas nuestra actriz
recibió la iniciación en esta bendita tierra.[47]

(She took such care over pose, gesture, costume and details that she
deserves our sincere congratulations. The impression I had of Señora
Xirgu – without any hint of adulation – was of an actress who, while not
yet having reached her peak, has improved by leaps and bounds since we
applauded her on previous occasions. She makes sure that she brings to
the theatre a true reflection of life without having recourse to rudeness or
stooping to the usual low tricks.

And we should be doubly satisfied by the fact that this should be so
and that she should be applauded and acclaimed as a result. After all, our
actress took her first steps in our blessed land.)

Once more, the image of the land is used in a hyperbolic fashion in
an article on Catalan theatre in the Barcelona press and is clearly a
sign of growing pride in Barcelona in the Catalan identity of their
stars.

Amichatis, on the other hand, writing in *El Día Gráfico* in 1914,
has somewhat mixed views on Xirgu, not so much for her acting as
for her Catalanness.[48] She belongs firmly to Catalonia, and her
youth was spent in a land which needed to demonstrate to the
outside world that its authors, politicians and actors were the best in
the world. In other words, it was a time when a resurgent Catalonia
was trying to reassert itself, and it needed people of the quality of
Xirgu to give it credence.

However, Amichatis finds that Xirgu's desire to rise in the world
gives her 'esa nota antipática y universal de los arrivistas' (that
unfriendly and universal characteristic of social climbers). Like
Dario Niccodemi, he writes, Xirgu seems to lack roots now. This
looks like a veiled criticism of her for leaving Catalonia and forming
her career in Madrid. She is a homely Catalan, and is not convincing
as a worldly international star:

Margarita Xirgu es catalana, tiene ese fondo de bondad, de aspereza y de
sencillez catalana. Es 'casolana', no puede, no debe andar por esos
vericuetos reservados para actrices que llevan una historia galante y
mundana, como base de sus triunfos teatrales. No puede Margarita
Xirgu, con toda su formidable fuerza de adaptación, vestir los ropajes de
la Réjane, de las actrices francesas. Fáltale esa mundanalidad, fáltale ver,

en la vida íntima, lo que en el teatro representa. Eso no puede verlo una actriz catalana, ni aún huyendo a París.

(Margarita Xirgu is Catalan, she has that fundamental Catalan kindness, harshness and simplicity. She is 'home-made' and cannot and must not follow the complicated route which is reserved for actresses whose stage triumphs are based on gallantry and high society. Despite her formidable powers of adaptation, Margarita Xirgu cannot wear the same costumes as Réjane or the French actresses.[49] She lacks that worldly quality, she cannot see, in her inner life, what that means for the stage. A Catalan actress cannot see it, even one who flees to Paris.)

Once more, Catalonia is associated with peasant values, and Catalans are deemed incapable of Parisian sophistication. Amichatis seems to resent the fact that Xirgu is gaining an international reputation and this sort of criticism suggests a much narrower vision on the part of some Barcelona critics than one might have expected. Like other eulogies of the Catalan soil already cited, the comment probably reflects the rejection by the now ascendant *noucentistes* of the 'northern', urban values associated with *modernisme* in favour of a more traditional Mediterraneanism.[50]

Vilaró i Guillemí, writing in *El Teatre Català* in the same year, is much more overtly critical of Xirgu for neglecting her Catalan roots and performing in Castilian.[51] We are familiar with this critic's rhetoric from his 1913 open letter to Borràs which was quoted earlier, but, whereas he urged the actor to be an ambassador of the beloved homeland, he accuses Xirgu of abandoning and despising her native Catalonia by performing only Spanish authors in the Spanish language. He compares her with Mimí Aguglia not for the usual reasons of acting quality but because both have betrayed their native lands – Sicily and Catalonia respectively. His tone is menacing, as he recalls that, the day after Aguglia had left Sicily, a black and red cross was placed at the door of her house there. He also refers to another, in his view, traitorous foreign actress, the Polish-born Edwige Mrozowska, who left Poland for Italy where she acted in Italian only to attempt to return to Poland later. However, according to Vilaró i Guillemí, she was rejected by the Polish public and obliged to abandon the stage. The author's conclusions are a mixture of menace and rhetoric, as he urges Catalan audiences to boycott Xirgu:

A Catalunya no hauríen de poguer recitar en altra llengua que la catalana, els artistes que'ns han deixat; no hi ha dret a befar-nos dintre de casa nostra mateix.

Ja que no som prou forts per a imposar un càstic, com fan en altres terres, tinguem al menys la dignitat de no anar a sentir-los si no vénen amb tot allò que a Catalunya tenim per més sagrat.

(The artists who have left us should be allowed to perform only in the Catalan language; they have no right to mock us in our own home.

Since we are not strong enough to impose a penalty, as they do in other countries, let us at least have the dignity not to go and hear them unless they come here with what we in Catalonia hold as most sacred.)

The tone of this article is aggressive, and once more reflects growing nationalist sentiments within Catalonia.[52]

The Catalan–Castilian debate is also aired by *L'Esquella de la Torratxa*, but, despite taking a similar line to Vilaró i Guillemí, *L'Esquella* makes the point obliquely and with irony: 'Tres funcions que constituiran tres solemnitats, doncs l'espectació per a admirar a la Xirgu en castellà es gran . . . entre'ls nostres catalanistes'[53] (Three performances which will constitute three solemn acts, for the anticipation of admiring Xirgu in Spanish is great . . . among our Catalanists). *L'Esquella* returns to the issue the following month, but this time at much greater length, more explicitly and without irony. In an article entitled 'La Xirgu, esperança nostra' (Xirgu, our hope), Yorick, having first praised her for her great qualities as an actress and having compared her with the Japanese actress Sada Yacco, who had captivated intelligent audiences the world over,[54] questions why Xirgu is not willing to include Catalan plays in her repertoire:

I nosaltres, fervents admiradors d'una i altra, ens preguntem: Perquè la nostra portentosa Marguerida es preocupa tant d'adaptar les seves sorprenents facultats a un teatre que no és el seu i a una llengua que no és la propia?

Es que la seva fama s'enxiquiria gens mostrant-se ingènua, escampant per l'estranger les flors perdudes del nostre repertori regional?

Perquè l'obsessió de l'idioma castellà l'esclavitza al punt – ella, tant catalana – de no volguer mai, no fòra de l'escena ni en l'intimitat, parlar en català per por del *rovellament*?

Aqueixa mania del castellà, segons afirma un notable crític madrileny, la perjudica al extrem d'obsessionar-la, a les mateixes taules, concentrant l'esperit en aqueixa injustificada temança, en detriment del reste de detalls.

I és una veritable llàstima que aqueixa basarda enguniegi a la nostra Xirgu, perque ningú, ni el més exigent espanyolista, pot dir d'ella que no *xafa* bé el castellà.

Temps a venir – i Déu vulgui que triguin forsa aqueixos temps – els veíns de Breda llegiran la consagració, la definitiva consagració de Marguerida Xirgu, la que únicament s'otorga després de la mort:
'Como artista, podía tener algún pequeño y perdonable defecto; pero su impecable pronunciación era un encanto, su límpido acento una maravilla. Al oirla nadie habría adivinado que aquella prodigiosa artista hubiese nacido en Cataluña'.

I els veíns de Breda en resteràn tots orgullosos i admirats.[55]

(As fervent admirerers of both ladies, we ask ourselves: why is our wonderful Margarita so concerned to adapt her surprising abilities to a theatre which is not hers and a language which is not her own?

Will her fame be diminished if she shows herself to be innocent, scattering abroad the lost flowers of our regional repertoire?

Does this obsession with the Spanish language enslave this most Catalan of ladies to the extent that she never wants to speak Catalan for fear it may be rusty – in private and away from the stage?

According to an important Madrid critic, she is so obsessed with Spanish that it adversely affects her, concentrating her mind on that unjustified fear to the exclusion of all else.

And it is a real pity that that fear should so trouble our Xirgu because no one, not even the most demanding Spanish specialist, can say that she does not speak Spanish well.

In the future – and, God willing, that will be a long time coming – the residents of Breda will read the dedication, the final dedication to Margarita Xirgu, the one that is permitted only after death:
'As an artist, she may have had a small and forgivable defect; but her impeccable pronunciation was a joy, her clear accent absolutely wonderful. You would never have guessed that that marvellous artist was born in Catalonia' (this paragraph is written in Spanish rather than in Catalan).

And the residents of Breda will be proud and full of admiration.)

J. Font de Boter, on the other hand, in his highly favourable *El Correo Catalán* review of *L'Aigrette*, simply points out that Xirgu went from Catalonia to

tierras lejanas. En ellas puede decirse que comenzó la metamórfosis de la actriz catalana en actriz castellana. Ha pasado un año y vuelve aquí consagrada por el público aplauso.[56]

(distant lands. It may be said that she began her metamorphosis from a Catalan to a Spanish actress there. She has spent a year there and she returns here consecrated by the public's applause.)

It is noticeable that this conservative Spanish-language daily does not censor Xirgu's change of tongue in the slightest, and, if Font de Boter is to be believed, the audience does not seem too bothered by it either. The only criticism the reviewer makes of Xirgu is when she tries to force her voice: she is better, he says, when she speaks naturally.

By the time Xirgu made a triumphant return to Barcelona in the mid-1930s, she was firmly established as an international star, and considered to be one of the best actresses in the history of the Spanish stage. The year 1935 was one of particular triumph for her in her native city, with the Barcelona premiere of García Lorca's polemical *Yerma*, her starring role in the revival of *Bodas de sangre* (*Blood Wedding*) and the Spanish premiere of *Doña Rosita la soltera* (*Doña Rosita the Spinster*). The reviews of *Yerma* will be considered in Chapter 6, but one should note that several newspapers had articles about her and interviews with her during the period when she was performing the García Lorca plays in the city. One such article appeared in *L'Esquella de la Torratxa* in November 1935, on the occasion of the announcement of the revival of *Bodas de sangre* at the Principal Palace. The article praises her and her choice of quality repertoire, but its main point seems to be to emphasize that Barcelona always welcomes quality:

> S'ha defensat amb obres dignes, i, en els moments pitjors per al teatre de Castella, ve a Barcelona després d'actuar a Madrid, amb un repertori de poetes i d'autèntics escriptors.
>
> I Barcelona li ha respost amb 'Yerma' i amb 'Fuenteovejuna', com la tornarà a respondre amb 'Bodas de sangre', teatre de dignitat i d'art, fet per qui sap què fa.
>
> Barcelona respon sempre, quan una actriu i una companyia se li presenta amb entusiasme i sense concessions.[57]

(She has got by with good plays, and, at the worst moment for the theatre of Castile, she comes to Barcelona after performing in Madrid, with a repertoire of poets and genuine writers.

And Barcelona has responded to her with *Yerma* and *Fuenteovejuna*, as it will respond again with *Blood Wedding*, which is dignified, artistic drama, by someone who knows what he is doing.

Barcelona always responds when an actress and a company performs before it with enthusiasm and without making any concessions.)

However, the attitude here appears to be defensive, as if the fact that Xirgu is now a really big star on the Spanish stage could be a threat to Barcelona's hegemony in matters of quality. Another, more bitter, article on Xirgu's abandonment of Barcelona for Madrid had been written by the Catalan art critic and defender of the avant-garde, Sebastià Gasch, in 1934.[58] Reporting on her 1934 season, he criticized various elements of her diction and declamatory style, but it is probable that Gasch's frustration with what he saw as Xirgu's desertion of Catalan theatre at a time when she was sorely needed in Barcelona was at the heart of his criticism.

As well as the question of how Xirgu is viewed in Barcelona, during her high-profile 1935 season Catalan journalists questioned her on how she viewed the use of Catalan in the theatre. In an interview with *La Rambla de Catalunya* in 1935 she makes it clear that the focus of her attention is on plays written in Spanish. In response to the question 'I si algun dia, temps a venir, hom reclamava el vostre talent, el vostre esforç, a benefici de l'escena catalana, què faríeu?' (And if one day in the future your talent and your effort are required for the benefit of the Catalan stage, what would you do?), she declares firmly that she would find it very difficult to abandon Castilian theatre:

> Pel rostre sereníssim de Margarida Xirgu passen les ombres de la perplexitat. Ens adonem, però, que l'actriu és incapaç de trair el seu pensament íntim. I, greument, ens diu:
> – Em costaria molt, molt, de desintegrar-me del teatre espanyol. Ho considero gairebé impossible. Vint-i-dos anys de contacte amb Castella! Penseu que em sento entranyablement lligada als pics de Gredos. Penseu que la visió d'Avila, per exemple, desperta dintre meu tots els ressorts de l'emoció . . .
> Per a nosaltres, les paraules de la senyora Xirgu, dites amb el to que ho han estat, no tenen rèplica. Així és que no se'ns acut altra cosa sinó dir:
> – Es llàstima.[59]

(Shadows of doubt cover Margarita Xirgu's serene expression. However, we realize that the actress is incapable of betraying her innermost thoughts. And, gravely, she tells us: 'It would be very difficult for me to break loose from Spanish theatre. I think it would be almost impossible.

Twenty-two years in contact with Castile! You must realize that I feel inextricably attached to the Gredos Peaks and that the vision of Avila, for instance, awakens within me all kinds of emotional stimuli . . .

As far as we are concerned, there is no answer to Senyora[60] Xirgu's words, spoken in the tone she has used. All we can say is: 'That's a shame'.)

Her identification with Castile is ironic in the light of her difficulties with the language when she first arrived in Madrid. She is also somewhat defensive in response to the interviewer's question as to why she performs only outdated Catalan plays when she does perform in her native language in Barcelona. The reason she gives is the lack of time to learn and rehearse new plays: performances are always improvised and hurried, she asserts. The exigencies of the commercial stage in Spain were such that companies worked in difficult conditions, often giving two daily performances. There was very little state subsidy for the theatre, making it especially difficult for creative practitioners, faced with the understandable demands of impresarios for marketable plays, to be able to develop their ideas or to experiment.

Indeed, in the same interview, Xirgu makes it clear that her heart lies not only with Spanish theatre, but also with the Spanish Republic, since she felt that, at last, there was some possibility of change. Previously, she claims, not a single peseta had been given to the theatre, whereas under the new government the situation had changed completely, a view confirmed by Rivas Cherif, who is also present at the interview and whose views on the kind of 'popular' audiences who are attracted to the theatre confirm Xirgu's own and are consonant with what García Lorca often said on the subject:

– [. . .] A nosaltres el gran públic, el públic popular, ens ha tractat sempre molt bé.

Ara el senyor Rivas Cherif intervé amb vivacitat, com aquell qui toca un tema que porta arrapat a l'ànima.

– El públic popular, cal dir-ho una i mil vegades, és allò millor que té Espanya. En totes les nostres actuacions, davant d'aquest públic hem trobat sempre una comprensió total, un entusiasme artístic remarcable.

– I allò que en diuen classes altes . . .

– A les classes altes – respon el senyor Rivas Cherif – no els interessa el teatre.

(We have always been very well treated by 'popular' audiences.

Now Senyor Rivas Cherif joins in with great liveliness, like someone who is dealing with a topic which is very close to his heart.

'The "popular" public, it has to be repeated a thousand and one times, is the best thing we have in Spain. We have always found total understanding and a remarkable artistic enthusiasm when we have performed before this public.'

'And what about the upper classes . . .?'

'The upper classes', replies Senyor Rivas Cherif, 'are not interested in the theatre.')

This was precisely the sort of radicalization of the theatre which distressed Marsillach in his 1933 article, considered in Chapter 2. Rivas Cherif had learned about Xirgu at Martínez Sierra's *tertulia*. He saw in her 'la única capaz de afrontar con decisión y posibilidades artísticas la aventura de la dignificación de la escena profesional'[61] (the only one with artistic possibilities capable of taking on the challenge of adding dignity to the professional stage decisively). Aguilera and Aznar sum up the contribution of talented individuals like Rivas and Xirgu who had to battle against all the defects which typified the Spanish theatre in the 1930s:

La colaboración entre Margarita Xirgu y Rivas Cherif, que abarca desde septiembre de 1930 hasta julio de 1936, iba a dominar cinco temporadas consecutivas en el teatro Español de Madrid, complementadas con importantes ciclos de representaciones en Barcelona, donde tuvieron lugar algunos estrenos importantes, y giras incansables por toda la geografía española. Esos cinco intensos años marcaron, sin duda, una de las etapas más brillantes de la vida escénica de nuestro país. Etapa que, ciertamente, se vio constreñida en sus logros por las deficiencias técnicas inherentes a un escenario anticuado, mal dotado de los recursos técnicos necesarios para una moderna concepción del espectáculo teatral, sin una infraestructura mínima para la disposición de tramoyas, escenografías y cambios rápidos de escenario habituales desde hacía tiempo en los principales teatros europeos, con una iluminación deficiente y arcaica; pero que, a su vez, estuvo avalada por una cuidadosa selección del repertorio, alejado del éxito fácil, para dar entrada a las obras más significativas del teatro clásico y moderno español, que alternaron con espectáculos representativos del teatro extranjero contemporáneo; por el espaldarazo ofrecido a jóvenes valores de la talla de Lorca, Casona o Alberti; por el cuidado con que se atendió la puesta en escena, con montajes, dados los recursos disponibles, espectaculares, tanto en escenarios convencionales como al aire libre, gracias al trabajo escenográfico de Fontanals, Burmann, Mignoni, Bartolozzi y Miguel Xirgu; por la calidad, en fin, de las propias representaciones, en las que la capacidad interpretativa se unía a la eficacia de la dirección escénica, tan poco habitual en el panorama teatral del momento.[62]

(The collaboration between Margarita Xirgu and Rivas Cherif, which covers the period from September 1930 to July 1936, dominated five consecutive seasons in Madrid's Teatro Español, complemented by important play cycles in Barcelona, where some significant premieres took place, and endless tours over the whole of Spain. These five intensive years were undoubtedly one of the most brilliant periods in the history of the Spanish theatre. A period whose achievements were constrained by the technical difficulties inherent in an antiquated stage, poorly endowed with the technical resources which are essential in the modern theatre, with a minimal infrastructure for the arrangement of stage machinery, scenery and rapid scene changes which had been common for many years in the main European theatres, with deficient and archaic lighting; but which was supported by a carefully selected repertoire, eschewing easy success, and bringing to the stage the principal classical and modern plays of Spain, which alternated with representative contemporary foreign drama; by the official support offered to young writers of the stature of García Lorca, Casona and Alberti; by the care devoted to staging what were, given the available resources, spectacular productions, in conventional and open-air theatres, thanks to the design work of Fontanals, Burmann, Mignoni, Bartolozzi and Miguel Xirgu; by the quality, in short, of the productions themselves, in which acting ability was combined with an effective direction which was so unusual in contemporary Spanish theatre.)

In the end, at least in some sections of society, Xirgu, like Borràs, was recognized as belonging to both Catalonia and Spain. In the words of the headline to her obituary in *Semana*: 'Ha muerto una gloria teatral de Cataluña y España'[63] (A heroine of Catalan and Spanish theatre has died). A writer of another obituary went a step further, describing her as 'una catalana de talla universal' (a Catalan of universal stature).[64] As the next three chapters will demonstrate, Xirgu was a key figure in raising the quality of the theatre in Barcelona, Madrid and elsewhere in the Hispanic world, whether she was performing Catalan, Spanish or foreign plays.

Foreign Theatre in Madrid and Barcelona

By the 1930s, thanks to the efforts of the likes of Xirgu and Rivas Cherif, who positively relished the challenge of new and difficult foreign plays as well as drama by the best young Spanish playwrights, Spain was at the forefront of Western theatre. However, one must guard against thinking that it was only in the 1930s that new foreign theatre was accessible to Spanish audiences. This was also the case earlier in the century and, as one critic puts it, 'el acceso al teatro extranjero constituyó uno de los principales cauces para la modernización de la escena española del primer tercio del siglo XX'[1] (access to foreign theatre was one of the principal channels for the modernization of the Spanish stage in the first third of the twentieth century). In this chapter the reception of a selection of specific plays and the impact produced by a unique ballet company will be discussed. As the chapter will also demonstrate, Barcelona and the Catalans played a key role in the diffusion and the modernization process in Madrid as well as in Barcelona.

Here we are not necessarily concerned with plays that were most popular with audiences but with the sort of – often minority – drama which changed theatre both inside and outside Spain.[2] The plays have been selected both to represent different dramatic styles and also to enable discussion of what the impact some of the most innovative foreign playwrights had in Madrid and Barcelona reveals about the theatrical environment in the two cities. Ibsen has been chosen as the most revolutionary playwright of the late nineteenth century, and one who especially caught the imagination in Barcelona. Wilde's *Salomé* has been selected for two reasons: because of its status as the most representative play in the non-naturalist mode during the period under discussion, and because Margarita Xirgu is the actress most associated with its production, both in Catalan and Spanish. The theatrical avant-garde of the 1920s and 1930s is represented by the German expressionist Georg Kaiser. Xirgu, Burmann and Rivas Cherif were all instrumental in the Madrid productions of two works of Kaiser.[3]

Exposure to foreign theatre in Madrid and Barcelona

A commonplace view is that Spanish theatre lagged behind that of the rest of Europe at the turn of the century. This is true to the extent that, as Chapter 1 demonstrated, the theatre in Spain lacked resources, was slow to introduce technical innovations and was in hock to the commercial interests of impresarios. However, it is untrue that Spain was not exposed to the outside theatre world or that its theatre practitioners were not *au fait* with developments in other countries. As Rubio has noted:

> De entrada, hay que acabar con la falsa idea de que existía retraso y aislamiento de la producción teatral en la península respecto a otros países europeos. Nada más lejos de la realidad. El sistema de producción teatral era deficiente y poco dado a novedades, pero no faltaron iniciativas de las minorías intelectuales españolas para conocer las nuevas tentativas escénicas y difundirlas en España.[4]

> (One has to begin by scotching the false idea that theatre production in the Iberian Peninsula was backward and isolated compared with other European countries. Nothing is further from the truth. The theatre production system was deficient and not open to new ideas, but the intellectual minorities in Spain were not afraid to undertake initiatives in order to get to know new trends in the theatre and disseminate them in Spain.)

Rubio's point, quoted in Chapter 1, that it was an intellectual minority who attempted to expose the Spanish theatre-going public to foreign plays, is largely true, although there were a number of ways in which Madrid and Barcelona audiences could become acquainted with them: the presence of touring theatre companies, mainly from France and Italy, normally playing in their native languages; translations into Spanish and Catalan of foreign works, some of which were performed but the majority of which were not; and press articles by informed individuals.

The Princesa Theatre was a focal point for visiting French companies. Sarah Bernhardt's company was there in October and November 1895 and November 1899. Félix Huguenot's company visited in April 1913, Cécile Sorel was there in 1899 and Albert Brasseur and Jean Coqueline in May 1916. Italian companies were also regular visitors to both Madrid and Barcelona in the late nineteenth and early twentieth centuries. The companies of such internationally known actors as Novelli, Zacconi and Grasso performed not only Italian plays, but also works by Spanish, Catalan and foreign playwrights. Novelli brought Ibsen's *Ghosts* (*Spettri*) to Barcelona in 1894, while Zacconi performed it in both cities in 1901. Grasso did *Juan José* in Barcelona and Madrid in 1907, while, as we saw in Chapter 2, Rusiñol wrote *Llibertat!* (*Freedom!*) for Italia Vitaliani, who premiered it in Italian translation in Barcelona in 1901.

In general, as Bonzi and Busquets demonstrate, the Italians were a lot more active in Barcelona than they were in Madrid during the first decade of the twentieth century.[5] Despite the presence of foreign (particularly French) companies in Madrid, this is what one would have expected since, as Chapter 1 demonstrated, Catalan intellectuals were steeped in European culture, and keen to promote internationalism as part of a new national consciousness. It was often through Catalonia that foreign theatre – and foreign culture more widely – became known in Spain.[6]

Wagner's concept of total theatre was particularly attractive to the Catalan *modernistes*, and Barcelona's Liceu Theatre became one of the principal Wagnerian centres in Europe. As was noted earlier, the production of Maeterlinck's *L'Intruse* at Rusiñol's *Festes Modernistes* in Sitges in 1892 is generally perceived as marking the penetration of symbolism into the Spanish theatre.[7] Regarding Zola, Ibsen and Maeterlinck, one critic's view is that, in contrast to Madrid,

> en Barcelona, los autores que adaptan las fórmulas de Zola, Ibsen o de Maeterlinck tenían algún público, ya que las obras tomaban acentos locales, dispuestas a expresar un regionalismo afirmado o una reivindicación social.[8]

> (in Barcelona there was an audience for playwrights who adapted the formulae of Zola, Ibsen or Maeterlinck, since their plays adopted local accents, and were prepared to give expression to a strong sense of regionalism or to social demands.)

Ibsen and Hauptmann had a particularly strong following in Catalonia, with several of their plays being performed in Barcelona at the turn of the century, mainly in Catalan.[9]

The awareness of European theatre in general and of these two dramatists in particular was due in no small measure to the efforts of the prolific Catalan critic and writer Josep Yxart. His was not the only press criticism of European theatre in the Spanish press of the period, and *La España Moderna*, in particular, frequently published articles on the subject by the likes of Unamuno, Gómez Barquero and Villegas. However, the chief source of information was Yxart, who wrote widely not only on European theatre but also on Catalan and Spanish drama. According to one of his contemporaries, Yxart was undoubtedly the leading contemporary Spanish critic,[10] while a 1982 study considers him to be the only person in Spain during his lifetime to be au fait with European theatre.[11] Another scholar regards his *Lo teatre català* (1878) as the first Catalan text to use the theories of Hegel and Taine in its analysis of Catalan theatre.[12] Yxart was a staunch defender of naturalism in the theatre, and a particularly keen advocate of Ibsen and Zola. He was not favourably disposed towards symbolist drama and, in complete contrast to the *modernistes*, had a particular aversion to Maeterlinck. He wrote in both Catalan and Spanish, his 1894 *El arte escénico en España (Scenic Art in Spain)* being especially widely read and influential. His critical views on the state of the contemporary Spanish theatre are summed up in the following passage:

En España, [. . .] un drama no es bello o detestable: es moral o inmoral, antes que todo. Para esa crítica, el género francés es, ya de antiguo, inmoral por sí . . . España y Francia pertenecen a dos latitudes, no ya diferentes, sino opuestas.[13]

(In Spain [. . .] a play is not beautiful or horrible: above all it is moral or immoral. For this type of critic French drama has long been intrinsically immoral . . . Spain and France belong to two spheres which are not just different but poles apart.)

Yxart also believed that innovations were taking place in the dramatic style of playwrights from other countries which were passing Spain by. Apropos of Hauptmann he writes:

Sin sentimentalismo alguno, conmueve tan sólo con el espectáculo del dolor presente; sin teorías ni tipos declamadores, presenta los verdaderos y distintos caracteres que intervienen hoy en la lucha social, resaltando con gran relieve, rebosando de vida.[14]

(With no sentimentality whatsoever, he moves one just through the spectacle of the grief that is present; with no theories or declamatory types he presents the authentic and varied characters who take part in the social struggle, standing out boldly, overflowing with life.)

Hauptmann was one of the most-performed foreign playwrights at Adrià Gual's Teatre Íntim. *Drayman Henschel* and *The Weavers* were put on in 1902, Margarita Xirgu played the lead role in *The Sunken Bell* in 1907, while *The Assumption of Hannele* and *Rosa Berndt* were performed in 1905 and 1908 respectively. Gual's choice of plays is interesting, as the naturalistic, socially critical Hauptmann is included along with plays in the symbolist idiom like *The Sunken Bell*. Gual was probably the major protagonist as far as actual performances of foreign plays are concerned, directing productions in which figures like Xirgu and innovative stage designers cut their teeth. According to one critic, Gual's production of *The Sunken Bell* represents a pro-European, sophisticated cultural renewal on the part of the Catalan bourgeoisie, and was watched by the sort of refined public who supported *modernisme* in architecture and the decorative arts.[15]

Naturalism in the theatre was better represented in other centres of a turn-of-the-century Barcelona hungry for novelty. Harsher examples than Gual's Hauptmann were the productions by Anarchist-inspired amateur theatre groups. Ibsen was probably their favourite playwright and *A Doll's House* received its Spanish premiere by one such group in 1896. *When We Dead Awake* and *The Pillars of Society* were performed in Catalan translation at the Teatre de les Arts in 1901, while the Avenir groups put on *Romersholm* in Felip Cortiella's Catalan translation at the Circo Español Theatre during the 1904–5 season. A contemporary reviewer, the influential Luis Araquistáin, linked its performance in Barcelona in 1915 with public concern over the condition of the River Llobregat, which enters the sea in Barcelona and which was believed to be responsible for a typhus epidemic in the city.[16]

Although Barcelona was dominant as far as the penetration of foreign theatre into Spain is concerned, there are instances of productions in Madrid. An early – but seemingly isolated – example of Zola's influence is *La taberna* (The Tavern), José Pina Domínguez's adaptation of *L'Assommoir*, which was performed at the Teatro de Novedades in Madrid in 1883.[17] In discussing the premiere, the *El Imparcial* critic reported that the play went down well with the audience, who were not as shocked by it as one would have expected. It is not, he declares, a typical Zola work, and in any case, many of the audience were already familiar with the novel. The reviewer finds that, like many melodramas based on novels, *La taberna* lacks a smooth structure, and that the transition between scenes is too brusque. In short:

> La obra podrá ser más o menos digna de censura, pero desde luego digna de ser vista y propia para excitar la curiosidad del público. Mucho nos engañamos o será para el empresario uno de los negocios más *realistas* de la presente temporada teatral.[18]

> (The play may or may not be worthy of censure, but of course it is worth seeing and just right to excite the audience's curiosity. If we are not very much mistaken, it will be one of the most *realist* box-office successes of the current season.)

The reviewer was sharply aware that, although the play may or may not be worthy of censorship, this particular venture represented not brave artistic experimentation but an opportunity for a good box-office return.

Ibsen

As a specific example of probably the major European dramatist of this period, I shall now consider two productions of Ibsen's *John Gabriel Borkmann*. As one would expect, a relatively early production took place in Barcelona within the Teatre Íntim's 1903 programme. M. y G.'s intelligent review in *La Ilustració Catalana* views it as an uneven play, but praises the quality of the production and the translation:

> Com en bona part de les produccions de d'Ibsen, lo que dona major interés a 'Joan Gabriel Borkman' no es precisament el drama que's desenrotlla a la vista del espectador, sinó'ls acontexaments que l'han precedit y dels quals es conseqüència [. . .] La traducció del senyor Roca y Capull acabadíssima y realisada ab ple conexement del original y de la llengua pròpia. Traductors de conciencia com ell son els que calen pera fer conèxer al nostre públich les obres d'altres paíssos.[19]

(As with many Ibsen productions, what lends *John Gabriel Borkmann* its main interest is not really the drama which unfolds before the spectator but rather the events which have preceded it and which control it. [. . .] Senyor Roca y Capull's translation is most polished and done with full knowledge of the original and of his own language. Conscientious translators like him are what are needed for our audiences to become familiar with plays from other countries.)

The reviewer's more general point about the need for high-quality translations of this sort to enable the Catalan public to become familiar with the theatre of other countries reflects the avid desire for new theatre that was typical of *modernisme*.

Other Barcelona newspapers generally praised both the play and the production. M.J.B., for instance, claims that the standard of the production was what one would expect from Gual: thoughtful and with careful attention to detail.[20] J.M. is impressed by Ibsen's masterful portrayal of Borkmann's struggle against his own impotence and solitude and by his immensely humane depiction of character.[21] N.N., however, is much more critical of Ibsen, accusing him of lacking discretion.[22] This review also contains a racial element, in the critic's view of the differences between Ibsen's and the Catalans' way of thinking:

L'obra en conjunt es producte de un art exótich, qual mérit no discutim; pero que está y estará sempre molt lluny de la nostra especial manera de pensar y de sentir. (p. 775)

(The work as a whole is the product of an exotic art, whose merit we are not questioning, but which is and will always be very far from our own special way of thinking and feeling.)

In common with all the other Barcelona reviewers, N.N. is impressed with the quality of the stage design by two important Catalan designers who, unlike Fontanals, remained in Barcelona: Miquel Moragas and Salvador Alarma.

It was not until much later that *John Gabriel Borkmann* was performed in Madrid.[23] As was observed earlier, a number of small alternative theatre ventures took place in Madrid in the 1910s. It was in the context of one of these, Ricardo Baeza's Atenea, that *John Gabriel Borkmann* was performed at the Princesa Theatre, in 1919, directed by Baeza himself.[24] Miquis described it as a serious enterprise on the part of Baeza and Miguel Muñoz.[25] The audience, he claimed, was generally attentive (with one or two exceptions). Miquis considered it a difficult play for Spaniards because of the very different environment in which it was set and the exotic figures and situations it evoked. He felt that it was well translated and acted, and praised the naturalness of the acting, a quality in short supply in Spain.

ABC's Floridor felt the work to be a 'prodigio de sobriedad y de técnica'[26] (a miracle of sobriety and technique). He saw it as an example of modern theatre, declaring that the Princesa had inaugurated 'su ciclo de teatro moderno en la más legítima expresión del concepto' (its modern theatre cycle in the most legitimate sense of the word). It seems odd to see Ibsen described as ultra-modern in 1919, but the comments perhaps indicate just how unused to seeing new foreign theatre the Madrid public was. Floridor suggests as much in the concluding paragraph of his review: 'La actitud del público fue en conjunto de interés [. . .] Es lógico, dadas las pocas ocasiones que tiene de admirar las obras maestras') (The audience was generally interested [. . .] This is understandable, given the few occasions they have to admire great works).

Manuel Machado, one of the most astute theatre critics of the time, as well as a leading poet, also highlights the fact that Spain lags behind the rest of Europe as far as its exposure to modern drama is concerned:

[La Empresa de Arte 'Atenea'] viene a intentar aquí, en los primeros días de la post-guerra, lo que allá por los años de mil novecientos noventa y tantos realizaba en París el teatro de l'Oeuvre, con Lugné-Pöe a la cabeza: una revisión general del teatro mundial para dar a conocer las grandes obras de los distintos países en la capital del mundo civilizado.[27]

(At the end of the [First World] War [the Arte Atenea Company] will be attempting here what L'Œuvre, led by Lugné-Pöe, was doing in Paris in the 1890s: a general revision of world theatre with the aim of introducing to the capital of the civilized world great works from different countries.)

Machado was extremely sympathetic to Baeza's project, and praised the translation, acting and *mise-en-scène*. He saw the Atenea as an oasis of artistic taste in the cultural wilderness that constituted the theatre scene in Spain. As far as the symbolism of *John Gabriel Borkmann* is concerned, Machado comments that it can be extremely simple – he approves of this and contrasts the simplicity with the way some Spanish intellectuals give what is vulgar and ordinary an undeservedly inflated importance. The most thorough review of *John Gabriel Borkmann* was José Alsina's in *El Sol*. He calls Ibsen the father of modern theatre and comments on how the production gripped the Princesa audience. He is especially complimentary about Mignoni's stage designs, which he felt captured the spirit of the play perfectly.[28] A much less intelligent appreciation of Ibsen is Manuel Bueno's 'Ibsen en España', which was part of 'Páginas teatrales' of *ABC*.[29] Bueno is hazy about Ibsen's introduction into Spain, claiming that he never really gelled with the Spanish people and was always a minority taste there. For Bueno, Ibsen represents individualism at a time when socialism is growing: he asserts that Spaniards are an outward-looking people and consequently not interested in the inner consciousness or in philosophical issues. These views border on the comic, and lack the serious and well-informed analysis of contemporary reviewers such as Miquis, Manuel Machado or Díez-Canedo. His conclusion – with its absurd racial stereotypes – is a case in point:

> Aquí no hay vida interior, porque no hay problemas trascendentales. El clima, las mujeres, la religión y el vino se oponen a que el español contraiga ese mareo filosófico, que es el martirio de los personajes de Ibsen. Asociémonos, pues a su gloria, pero reconociendo que no es intelectualmente mucho más extraño que Buda, porque, al fin, Buda es, ante todo, el dios de la pereza, y la pereza es aquí una virtud nacional.

> (There is no inner life here, because there are no momentous problems. Our climate, our women, our religion and our wine militate against the Spaniards' contracting this philosophical sickness, which torments Ibsen's characters. Let us share, then, in his glory, but let us also recognize that intellectually he is not much stranger than Buddha since, when all is said and done, Buddha is the god of laziness and laziness here is a national virtue.)

According to Gregersen, it would appear that this was the typical view of Scandinavian literature in Latin countries: 'this marked antipathy to what the Latins popularly regard as the dominant note of Scandinavian literature (i.e. its gloominess)'.[30] This perceived attitude is in marked contrast to that of the Catalan *modernistes*, which would account for the earlier and much more enthusiastic acceptance of Ibsen in Barcelona than in Madrid. We should also note the following comments of the Catalan Pompeu Gener, who translated *Ghosts* into Spanish:

> Sin ser, precisamente, un drama *a tesis*, Los Espectros de Ibsen defienden una causa tan noble como la de la buena procreación, por medio de las condiciones adecuadas y del amor en las uniones sexuales, presentando en escena los desastrosos resultados de estas nefandas uniones legales registradas por el Estado y bendecidas por la Religión, pero exentas de amor y de condiciones de vida, resultados agravados por el miramiento a las conveniencias sociales y a las preocupaciones públicas.
>
> Así se explica el entusiasmo que este drama ha producido en todos los públicos ilustrados de Europa y de América. En vano que la censura inglesa lo haya prohibido con hipocresía protestante: hasta en la misma Inglaterra ha sido introducido y leído con avidez por todos los que piensan y sienten libremente. En Francia, en Italia, en Alemania y aun en Rusia, se han agotado varias ediciones de Los Espectros, a más de la innumerables representaciones, que ha tenido sobre la escena.
>
> Nosotros creemos haber hecho un bien a España y a los países americanos de lengua española al traducir el presente drama de Ibsen, dirigido al mejoramiento de nuestra especie sobre el planeta.[31]

(Although it is not exactly a thesis play, Ibsen's *Ghosts* defends a cause as noble as that of decent procreation, through adequate conditions and love in sexual union, by presenting on stage the disastrous results of those heinous legal unions registered by the State and blessed by the Church, but lacking love and living conditions, results which are aggravated by regard for social convenience and public opinion.

This explains the enthusiasm which this play has elicited amongst all the erudite audiences in Europe and America. The English censors, acting with Protestant hypocrisy, have banned it in vain: it is being circulated even in England and is being read avidly by all free thinkers. In France, Italy, Germany and even in Russia several editions of *Ghosts* have gone out of print, and the play has been performed on countless occasions.

We believe we have done Spain and Spanish America a favour by translating Ibsen's play, which is aimed at the improvement of our human race.)

In a 1920 review of the play, Critilo declares that it is still very difficult to see an Ibsen play put on in Spanish.[32] The most performed Ibsen plays, according to this critic, are *Ghosts* and *A Doll's House*, while a very poor production of *John Gabriel Borkmann* had been put on recently (p. 13). However, las obras restantes, entre las que están las mejores, son aún desconocidas de nuestro público, aunque ya pueden leerse en traducciones, a veces aceptables [. . .]Enrique Ibsen, es poco menos que desconocido entre nosotros. (pp. 13–14)

(our audiences are still unfamiliar with the remaining plays, although they may be read in translations which are sometimes acceptable [. . .] . Heinrik Ibsen is almost unknown here.)

In Barcelona, on the other hand, Ibsen was already considered to be passé by the 1920s, as reviews of an Ibsen centenary production of *Solness* in 1928 demonstrate.[33]

The Ballets Russes

Of all the foreign companies to visit Spain, the one which had the most profound effect on the avant-garde minority not only of theatre people but more generally of writers and artists was not a theatre company in the traditional sense but Serge Diaghilev's Ballets Russes. The involvement in the group of avant-garde writers, artists and composers of the stature of Cocteau, Picasso, Stravinsky and Satie is well documented. Productions like *Parade* and *Petruchka* suggested ways in which the theatre might break with naturalism in a radical and striking way. Picasso's designs for *Parade*, for instance, indicated the new directions that design could take and pointed the way for the involvement in stage design of two great Catalan avant-garde artists, Salvador Dalí and Joan Miró.[34]

The extension into dance, spectacle and music is indicative of a move against naturalism in the theatre in Western cultures in general during the late nineteenth and early twentieth centuries. Spanish audiences were used to a blend of dance, music and speech in the *zarzuela*, *género chico* and gypsy flamenco traditions,[35] but the Ballets Russes were a new phenomenon. They were, of course, central to the growth of interest in ballet as an avant-garde art form in Europe, and a number of Spanish writers explored the liberating possibilities of dance. In Gómez de la Serna's plays, for example, dance and mime are vehicles for the release of suppressed sexuality. Dance and mime are intimately connected in his one-act pantomime *La bailarina*, which contains a constant juxtaposition of female sexuality and virginity, free movement and constraint, and dream and disillusion. Linguistic logic is frequently broken, and mime is juxtaposed to lyricism.[36] As one would expect, other men of the theatre to show an interest in the Ballets Russes were Gual and Rivas Cherif. In a *La Veu de Catalunya* article, Gual claims that he is not terribly familiar with their work, but, from what he has seen, 'la característica dels seus conjunts, serà la vibració dels sons, de tons i de moviments excelsament combinats'[37] (the characteristic feature of their ensembles is the vibration of sound, of tones and of sublimely-blended movements). He recognizes that the theatre is in the early stages of what he describes as 'una marcada revolució en les manifestacions d'art plàstico-teatral' (a significant revolution of plastic arts in the theatre), but urges caution to ensure that the lesson of the Ballets Russes is properly digested and does not become a passing fad.

For Rivas, the Ballets Russes opened up new horizons for Spaniards who were accustomed to such poor quality.[38] However, as we have seen, even before the group toured Spain, some of its ethos had already been felt in the development of non-naturalist theatre, especially in Barcelona. Wagner's presence in Barcelona has been noted as has the excitement playwrights like Maeterlinck provoked among the *modernistes*. The Ballets Russes represented an extension of an anti-naturalist aesthetic which was already deep-rooted in the city's culture.

Oscar Wilde's Salomé

This was perhaps the most emblematic play in the development of a modernist aesthetic in the theatre. Originally written in French in 1892, the play was published simultaneously in French and in English translation in 1893, and in 1894 an English edition appeared with illustrations by Aubrey Beardsley.[39] It was first performed in 1896, at Lugné-Poë's Théâtre de l'Œuvre in Paris, but did not receive its first public performance in England until 1931. English public opinion had been scandalized not only by the content of the play, but also by Wilde's personal life. *The Times* reviewer of 23 February 1893 is scathing in its criticism of the play, calling it 'an arrangement in blood and ferocity, morbid, bizarre, repulsive, and very offensive in its adaptation of scriptural phraseology to situations the reverse of sacred'.[40]

Wilde was not the first or the last writer to take up the Salomé theme. It inspired a whole range of artistic creations – literary, pictorial and musical – the best-known of which is probably Richard Strauss's opera of 1905. However, it is Wilde's play that really gave Salomé her status as 'le "Mythe fin-de-siècle" par excellence'.[41] The play lies at the opposite end of the scale to naturalism and is, according to one critic, 'the first triumphant demonstration of the symbolist doctrine of total theatre'.[42]

In the Iberian Peninsula too, such issues as the development of a symbolist aesthetic and a search for alternatives to naturalist theatre were motives for an interest in the Salomé theme. Delfina P. Rodríguez has catalogued its influence on Spanish and Spanish-American writing, including poetry and prose as well as theatre.[43] Writers who were attracted to the figure of Salomé include Darío, Villaespesa, Goy de Silva, and the two Ramóns, Gómez de la Serna and Valle-Inclán, all of whom were instrumental in bringing about the penetration of modernism into the Iberian world.

As for as actual performances, it is hardly surprising that it was Margarita Xirgu who was responsible for staging this complex and controversial play. She premiered the play in Catalan on 5 February 1910 in the Teatre Principal in Barcelona, and in 1913 it formed part of her touring repertoire (in Spanish, of course) in Malaga, Santa Cruz de Tenerife and Latin America. Xirgu first performed the play in Madrid on 20 May 1914 at the Teatro de la Princesa, its first performance in the city in Spanish.[44] Regarding the Barcelona premiere, one reviewer tantalizingly writes: 'en la memoria está todavía fresco el recuerdo de representaciones recientes'[45] (recent performances are still fresh in the memory), without saying which ones. As far as I can ascertain, this was the first time the play had been performed in Barcelona, so the critic may have been referring to productions elsewhere in Spain or Europe. It is more likely, I feel, that he had in mind Richard Strauss's opera, which was playing at the Liceu in Barcelona at the same time as Xirgu was performing the Wilde original.

There are perhaps four reasons why the Catalan actress should have been attracted to *Salomé*. First, precisely because it *is* difficult, a poetic work a world away from the naturalist well-made play. A second reason is that it is a tragedy, an early manifestation of a genre Xirgu was to cultivate later in her career, in such plays as Seneca's *Medea*, and, most famously, García Lorca's folk tragedies. A third motive is that Salomé is a shocking female part, one whose challenge Xirgu was not alone in accepting. Sarah Bernhardt had made the role her own, while Valle-Inclán's version of the Salomé legend, *La cabeza del Bautista*, was to owe much of its impact when first performed in 1924 to Mimí Aguglia.[46] The importance that the leading actor or actress still had in Spain is exemplified as much by Xirgu as by María Guerrero before her. Fourth, there is the central importance of dance to the play. What gave the play much of its fame – or made it infamous – is the dance of the seven veils which Salomé performs for her step-father. Dancers as well as actresses were attracted to the part. Xirgu's cultivation of dance as avant-garde form in *Salomé* places her firmly in the camp of international modernism, and serves to underline our conclusion that she was a key figure in bringing modernism to the Spanish theatre at a relatively early date. Whatever her motives were, it has to be said that in her choice of *Salomé* Xirgu shows a remarkable maturity, as she was only twenty-one at the time.

As far as Barcelona is concerned, the reception of *Salomé* was as mixed there as it was in the rest of Europe, and, as with García Lorca's *Yerma*, over twenty years later, Xirgu provoked controversy in her native city (see Chapter 6). Domènec Guansé describes the situation graphically:

> Si el éxito de *Salomé* fue enorme, aún mayor fue el escándalo. Los artistas que, llenos de orgullo, se habían imaginado que en Barcelona podían atreverse impunemente a todo, sufrieron un buen desengaño. La reacción contra la obra se desató con tanta violencia que el Teatre Principal tuvo que cerrar las puertas. La compañía, al verse en la calle, buscó refugio. Lo encontró en uno de los locales del Paralelo: El Teatre Nou.[47]

> (If the success of *Salomé* was huge, the scandal it caused was even greater. Those artists who in their pride had imagined that they could try anything in Barcelona received a rude shock. There was such a violent reaction against the play that the Teatre Principal was forced to shut its doors. Out in the street, the company sought refuge. It found it in one of the theatres of the Paral.lel: the Teatre Nou.)

The Paral.lel, as earlier chapters have demonstrated, is an area of Barcelona which in the early part of the century was famous both for its left-wing politics and for its criminality, prostitution and low life. It was home to vaudeville theatres, where risqué spectacles scandalized the bourgeoisie.[48] The type of middle-class audience which was accustomed to attending theatres like the Principal – one of what Enric Gallén refers to as the great 'coliseums' of the old part of the city[49] – did not take kindly to plays like *Salomé*, and probably felt that they were more at home in an area like the Paral.lel. The play, as we have seen, was no stranger to scandal, to which Xirgu added by playing the part with her midriff exposed.[50] The fact that 1910 was a year of relative radicalism in Barcelona and Spain, as in the rest of Europe – it marked the formation of the government of the radical anticlerical Canalejas,[51] and the Tragic Week in Barcelona had taken place during the preceding year – did not alter the city's underlying conservatism, reflected in the *Diario de Barcelona*'s description of *Salomé* as a 'detestable' play.[52]

Two other contemporary reviewers were, on the other hand, full of praise for the play. *La Escena Catalana* claims that the audience was most enthusiastic, and that the play received numerous curtain calls. Josep M. Jordà, writing in *La Publicidad*, confirmed this view, adding that it had the qualities needed to win over audiences of all cultural levels. Jordà's is an especially sensitive and intelligent – if somewhat over-enthusiastic – review, illustrating that the standard of theatre criticism and the knowledge of foreign theatre in Spain at this time was not always as poor as is sometimes supposed. He admired the play's daring, and its poetic, plastic and dramatic qualities, considering that the scene between Salomé and Johanan (presumably the final one) was incomparably sublime. He was most impressed by the acting, and went into raptures about Xirgu.

> Margarita Xirgu, la eminente, la más grande de nuestras actrices dramáticas, alcanzó un gran triunfo, un triunfo inmenso. Era para ella la velada de anoche, velada de prueba y lo fué de triunfo. Alcanzó en toda la obra la grandeza trágica y sus acentos estremecían al público que admiraba su genio, su asombroso instinto, sus adivinaciones, su arte admirable. ¿Qué más decir de ella? Para su labor alcanzó aquella altura artística donde sólo llegan los escogidos.[53]

> (The eminent Margarita Xirgu, our greatest actress, achieved a great triumph, an immense triumph. Yesterday evening's performance was a test for her, and it turned into a triumph. She achieved a tragic greatness throughout the play, and her voice sent shudders through the audience, who admired her genius, her amazing instinct, her intuition, her

wonderful art. What more can one say about her? She reached artistic
heights which only the chosen few achieve.)

Jordà's view is that the play's appeal extends beyond class divides:

> No ya ante un público inteligentísimo y culto como el de anoche, sino
> ante un concurso cualquiera, ante cualquiera [*sic*] colectividad de mucho
> más bajo nivel intelectual ha de imponerse forzosamente por su
> grandiosidad, por su genial audacia y por los raudales de poesía que en
> ella viven.

> (It would impose itself through its grandeur, through its brilliant
> boldness and its torrents of poetry not just on yesterday evening's highly
> intelligent and cultured audience but on any gathering, on any group
> with a much lower intellectual level.)

Here is one critic who appreciated both the boldness of the venture
and its poetic qualities. Jordà clearly approved of the radical break
with prevailing naturalism that *Salomé* represents. Finally, he is one
of the few critics who considered the Wilde play to be superior to the
Strauss opera.[54]

To judge from contemporary newspaper reviews, Xirgu's performance of *Salomé* seems to have caused less scandal in Madrid
that it had done in Barcelona. First-night reviewers concentrated
exclusively on artistic issues and, in general, were enthusiastic about
Xirgu. Even the normally conservative daily *ABC* described *Salomé*
as her most complete creation.[55] For Tristán in *El Liberal* 'la
sensación de arte serio, sincero y grande que se experimenta viendo
a la Xirgu en "Salomé" es extraordinaria' (the sensation of serious,
sincere, great art which one has when one sees Xirgu in *Salomé* is
extraordinary). This critic's view is that Xirgu was able to add a
poetic dimension of which only great actresses are capable,
especially in the seduction scene.[56] García de Candamo in *El Mundo*
praised the subtlety with which Xirgu conveyed the complexity of
Salomé's psychological make-up, as well as her use of gesture, which
'añade belleza a la figura y completa de una manera perfecta la
emoción de las palabras'[57] ('adds beauty to the figure and completes
the emotion of the words in perfect fashion').

The play seems to have been an unqualified success with the
Madrid audience. García de Candamo wrote: 'Anoche el triunfo que
la admirable actriz logró fue extraordinario y ruidosísimo . . . El

público premió la labor de la artista con aplausos' (Last night, the triumph achieved by the splendid actress was extraordinary and very noisy . . . The audience rewarded the artist's endeavours with applause). Tristán also highlighted the favourable reception of the play by the audience, as attested by the numerous curtain calls. Xirgu was certainly well-known in Madrid by this time, but was not yet based in the Spanish capital. Tristán uses his *El Liberal* review of the last night of Xirgu's short season to call for her company to have a permanent base in Madrid, preferably at the prestigious Teatro Español: 'Todo, menos que una actriz de los méritos de Margarita Xirgu se vea obligada a actuar durante el invierno en provincias, por falta de teatro en la Villa del oso'[58] (Anything except that an actress of the quality of Margarita Xirgu should have to act in the provinces during the winter because of the lack of a theatre in Madrid). This attitude was typical of Madrid critics (as it is probably of critics in most nations' capital cities): they appreciated playwrights and other theatre practitioners in Barcelona, but felt their talents should not be wasted there or in other 'provincial' cities.

Although Xirgu's performance in *Salomé* received almost unanimous acclaim from the Madrid critics, the translation of the play most certainly did not. The general critical view was that Xirgu saved a play which had been very badly translated by Joaquim Pena, despite Ricard Salvat's description of him as a mythical figure in the world of Catalan translation.[59] By far the harshest critic, not only of the translation, but also of the quality of the acting, was Alejandro Miquis, one of the best-known, best-read, most informed, but also the most demanding theatre critic in early twentieth-century Madrid. His review in *Diario Universal* was vitriolic, and not merely about the translation:

> La traducción que anoche vimos de la obra de Oscar Wilde es de las más lamentables que hemos padecido aquí, donde es tan frecuente el caso de traductores que desconocen los dos idiomas entre que se colocan como 'trait d'union'.
>
> Del espíritu del traductor al del actor hay un abismo, y el público sufrió anoche la tortura de verse suspendido sobre ese abismo durante una hora.
>
> La interpretación tampoco fue recomendable: cada cual [de los actores] hablaba en el que mejor le parecía, y así, la orquesta sonaba de un modo lamentable y además, muchos actores habían olvidado sus papeles, y los esfuerzos del apuntador no bastaban para evitar baches lamentables.[60]

(The translation of Oscar Wilde's play which we witnessed last night was one of the most lamentable we have suffered here, where instances of translators who do not know either of the two languages are so common.

There is an abyss between the spirit of the translator and that of the actor, and last night the audience had to suffer the torture of being suspended over that abyss for an hour.

The acting wasn't much good either: each of the actors spoke as best he saw fit with the result that the orchestra sounded terrible and, what is more, many of the actors had forgotten their parts, and the efforts of the prompter did not suffice to avoid deplorable gaps.)

It is curious that no other critic should mention what seem to be such obvious defects in the production. It is impossible to speculate whether Miquis was exaggerating, but, as we have seen, he was normally reliable and fair if demanding. Miquis's view was that Xirgu's acting just about saved the day, but he took her to task for certain defects in her delivery:

Sólo la Sra. Xirgu logró convencernos a ratos; pero con la 'pose' y con el gesto, no con la palabra: la Sra. Xirgu necesita aprender a matizar y entonces será una actriz completa. Entretanto, lo repetimos, sólo con los gestos y las actitudes, logra convencer, y no siempre'[61]

(Only Señora Xirgu managed to convince us with her 'pose' and with her gesture, but not with her voice quality: Señora Xirgu needs to learn to be more subtle in this aspect and then she will be a complete actress. Meanwhile, I repeat, she managed to be convincing only with her gesture and her pose, and then not all the time.)

Miquis seems to be expressing qualified approval of the physicality of her performance – associated with the new style of acting and, of course, with dance – but did not like her voice quality, a central element of the type of naturalistic theatre with which Xirgu, at least to an extent, was attempting to break.[62]

Despite Miquis's serious reservations, Xirgu's *Salomé* was undoubtedly a critical success. However, perhaps more important was the fact that the play was actually performed at all. It was relatively rare in Spain at this time to see symbolist or poetic plays of this kind performed, certainly in the commercial theatre, and even to a large extent in small art theatres. The case of *Salomé* reveals that, as far as the reception of recent foreign theatre was concerned, Barcelona and Madrid were not dissimilar. The role of Xirgu – a Catalan who exported her talents to Madrid, the rest of Spain and Latin America – was crucial in its diffusion. Along with Xirgu, the other theatre practitioner most responsible for exposing the Spanish public to foreign plays was, of course, Rivas Cherif.[63] In the 1920s his small theatre groups performed several foreign plays, such as Cocteau's *Orfeo* with El Caracol in 1928. During the 1930s, Rivas's experience and persistence continued to allow Madrid's theatre-going public to be able to see some of the most innovative and revolutionary theatre in Europe.

Georg Kaiser

One of the leading European avant-garde playwrights – although by no means the most extreme – was the German expressionist Georg Kaiser. The first of his plays to be performed in Madrid in the 1930s, *Un día de octubre* (Spanish translation of *Oktobertag*), was staged by El Caracol at the Muñoz Seca Theatre in 1931, in the middle of the elections which brought the Second Republic to power and in the post-election euphoria.[64] Two influential figures who were either from Catalonia or had spent an important period there were involved in the production: Xirgu as actress and Burmann as stage designer. Díez-Canedo gives the background to *Un día*, and sees Strindberg and Wedekind as Kaiser's precursors. The critic considers him to be the leader of expressionism, but believes it hard to pigeonhole him. It is a sensitive review, which demonstrates its writer's familiarity with contemporary theatre and his ability to appreciate the peculiarities of individual texts and to relate them to the author's œuvre:

> Como todas las comedias de Káiser, 'Un día de octubre' tiene su atmósfera peculiar, a la vez fría y apasionada. Para desarrollar su pensamiento, de arrebatado vuelo místico, viene a una forma clara, recortada, como medida a regla y compás. Sus diálogos parecen esquemáticos, si no se quiere ver en torno a las palabras precisas un halo trascendental.[65]

> (Like all Kaiser's plays, *Oktobertag* has its own peculiar atmosphere, at once cold and passionate. In order to develop its thought, with its

impassioned mystical flight, it has a clear, clipped form, as if measured by ruler and compass. Its dialogues seem schematic, if one does not wish to see a transcendental halo around the words.)

Juan G. Olmedilla was also impressed by *Un día de octubre*, especially with Xirgu's performance: she was 'prodigiosamente compenetrada con su papel, al que dio un relieve excepcional y que le valió uno de los triunfos más considerables de esta temporada'[66] (amazingly in tune with the role, to which she gave exceptional prominence and which provided her with one of the major triumphs of the season).

Alejandro Miquis, however, writing now in *Nuevo Mundo*, does not see anything especially new about the play.[67] He detects in it a typically ironic vein and, in a characteristically succinct summary, recognizes that Kasier's success in Madrid is well deserved, but that this particular play is not really representative of his work as a whole and is not a suitable model for new drama:

> *Un día de octubre* me parece, en suma, una comedia interesante, por lo que intriga a los espectadores, y en ese sentido y en alguno más digna del buen éxito que ha logrado en Madrid; pero no creo que sea ni la más representativa de la dramaturgia de su autor, en que hay obras de interés literario y social más elevado, ni creo tampoco que sea un modelo, ni siquiera una muestra del arte teatral nuevo.

> (In short, *Oktobertag* seems to me to be an interesting play, and for this reason intrigues the spectators. In this and other senses it is worthy of the success it has achieved in Madrid. However, I do not think that it is the author's most typical play, in that there are others with a greater literary and social interest, nor do I think it a model, or even a representative example, of the new theatre.)

Unlike Miquis, Fernández Almagro, writing in *La Voz*, considered it to be one of the most suggestive plays in contemporary world theatre.[68] Although it might seem to be a kind of vaudeville piece or a melodrama, opines Fernández Almagro, *Un día de octubre* is, in fact, political theatre, in which 'de la verosimilitud ascendemos a un plano abstracto de realidad estética que nos convence del todo' (from verisimilitude we ascend to an abstract plane of aesthetic reality which is completely convincing).

Sensitive as Díez-Canedo, Fernández Almagro and Miquis are as reviewers, their style of writing is traditional. A snappier, more modern kind of criticism is Arturo Mori's in *El Liberal*, rather in the style of the *Guardian*'s 'Pass Notes':

> – ¿Kaiser? ¡Ah, sí! El autor de 'El incendio de la Opera'. Enjundia y teatro.
> – 'Un día de octubre' es el punto más firme de Kaiser en la escena. Una estilización lógica y humana.
> – ¿Nada de realismo?
> – Nada de realismo. Reacción cerebral. Concepto idealista del drama. Pero asequible al público.[69]

> (– Kaiser? Ah yes! The author of *Fire in the Opera House*. Very weighty theatre.
> – *Oktobertag* is Kaiser's strongest work. A logical and human stylization.
> – No realism?
> – No realism. Cerebral reaction. Idealist concept of drama. But accessible to the public.)

Mori provides the salient features of the plot in an equally concise manner, as he does in his discussion of Kaiser's latest works, the translation of *Oktobertag* and the quality of Xirgu – who leaves the main interlocutor uttering 'unique!' – and the other actors, and audience reaction.

The second of Kaiser's plays to be performed in Madrid was *Gas* (presumably a Spanish translation of *Gas I*), one of the *Gas* trilogy which deals in a strikingly anti-naturalist way with such themes as the mechanization of modern society and offers a vision of an idyllic rural alternative to it.[70] This time Xirgu made just a single guest appearance in one performance of the play, but Rivas Cherif was once again the moving figure behind the production as his TEA (Teatro Escuela de Arte, Theatre Arts School) staged it in March 1935.[71] Juan G. Olmedilla uses his *Heraldo de Madrid* review of *Gas* at the María Guerrero to make general observations about the state of Spanish theatre. He informs his readers that this is the fourth Kaiser play to be translated into Spanish, but only the second to be performed.[72] Olmedilla's main point is that good theatre does not have to be minority theatre, but that this is not happening in Spain:

> Confiar en el empresario inteligente que quiera darlas a conocer, convencido de que pueden hermanarse en un gran autor internacional el decoro artístico y el negocio, es ilusión vana.[73]

TEATRO ESPAÑOL

BENEFICIO DEL HOGAR DEL ACTOR

EL MARTES, 19 DE MAYO DE 1936

A LAS SEIS Y MEDIA DE LA TARDE

UNICA REPRESENTACION de la obra mundial de GEORG KAISER, traducida al castellano por Alvaro Arauz y Luis Fernández Rica,

" G A S "

Por el cuadro artístico Teatro Escuela de Arte (T. E. A.).

COMPLETARA EL PROGRAMA LA INTERVENCION DE NOTABLES ARTISTAS.

ENCARGOS EN CONTADURIA.

DONATIVOS MINIMOS

	Pesetas.		Pesetas.
Palcos plateas con entradas	25,—	Butacas de anfiteatro principal..	2,50
Palcos entresuelos con idem	25,—	Delanteras de anfiteatro segundo.	2,50
Palcos principales con idem......	15,—	Butacas de anfiteatro segundo....	2,—
Palcos segundos con idem........	12,—	Delanteras de paraiso...........	2,—
Butacas con entrada	5,—	Butacas de paraiso.	1,50
Delanteras de entresuelo	5,—	Delanteras laterales de paraiso .	1,50
Butacas de entresuelo.	4,—	Entrada de palco......	1,50
Delanteras de anfiteatro pral ...	3,—		

Imp. TORERIAS, Bravo Murillo, 30.-Madrid

Figure 1. Playbill for *Gas*.

(It is a vain illusion to believe that an intelligent impresario will make them known to the public, convinced that, in a great author, artistic standards can be combined with business).

Gas is the sort of social drama which needs to be seen by a wide audience in order to convince those responsible for theatrical activity in Spain that mass theatre can be of high artistic quality. Olmedilla looks for a balance: he rejects both the type of theatre that panders to popular taste and so-called art or minority theatre. *Gas* is precisely the sort of play that is needed:

> 'Gas', de Kaiser, es precisamente lo que debe ser una representación del Teatro Escuela: una lección, bien elocuente por cierto. Modernidad en la forma, profundidad en la intención, equilibrio perfecto entre el arte y la eficacia, que permite al autor granjearse la estimación de los mejores y el aplauso de la muchedumbre. Teatro, en suma.

> (Kaiser's *Gas* is precisely what a production of the Teatro Escuela should be: a lesson, and an elegant one at that. A modern form, a profound objective, a perfect balance between art and effectiveness, which allows the author to earn the respect of the elite and the applause of the masses. In short, theatre.)

Antonio Espina in *El Sol* also praises Kaiser's qualities: like Toller, his plays have a sharp social message, but they are both great artists and intellectuals with a strong literary personality. Espina, like Olmedilla, explains that a translation of *Gas* had been published previously in *Revista de Occidente*, but that this new version – by Fernández Rica and the young poet Alvaro Arauz – was sharper and snappier. Espina believes that translations should be faithful to the original, but in this case, he observes, the translators were justified in cutting passages, since the original has a number of dialogues on the same theme. Like Olmedilla again, Espina uses his review to make general points about the Spanish theatre. He criticizes the lack of attentiveness of Spanish audiences: they must be taught to listen and to pay attention, and 'esta insuficiencia de la capacidad de atención del público abre la puerta a otros muchos defectos y corruptelas de que está lleno nuestro teatro'[74] (this lack of attention span on the part of audiences opens the door to many other defects and abuses of power which prevail in our theatre).

A.M., writing in *El Liberal*, is another critic who uses his review of *Gas* to make general comments about the state of Spanish theatre.

He declares that Kaiser is known in Spain for his more accessible plays (presumably he is thinking of *Un día de octubre*), and that no one has dared to put on plays like *Gas* because of box-office issues.[75] A.M. cannot understand the refusal when everyone says that Spanish theatre is going through such an awful crisis.[76] *Gas*, he maintains, is a wonderful play, one of the best in the world during the last decade. The reviewer praises all concerned, Rivas Cherif, the translators, the actors and the young composer, Enrique Casal, who was a nephew of Chapí, one of the most famous composers of *zarzuelas*. A.M. emphasizes that the audience gave the play a thundering ovation at the end of each act. He ends his review with a polemical rallying call: 'Empresarios, ¿hasta cuándo continuaremos en el "limbo"?' (Impresarios, until when will we remain in limbo?).

Díez-Canedo, writing in *La Voz*, praises TEA for putting on the play, which would have been beyond the means of any other group. He summarizes its action, and explains its part in the trilogy. He contrasts *Gas* with other stereotypical social plays which they are so used to seeing in Spain. For Díez-Canedo, Kaiser

> extrema sus notas desoladoras, en la técnica del autor, cortada, elíptica, mecánica, evadida en el tono del naturalismo, ya caduco, hacia un arte literario diferente, cuya plástica incide en la de las más avanzadas artes figurativas.[77]

> (maximizes its desolate details, using a technique which is clipped, elliptic, mechanical, avoiding out-of-date naturalism and moving towards a different literary art, whose plasticity has a bearing on that of the most advanced figurative arts.)

Not only does this review indicate that there were people in Spain capable of understanding the most demanding kind of new play, but Díez-Canedo's comment that 'así lo han entendido y realizado los jóvenes actores de la Tea, dirigidos esta vez por Felipe Lluch Garín' (this is how it has been understood and executed by the young actors of the TEA, directed on this occasion by Felipe Lluch Garín) indicates that, at least in his view, Spain had a group capable of rising to the challenge presented by Kaiser. He believes that the cuts made by the translators were judicious in that they have avoided repetitions, which Spanish audiences would have found irritating. Díez-Canedo was particularly impressed by the evocation of the mass, especially when the group of workers comes on stage from out of the audience, and in the meeting scene. He considers the acting, the music and the staging to be splendid, and the only pity was that it was seen by such a small proportion of the population.

Another of this well-informed, cultured generation of Spanish critics, E. Estévez-Ortega, uses the occasion of the production of *Gas* to write more generally on Kaiser. He demonstrates his wide reading by citing an article on Kaiser in *Theatre Arts Monthly*, which claimed that the German was the greatest of the contemporary dramatists. Estévez-Ortega analyses the cinematic techniques of his plays, and examines what he calls Kaiser's telegraphic style.[78] He also discusses what some may consider Kaiser's surprising preference for the melodramatic form (the *folletín*). However, writes Estévez-Ortega,

> dentro del folletín tiene siempre grandes inquietudes intelectuales, que culminan en *Gas*, en *De mañana a media noche*, derivando hacia el drama social y a los conflictos que el maquinismo acarrea a la sociedad moderna.

> (within this melodramatic form he is engaged in intellectual exploration, which culminates in *Gas*, in *From Morning to Midnight*, leading to social drama and the conflict which the machine culture gives rise to in modern society.)

TEA continued to perform *Gas* during the spring of 1935 and, as the playbill in Fig. 1 demonstrates, into the spring of 1936. Margarita Xirgu played a role in a performance of the play on 22 June, demonstrating once more her commitment to new theatre.[79]

In conclusion, there was an awareness at a comparatively early date in both centres – albeit by an educated minority – of new movements in European theatre, and of manifestations of symbolist theatre as an alternative to naturalism. Margarita Xirgu, a key figure in the success of internationally known Spanish dramatists like García Lorca and Alberti, cut her teeth on *Salomé*, and it is perhaps not stretching things too far to see this play as a precursor of her much better known and acclaimed successes such as *Bodas de sangre* (*Blood Wedding*). Although Spain lacked a theatre of the stature of the Théâtre de l'Œuvre, the largely unsung efforts of Anarchist theatre groups in Barcelona, the vision of such figures as Gual,

Xirgu and Rivas Cherif, as well as some of the theatre critics in Madrid and Barcelona, meant both that early twentieth-century Spain was not such a theatrical backwater as is sometimes assumed and that the contribution of Catalan theatre practitioners to the development of a poetic and avant-garde theatre movement in Spain as a whole was vital. Barcelona, through the likes of Gual and Xirgu, was at the forefront of the penetration of foreign theatre into Spain in the early twentieth century. During the early 1920s, the efforts of the impressario Josep Canals, with the help of such Catalan intellectuals as Carles Soldevila and Josep Millàs-Raurell, meant that foreign playwrights of the stature of O'Neill and Pirandello were performed in Barcelona. However, it is clear that, with the possible exception of Pirandello, the impact of new foreign drama in Barcelona was much less than it had been at the turn of the century, when Ibsen, Hauptmann, Maeterlinck and Wagner were so influential.[80] The new European playwrights of the late nineteenth century were generally performed earlier in Barcelona than in Madrid. Towards the end of the period under study, this seems no longer to be the case. As far as the reception of foreign theatre in the two cities is concerned, our study has allowed us to appreciate a variety of critical views – sometimes depending on the political sympathies of the reviewer and the newspaper – but there is sufficient evidence to suggest the existence of a body of critics in both Madrid and Barcelona who were open to productions of new and challenging plays. This impression will be confirmed as we now move to consider, in Chapters 5 and 6 respectively, how Catalan and Spanish theatre was received in the two cities.

Reception of Catalan Theatre in Madrid and Barcelona

Guimera, Terra Baixa

Author: Àngel Guimerà
Title: *Terra baixa*
Madrid premiere: November 1896 at the Teatro Español by the Guerrero/Díaz de Mendoza Company
Barcelona premiere: May 1897 at the Teatre Romea by the Romea's resident company headed by Borràs
Plot outline: The play is a harsh critique of how a landowner (Sebastià) sexually abuses a young orphan girl for whom he is meant to be caring (Marta), and arranges a marriage between her and an untutored shepherd (Manelic) in order to cover up his relationship with the girl and hence prevent his own disinheritance. His plan backfires as Manelic and Marta fall in love, and defy the tyrannical Sebastià. With the help of the acquiescent villagers, who depend on the landowner for their livelihood, Sebastià ejects Manelic from the village, but the latter returns and strangles him, before escaping with Marta to the mountain lands from which he came. The mountain, or 'high lands', represents a kind of Arcadia which purifies individuals of the narrow-minded pettiness acquired in the lowlands. The portrayal of the villagers is negative, with the exception of the innocent young girl Nuri, who seems to be Marta's only true friend.

El teatro catalán, pese á la prevención que existe en Madrid contra todo lo que no es arte castellano y hablado en castellano, ha tenido un gran éxito en esta capital de España.[1]

(Despite the prejudice that exists in Madrid against any art which is not Castilian and spoken in Spanish, Catalan theatre has been very successful in the Spanish capital.)

This statement by an admittedly pro-Catalan writer sums up what was a major achivement on the part of the renascent Catalan theatre. Although the critic was writing about Ignasi Iglésies, the real breakthrough had been made in the 1890s by Àngel Guimerà, the first Catalan dramatist to attract widespread and sustained interest in Madrid, particularly in his best-known play, *Terra baixa* (*Marta of the Lowlands*). As was observed in Chapter 2, the play was translated by the Spanish dramatist José Echegaray. It is preceded by a notice to the actors on how to pronounce certain words. As with an earlier translation of Guimerà's *Maria Rosa*, most of these seem to concern Madrid dialogue, especially the replacing the 'ado' and 'ido' endings of past participles with 'áo' and 'ío'.[2] It is interesting that the best known of all the Catalan plays should be 'Madridified' for the audiences of the Spanish capital. This suggests that the Madrid perception of Catalan theatre as merely 'regional' was not justified, but rather that one is dealing with 'foreign' theatre which had to be translated and localized for the benefit of actors and audiences in the nation's capital.

The play was premiered at the Teatro Español in November 1896 by the Guerrero/Díaz de Mendoza company. It is a sign of the regard in which the play was held in Madrid theatrical circles that it should be performed by the capital's leading company in one of its most prestigious theatres. It clearly was an immediate hit with Madrid audiences. The *El Imparcial* reviewer mentions that author and translator received five or six curtain calls, but he does not like its sombre, gloomy atmosphere. For him, it is 'lánguido muchas veces y falso casi siempre'[3] (often languid and almost always false). Likewise, Eduardo Bustillo, having praised *Juan José* unreservedly, opines that the Guimerà play lacks a realistic base, and accuses it of dramatic falseness.[4] Enrique Sepúlveda, writing in *Nuevo Mundo*, is also critical of a certain lack of realism in the play, and happier about the first act than the others. However, his review is favourable overall, and he particularly praises Díaz de Mendoza

> que ha hecho de su papel una verdadera creación, y encontrado para llevarla a término, gesto, expresión, sentimiento, arranques, naturalidad, todo lo que un primer actor debe tener.[5]

> (who has turned the role into a true creation. To bring it to fruition he has discovered everything a leading actor must have: gesture, expression, feeling, energy, naturalness.)

Interestingly, the role of Manelic was well established by Díaz de Mendoza before Borràs made it his own.

Federico Urrecha was another Madrid critic who had mixed feelings about the play. He writes approvingly of Guimerà, although he is not entirely convinced by the play:

> Si no creyese como creo que la musa de Guimerà ha de ejercer gran influencia sobre nuestro teatro, con provecho mío y aun del lector, cumpliría diciendo que el primer acto gustó mucho, que el segundo gustó más, y que el tercero gustó poco. Pero Guimerà tiene derecho a todo nuestro respeto.[6]

> (If I did not believe as I do that Guimerà's muse will exercise a great influence on our theatre, to my benefit and to that of the reader, I would simply say that the first act went down well, the second went down better and the third didn't go down at all well. But Guimerà deserves our total respect.)

He believes that there were too many characters gossiping about Manelic – it would have been sufficient, he believes, for Guimerà just to have used Nuri to bring him to realize what was happening. Nonetheless, Urrecha believes that she is the best-drawn character in the play. For this critic the performances were uneven, and he even criticizes Guerrero, who tried hard, but found Marta a difficult role to play. Díaz de Mendoza had studied the role of Manelic fully and pulled off the difficult scene in the second act well.

Juan Palomo in the 'Gacetillas teatrales' section of *El Globo* also liked Nuri, and confirmed the popularity of the play with the audience as author and translator took many curtain calls at the end, while Acts 1 and 2 provoked special applause. In contrast to Urrecha, Palomo is full of praise for the portrayal of the 'white peasant slaves', as he calls them, for whom gossip represents an escape of sorts from their sad lives. There are things the critic does not like about the play, but overall he is very positive:

> *Tierra baja* no es un drama perfecto, pero tampoco una obra vulgar. Es de las producciones que se analizan para admitir sus bellezas y reconocer sus errores, no de las que pasan por el escenario sin dejar huella. *Tierra baja* deja la huella que puede imprimir sólo un talento extraordinario.[7]

> (*Marta of the Lowlands* is not a perfect play, but nor is it a vulgar work. It is one of those productions which one analyses in order to recognize its

beautiful features and to admit its errors, not one which is performed without making its mark. *Marta of the Lowlands* leaves the mark which only an extraordinary talent can do.)

Palomo's is typical of the generally balanced view of Madrid critics, who judge the play on its merits rather than on political grounds. The contrast with Martínez Olmedilla's ravings about Catalan theatre (discussed in Chapter 3) could not, on the face of it, be more marked. However, Palomo believes that the distinction between Castilian and Catalan men of letters was a false one, and that they were all simply Spaniards:

> ¿Quién habla de literatos castellanos y de literatos catalanes? Si alguien hiciera tales distinciones, se le podría contestar recordando cómo ante el público abrazados aparecieron Echegaray y Guimerà. No hay más que literatos españoles.

> (Who speaks of Catalan men of letters and Castilian men of letters? If anyone made such a distinction, one could remind them that Echegaray and Guimerà appeared on stage together in an embrace. There are only Spanish men of letters.)

So although his review is balanced as far as questions of artistic quality are concerned, he is not prepared to accept a distinctive Catalan theatre culture and tries to appropriate Guimerà for Spain. However, as was observed above, the fact that the play had to be translated and annotated for the benefit of the Madrid-based actors and audiences suggests that Spanishness (or at least 'Madridness') is not an appropriate label for Guimerà.

Terra baixa was not performed in Barcelona until 10 May 1897, and attracted rather less favourable criticism from the Barcelona press than it had done in Madrid. Part of the reason could well have been that, like other plays by Guimerà and his contemporaries, it was performed in Madrid in Spanish translation before receiving its Catalan premiere.[8] To add insult to injury as far as Barcelona was concerned, the play was performed in Catalan provincial towns like Tortosa and Reus before Barcelona.

La Vanguardia makes the point that many people will already have read it, with the result that the novelty aspect enjoyed by Madrid audiences would have been missing in Barcelona. Nevertheless, according to this newspaper, the play produced a profound impression on the Romea first-night audience.[9] Borràs played the role of Manelic, which was in no small measure responsible for his fame. The *La Vanguardia* reviewer is generally quite impressed by the actor, although he does criticize him for adopting a histrionic rather than a naturalistic style and for playing to the gallery:

> El señor Borrás, que representaba el humanísimo *Manelich*, logró anoche algunos aplausos francos y entusiastas, pero cayó con tanta frecuencia, en el decir, en amaneramientos de tan mal gusto, que quedó completamente deslucida su labor de conjunto. No es a gritos, ni lanzando al aire los brazos, como se conquistan en un teatro los aplausos buenos, aquellos que fortifican al actor, que le alientan y le llegan al alma, porque su conciencia de artista señala en ellos el premio debido a su mérito y a su esfuerzo . . . No olvide esto el señor Borrás, y no sacrifique en aras de una pequeña parte del público, las cualidades que posee para llegar a ser un buen actor.

(Yesterday evening Señor Borràs, who played the very human Manelic, won frank and enthusiastic applause, but he fell so frequently into such tasteless mannerisms in his verbal expression that his overall performance was completely spoilt. In the theatre it is not by shouting or by waving one's hands in the air that one achieves genuine applause of the sort that fortifies the actor, encourages him and reaches his soul, because his artistic awareness indicates in that applause the recognition which is due to his merit and his effort . . . Señor Borràs should not forget this nor should he sacrifice in the name of a small section of the audience the qualities he possesses in order to become a good actor.)

It must be remembered that Borràs was still a young and relatively unknown actor at this time, and the lecturing tone of the above passage was certainly not to be found once he had acquired renown both inside and outside Catalonia, particularly following his highly successful 1904 Catalan season in Madrid which is discussed below. The *La Vanguardia* reviewer is also less impressed generally by what he describes as the wooden acting in the splendidly written final scene. He then criticizes individual actors and actresses for certain defects: in short, his review was full of praise for the quality of the play – especially for its beauty and its human qualities – but was highly critical of the acting.

Lluís Via in *La Renaixensa* also criticizes Borràs for being excessively demonstrative and the rest of the cast for their lack of preparation, a situation he trusts will be quickly rectified.[10] However,

Figure 2. The actor Enric Borràs in the role of Manelic in Guimerà's
Terra baixa.

he staunchly defends Guimerà against accusations of Romanticism and the criticism levelled at the play by 'un crítich molt sábi y molt madrileny' (a very wise and very Madrid critic) – he does not specify who the critic is – that the play lacks substance (p. 408). Via is particularly enthusiastic about Manelic and claims that *Terra baixa* is not a social drama, but more of a psychological study, a dramatic poem and a play which is 'tractat ab una elevació poch coneguda en lo teatro' (pp. 408–9: treated with a nobility which is infrequent in the theatre). According to Via the play was an almost unparalleled success:

> Lo públich, distingit y numerós; l'entusiasme aumentant en cada escena. Se cridá al autor infinitat de vegadas. Un éxit, en fí, com no s'havia vist de molt temps en lo teatre catalá. (p. 410)

> (The audience was distinguished and large; the enthusiasm increased with each scene. The author was called countless times. In short, it's a very long time since Catalan theatre has seen such a successful production.)

N.N. in *L'Esquella de la Torratxa* considers that 'en sas concepcions sempre grandiosas é hiperbólicas, en Guimerá es tal vegada 'l poeta dramátich menos catalá de Catalunya'[11] (In his constantly grandiose and hyperbolic creations, Guimerà is perhaps the least Catalan poet in Catalonia). However, in his creation of secondary characters and use of language, N.N. considers him to be a true Catalan, without specifying exactly how he fulfils these racial conditions. The reviewer considers that the third act of *Terra baixa* could have been suppressed, as he finds it unconvincing that the villagers would have supported Sebastià in his evils plans and expelled Manelic from his house: 'Això no passa mes qu'en lo pais dels somnis melodramátichs' (This happens only in the land of melodramatic dreams). Is this a refusal to accept that Catalan peasantry would be capable of vile deeds, one wonders? He feels that the overall effect of the play is powerful and that the audience admired Guimerà's poetic imagination despite not identifying with the action. N.N.'s concluding remark is that the play will achieve extraordinary success despite a flawed production.

Towards the end of 1897, *Terra baixa* was performed again in Barcelona, this time in its Spanish translation by the Guerrero/Díaz de Mendoza company at Barcelona's Principal Theatre in late

Figure 3. Salvador Alarma's stage design for Guimerà's *Terra baixa*.

November. *La Vanguardia* describes the usual distinguished audience who watch 'serious' theatre in Barcelona, but, as in the review of Borràs's *Terra baixa* the previous year, is critical of the performance of the final scene.[12]

La Renaixensa makes only the briefest allusion to the fact that the play is a translation of *Terra baixa*,[13] while *L'Esquella de la Torratxa* – like *La Renaixensa* a pro-Catalan publication – does not even mention that the play is written in Spanish and does not even refer to Guimerà by name. It simply forms part of a review of the whole season by the Guerrero/Díaz de Mendoza company. The reviewer praises *Tierra baja*'s artistic qualities – its polished care is not seen very often in Spanish companies and its rich and appropriate *mise-en-scène* is a novelty.[14] If, through its quality, it could attract audiences who had grown accustomed to the bad taste of much Spanish theatre, then credit would have to be given to Guerrero, says the reviewer, even if her intention was to please a foreign audience. The only barbed comment in the review comes in the final paragraph – the company should learn to begin their performances on time and cut the length of the intervals. This is what foreign companies do, and it is appreciated by audiences. The audience for the five performances of the Díaz de Mendoza/Guerrero season was large, enthusiastic and brilliant. These reviews are concerned with issues of theatrical and artistic quality rather than with Catalanness.

The international interest in *Terra baixa* and the willingness of Barcelona to accept foreign as well as Spanish translations of plays by their favourite dramatists is evinced in the production of a Sicilian version of *Terra baixa*, which was performed at the Teatre Novetats in Barcelona by the Grasso/Aguglia company in January 1907: this was the version that inspired the opera *Tiefland*, an international hit some three years later.[15] The *La Veu de Catalunya* reviewer uses character names from the original Catalan text rather than those of the Sicilian adaptation for the greater clarity of his readers.[16] According to *La Veu*, Nuri, who is such an important figure in the original, has an almost insignificant part in the adaptation, which lacks the poetic quality of the Catalan and is subject to more violent changes. The reviewer is full of praise for Aguglia as Marta and Grasso as Manelic.

Jori in *La Publicidad* makes some of the same points as the *La Veu* reviewer.[17] He informs his readers that the Sicilian work is an adaptation by A. Campagna, and gives the names in Sicilian rather than in Catalan. Jori is enthusiastic about the acting, but does not approve of the scenes which have been added or omitted. The audience, he reports, despite finding the names strange, applauded enthusiastically. At the end of the play, Guimerà came on stage and emotionally embraced Grasso and Aguglia, which suggests that the author, at least, was happy with their adaptation.

My consideration of the reception of the various versions of *Terra baixa* in Madrid and Barcelona has revealed its popularity among audiences and critics alike. Perhaps surprisingly, the Barcelona press was less warm than their Madrid counterparts. This could have been because they were more critical of one of their 'own' works than the Madrid-based press were. Another motive was possibly a sense of pique that the play had been performed in the Spanish capital before receiving its premiere in the capital of Catalonia. A kind of mini tug-of-war over the identity of Guimerà – an ardent Catalanist born in the Canary Isles – seems to characterize some of the press reviews. On the other hand, the Barcelona reviews reveal a certain nonchalance at the fact that the play could be performed in Spanish and Sicilian translation as well as in the original Catalan. This suggests the permeability of Barcelona as far as the language question is concerned, as well as its sense of internationalism.

Terra baixa is arguably the most popular and durable Catalan play of all time. It continued to be put on in Madrid into the 1920s and 1930s by a variety of companies, including relatively little-known Spanish ones.[18] It still continues to be performed in Barcelona, with a new production forming part of the 2001–2 season of the National Theatre of Catalonia (Teatre Nacional de Catalunya) in Barcelona. However, as Chapter 3 demonstrated, it was Enric Borràs who really gave the play its renown, beginning with his production in his remarkable 1904 Madrid season.

Borràs's 1904 season

Despite the continuing and long-lasting success of *Terra baixa* with the public of Madrid and Barcelona, by the end of the nineteenth century, among Madrid intellectuals and theatre critics at least, Guimerà was considered to be old hat, and their attention had switched to the new group of *modernistes* which included Gual, Rusiñol and Iglésies. The interest culminated in 1904, when Tirso Escudero brought Enric Borràs to Madrid to perform a short season of Catalan plays in the original Catalan at the Teatro de la Comedia. In the rather barbed words of Miquis,

> no podrán quejarse los catalanes; el público de Madrid ha soportado pacientemente, por estar escritas en catalán sin duda, una porción de obras que en castellano no hubieran pasado sin protesta.[19]

> (the Catalans can't complain; the Madrid public has patiently sat though some of the plays, no doubt because they were in Catalan: had they been in Spanish, there would have been protests.)

Escudero's was a particularly bold venture, as this was a period of conflict between Madrid and Barcelona. The hostility culminated in 1905 in the assault by 300 army officers of the Barcelona garrison on two Lliga Regionalista publications, the satirical magazine *Cu-cut!* and the daily *La Veu de Catalunya*. The attack was in retaliation for satirical articles written about the army after the Cuban defeat and, in its turn, was an important contributory factor in the formation of Solidaritat Catalana in the same year. Balcells refers to the 'anti-Catalan atmosphere that reigned in Madrid' at this time,[20] which makes the bravery of those concerned all the more noteworthy and the success of the venture all the more surprising.

Borràs performed mainly plays by the young Catalan playwrights who were viewed in Madrid as indicating the new direction Spanish theatre should take. According to Vila San-Juan, Borràs was more interested in exposing the Madrid theatre-going public to a representative selection of contemporary Catalan plays than in either his own personal achievement or box-office success.[21] As well as works by younger playwrights, he also played some Guimerà – *Maria Rosa*, *La festa del blat* (*Wheat Festival*) and, of course, *Terra baixa*. *La festa del blat* – which concerns the violent revolt of a repressed peasant community – attracted some negative reviews. Miquis did not like it, feeling that it was not modern like the plays of Rusiñol, Iglésies and Crehuet,[22] especially the latter two. Ángel Guerra was enthusiastic about *Terra baixa*: 'siempre conmoverá hondamente este drama de pasión, que lleva el escalofrío hasta los huesos' (we will always be moved by this drama of passion, which chills one to the bone), but thinks that *La festa del blat* is the worst thing Guimerà has done.[23]

In what turned out to be a shrewd move by Borràs, as part of his season he performed the big Madrid hit of previous years, Dicenta's *Juan José*.[24] His boldness in playing this Madrid working-class icon paid dividends as he won over his audiences and even Dicenta himself:

> Su perfecto castellano, su gentileza para el pueblo de Madrid, ofreciéndole una obra de palpitante actualidad, y su soberano gesto y brío en el papel de obrero enamorado madrileño, acabó de atraerse a toda la ciudad. Un periódico tan serio como *El Heraldo de Madrid*, al comentarlo con elogio, recogía un impresionante incidente: en medio de las ovaciones y bravos que rodearon su parlamento, un espectador, entusiasmado y de pie en las butacas, había exclamado a voz en grito:
> – ¡Ya es nuestro! ¡Ya es nuestro Enrique Borràs!
> [. . .] *Juan José* era entonces la obra del momento, constituyendo la consagración definitiva del buen dramaturgo don Joaquín Dicenta.
> [. . .] Don Joaquín Dicenta, el autor de la obra, dijo a gritos que aquel era su verdadero *Juan José*.[25]

(The whole city was won over by his perfect Spanish, the courtesy he showed to the Madrid people by offering them a vibrantly contemporary work and his supreme gesture and energy in the role of the passionate Madrid worker. A serious paper like *El Heraldo de Madrid*,[26] praising his role, reported an amazing incident: in the midst of the ovation and shouts of 'bravo!', a spectator climbed on a seat in his enthusiasm and shouted: 'He's ours! Enric Borràs is ours!' [. . .] *Juan José* was the play of the moment, and the one which really established Joaquín Dicenta's reputation. [. . .] Dicenta, the author of the play, shouted that this was his real *Juan José*.)

It is very interesting that Borràs, a Catalan 'outsider' in Madrid, should play the role of Juan José, himself a rejected and eventually vengeful outsider.[27] However, it seems that this play persuaded Madrid audiences that Borràs was one of their own, and what appears to have been his accomplished Castilian accent is in marked contrast to Xirgu's strong Catalan accent and imperfect use of the Spanish language when she first appeared in Madrid. If the 'he's ours' comment is to be believed, here is another example of Madrid's desire to appropriate a Catalan theatre practitioner.

The *Diario Universal* recognized Borràs as a kind of link between Madrid and Barcelona, and between Catalonia and the rest of Spain, and claimed that the theatre could break down barriers created by politicians.[28] The critic Zeda, on the other hand, a hard-line positivist who believed in Taine's determinism, had a rather different perception. In an article in *El Teatro*, he claimed that, despite the quality of Borràs's Spanish, the audience was not convinced by his *Juan José*.[29] Zeda thinks that one must not judge his ability to perform in Spanish from this play: Borràs lives in Catalonia and is therefore not sufficiently in tune with the style of the Madrid working classes. However, Zeda begins his article with sentiments which were echoed by much of the Madrid press, as he urges applause for Borràs and his Catalan company. They have created an excellent impression in Madrid with both public and critics. He praises Borràs's ability to play convincingly totally different roles:

El artista catalán posee en absoluto la cualidad más importante que puede exigirse a todo actor, la de transformarse de tal modo que apenas es posible reconocer en el personaje de hoy al personaje de ayer.

(The Catalan artist possesses fully the most important quality that can be demanded of any actor, namely the ability to transform himself so completely that it is hardly possible to recognize yesterday's character in today's.)

Zeda's main point is that contemporary Catalan theatre does not reflect the spirit of Catalonia, but is instead a version of its counterpart in northern Europe. Like a number of his contemporaries, Zeda tries to explain his point in what seem to be simplistic racial terms. Just as Bueno feels that Ibsen cannot be popular in Spain because of certain characteristics of the Spanish people, so the sadness which Zeda identifies as typical of contemporary Catalan theatre

> no puede proceder de la hermosa región catalana, cuyos frondosos jardines, su cielo despejado y su mar azul son más a propósito para evocar en el alma de los artistas las vehementes pasiones, los poéticos idilios, la riente hermosura del arte latino que las tétricas creaciones de la musa septentrional.

> (cannot come from the beautiful Catalan region, whose leafy gardens, clear sky and blue sea are more suited to evoking in artists' souls powerful passions, poetic idylls and the smiling beauty of Latin art than the dismal creations of the northern muse.)

As usual, the Madrid critic who devoted most space to the season was Alejandro Miquis. He was generally positive about it, but was also his customary critical self. As well as briefer reviews in *Diario Universal*, he wrote a long and detailed article in *El Teatro*,[30] which demonstrated once more his knowledge and appreciation of theatre. The detailed and serious attention given to the Borràs season in the Madrid press is a sign that it made a real impression in the Spanish capital.

Miquis begins his *El Teatro* article by stating that this year unusually no foreign company has played in Madrid, which has allowed them to discover a new actor without having to leave Spain: 'un actor insigne digno de colocarse con los más famosos y que, sin embargo, en España vivía poco menos que desconocido' (p. 9: a notable actor worthy of a place among the most famous, but who was virtually unknown in Spain). He wonders why the Catalans have not wanted to reveal this treasure to the outside world, and concludes it is because they themselves do not appreciate him. According to the critic, Borràs has been forced to perform in a minor theatre in Barcelona. No one told Castilian visitors to Barcelona of the existence of this great actor, claims Miquis, and the Catalan intellectuals were amazed if anyone actually praised him. Miquis finds this curious, since 'a los catalanes *curages* les ha preocupado siempre cultivar su jardín, y más de una vez han empleado cuidados excesivos en plantas de vida efímera' ('true' Catalans have always been concerned to cultivate their gardens, and on more than one occasion they have spent too much time looking after plants that don't last). The Catalans cannot offer the excuse that they have had nothing to compare Borràs with, since the foreign companies that visit Madrid habitually play in Barcelona too. According to Miquis, visiting Castilian actors are more enthusiastically applauded than Borrás, despite being inferior to him (p. 10).

Miquis then polemically asserts that Borràs is not playing more than twenty shows in his Comedia season due to the 'conveniencia de llevarle a Barcelona donde una empresa conocedora de sus intereses puede ahora explotarle ¡como una novedad!' (p. 11: the convenience of taking him to Barcelona where a company which is aware of its own interests can now exploit him him as a novelty!). In other words, Miquis is claiming that Borràs has been discovered in Madrid before Barcelona, although the Catalans are happy to turn their shortsightedness to their advantage. He is another Madrid critic who seems to appreciate individual Catalan theatre practitioners, while implying an unfavourable view of the Catalans in general. This is another example of attempts to appropriate Catalan individuals for Spain, while showing disdain for the society of their origin. Such attitudes are a manifestation of a sense of cultural superiority, born of the fact that Madrid was the centre of the Spanish theatrical (and political) world. Displays of otherness were regarded as suspicious, even by such erudite and open-minded critics as Miquis.

In his discussion of individual plays performed by Borràs, Miquis opines that Manelic is synonymous with the actor,[31] who has changed him from an idiot into an innocent whose actions are conditioned by his isolation from the real world. Miquis admires the way Borràs is able to change his character completely to play the main part in *Els vells*, to the extent that the first-night audience applauded without realizing who he was (p. 10). He then goes on to affirm that Borràs is an excellent director as well as an actor (p. 12), before discussing the development of contemporary Catalan theatre. He sees it as not characteristically regionalist theatre, but as heterogeneous and marked by the influence of foreign drama.

In his *Diario Universal* review of *Els vells* within the Borràs Catalan season, Miquis makes the point that Spaniards, accustomed as they were to the conventions of melodrama, could not understand how the character could reason about his problems rather than allow himself to be dragged along by the violent impulses of his amorous passion.[32] He likens Iglésies's realist technique in this play to that of Pérez Galdós; Iglésies does not theorize and his plays are not sociological tracts, but are based on his observation of ordinary people. Miquis declares that the only reason he is not bothered about the lack of an appropriate translation of *Els vells* is because there is no Castilian actor who is good enough to perform it. Miquis is less impressed with *El místic*, although once more he feels that Borràs was magnificent.[33] His view is that one would have expected something better from a dramatist of Rusiñol's quality,

> un drama que encajase menos en los moldes viejos de la retórica tradicional y nos diese una visión de la vida más amplia, más clara, menos cubierta a ratos por foliaciones que sólo brotando muy naturalmente pueden tener verdadera belleza.

> (a play which would fit less into the old moulds of traditional rhetoric and give us a vision of a broader, clearer life, one less covered by foliation which merely by sprouting naturally can possess a true beauty.)

Zeda, on the other hand, in his *El Teatro* review, thinks *El místic* is one of the best modern plays while *Els vells* grieves the spectators' souls. However, he concludes: 'Lástima que en esta obra, verdaderamente notable, haya que lamentar la montonía de una misma situación en casi toda ella, el pesimismo sin atenuaciones que la informa' (It is a pity that in this truly notable play one should have to lament the monotony of the same situation throughout, the unrelenting pessimism which informs it).

In short, although not all the plays pleased all the critics all of the time, Borràs's season made a deep impression in Madrid, and led to his permanent move there in 1905. Although the younger playwrights attracted the attention of the critics, the season established Borràs's fame in the role of Manelic, a part to which, as was observed in Chapter 3, he was to return time after time to great popular acclaim. He was performing the role once more at the Comedia, this time in Spanish, as early as October 1904. Like Ángel Guerra, whose review of *Terra baixa* was mentioned earlier, José de Laserna commends Borràs for the quality of his Spanish: 'Respecto a la pronunciación, no se le nota a Borrás ni el más ligero asomo de acento o dejo catalán: su dicción castellana es pura y natural'[34] (As far as pronunciation is concerned, there is no trace of a Catalan accent in Borràs: his Spanish diction is pure and natural). It is as if Borràs had effaced signs of his otherness in a way Xirgu, for instance, who never lost her Catalan accent, did not do. The irony is that, as Chapter 3 demonstrated, during the 1920s and 1930s it was Borràs who maintained closer contact with his Catalan repertoire and public than Xirgu did. Laserna makes it clear that Borràs had made a tremendous impression in his Catalan season in May, and that expectations were high for his performance of *Terra baixa* in Castilian. Naturally, the premiere was a sell-out. Laserna is enthusiastic about Borràs's performance, and uses a rather unexpected image when he claims that the emotion generated in Act 1 provoked 'a true orgasm'. Laserna is unable to resist a sly aside about people in Barcelona who resented Borràs's performing in Madrid:

el insigne actor catalán don Enrique Borrás, que el público y la prensa de este odiado *Madrit* sacó de la oscuridad y del anónimo en que sus mismos paisanos lo tenían confinado entre Sitges y Sabadell para lanzarlo al aplauso y a la admiración universal, debiéndose principalmente tan fausto suceso a la generosa iniciativa del activo y emprendedor empresario de la Comedia, D. Tirso Escudero.

(the famous Catalan actor Enric Borràs, whom the public and the press of the hated Madrid rescued from the obscurity and anonymity to which his fellow countrymen had confined him between Sitges and Sabadell and launched him into universal applause and admiration. This happy occurrence was due mainly to the generous initiative of the active and enterprising impresario of the Comedia, Tirso Escudero.)

Laserna's assertion that Escudero rescued Borràs from obscurity is yet another example of a Madrid critic's appreciating the qualities of an individual Catalan theatre practitioner while criticizing the society from which he emanated. It was not that Madrid was not interested in or did not admire Barcelona's theatre culture (Chapter 2 demonstrated that it certainly did). It was when this took on a specifically Catalan dimension that it seems to have been resented. With an air of superiority characteristic of critics based in a nation's capital city, Laserna lauds the sophisticated nature of Madrid audiences.

Rusinol, El Místic

Author: Santiago Rusiñol

Title: *El místic*

Madrid premiere: Within Enric Borràs's Catalan season at the Teatro de la Comedia in May-June 1904; as a single listing in December 1904 at the Teatro de la Comedia by the Enric Borràs Company

Barcelona premiere: December 1903 at the Teatre Romea by the Romea's resident company

Plot outline: Ramon is a young trainee priest in a small, remote Catalan mountain village. He has high ideals and takes literally a comment by the bishop that Jesus's teaching involved taking the Christian message to the wider outside world: having gone to the mountain to find the apostles, says the bishop, Christ then took them to Jerusalem. By Act 2, Ramon has been ordained and has moved to the city (Barcelona in the original Catalan version, but a Spanish provincial capital in Dicenta's translation), where he attempts to help the poor, but there is a conflict between his idealism and their practical needs.

Ramon's second cousin Marta has followed him to the city. She has been abandoned with child, and has come to Ramon to ask for help. However, she has always loved Ramon, and it is clear that he has felt the same about her. The celibacy demanded of priests obviously does not permit him to pursue his love, as a familar Rusiñol theme unfolds, namely the impossibility of reconciling ideals and human frailities. Ramon's failure leads to his illness and death, and although, in typically *modernista* fashion, a Rusiñol work usually portrays the superiority of idealism over prosaic reality, at the end of *El místic* the audience is left to ponder the limitations of spirituality, as the dying Ramon confesses his feelings for Marta.

The play also explores the hypocrisy of the Church in rural communities and amongst the urban rich. The Baroness aims to organize a fund-raising party for the poor but does not want them present at it, which introduces another of the play's themes: how should society deal with the poor? Miquel, an ex-prisoner whom Ramon attempts to help, is as much of an idealist as the priest, and also falls in love with Marta. His social idealism proves ultimately as futile as Ramon's mysticism, and he is murdered for attempting to organize social protest. Underlying his examination of social and spiritual issues is the irony which is so characteristic of Rusiñol. Although he is associated with liberalism and is known for his biting satire of the bourgeoisie, in *El místic* he also directs his satire against liberals' willingness to protest for protest's sake

By December 1904, Borràs was performing in Spanish translation another of the Catalan plays with which he had taken Madrid by storm in the spring, Rusiñol's *El místic*, in Dicenta's translation, again in the Comedia Theatre. Various critics comment on the quality of the translation, which was they felt contributed significantly to its success.[35]

The critics also highlight the audience's enthusiastic reception of the play. *El místic* was obviously something different as far as the Madrid theatre-going public was concerned.[36] Arimón declares that 'no hubo ni un solo instante de vacilación, ni decayó jamás el interés extraordinario que el drama inspiraba'[37] (there was not a second's hesitation, nor did the extraordinary interest which the play inspired wane for a moment). The play was interrupted by spontaneous bursts of applause, while Rusiñol, together with Borràs and Rosario Pino, had to take many curtain calls at the end. The leading actor and actress received rave reviews from the critics. According to Arimón, Borràs reached heights of which only really great actors are capable, while Pino was also incomparable in the role of Marta. Miquis's positive opinion of Borràs, which was clear in his reviews of the May–June season, is confirmed by this production: he considers him to be at least the equal of Zacconi, while *El místico*, writes Miquis, will give him international fame. He also praises Pino, opining that 'Ella y Borràs son dos grandes artistas que aciertan siempre' (She and Borràs are two great artists who always get it right). Miquis's view is that the play will bring well-deserved revenue to the Comedia, whose management is to be praised for its endeavours.

The Barcelona press had been rather more concerned with the moral issues raised by *El místic* than their Madrid counterparts. Ramón Pomés, writing in *La Vanguardia*, takes issue with the view that the play is about ordinary people – it is, he affirms, much more than this. For him the 'labor [de Rusiñol] es indudablemente una de las más valiosas e interesantes dentro de nuestro moderno teatro regional'[38] ([Rusiñol's] work is without doubt amongst the most worthy and interesting in our modern regional theatre). The words 'nuestro' (our) and 'teatro regional' (regional theatre) are another illustration of the way in which Catalan theatre is viewed – probably unconsciously – as an adjunct of Spanish theatre in general. Pomés considers that Ramon is not a real mystic: a real mystic would neither argue and debate nor fall in love the way Ramon does, the chief defect of the play, according to the reviewer. However, he likes Ramon's calm and tranquil exposé of the 'tremenda y lamentable desviación que está sufriendo en nuestros días la moral evangélica' (extraordinary and lamentable deviation which the evangelical doctrine is suffering today). Many scenes are beautiful, but he finds the final scene almost pitifully grotesque and totally unacceptable, although it did not merit the sniggers it received from a section of the audience. If Pomés is to be believed, perhaps this is another example of a rather detached and sceptical Barcelona audience not liking the baring of the soul. Pomés also condemns one of the scenes of Act 2 (he does not specify which one) for being 'dramáticamente una gran mentira' (a great lie, dramatically speaking) – despite this, it was (mistakenly) applauded by the audience. Somewhat mysteriously Pomés declares that he is deliberately not commenting on a number of the scenes, since 'no son de muy fácil cumplimiento en la cotidiana labor periodística' (they are not very easy to deal with in one's everyday journalistic work). There is very little on how the play functions as theatre: once more the preoccupation is with moral issues.

The *La Publicidad* reviewer informs his readers that the theatre was full well before the curtain rose on *El místic*, which he considered to be the best conceived and developed of all Rusiñol's plays, and one of the best in Catalan theatre.[39] This reviewer regards Ramon more sympathetically than Pomés, declaring that Rusiñol's character reflects not those Catholic priests who are devoid of Christian altruism but the ones who empathize with the meek and the suffering, in other words those at whom an allegedly sophisticated Barcelona audience would laugh. The *La Publicidad* critic reprimands the Pharisees who attack evangelists of Ramon's ilk, who, like the Catalan poet/priest Jacint Verdaguer,[40] 'pasó también en esta vida el calvario que reservan los malvados y los hipócritas, a todas las almas sinceras' (had also to bear in this life the cross which evil hypocrites reserve for all sincere souls) .

This review is much more sympathetic than Pomés's to the play's main character, but some of the comments on the play as theatre are banal and general, as in

> la arquitectura teatral de 'El mistich' es sólida, conservando las proporciones justas, que dan a la obra aquella harmonía característica de las creaciones artísticas bien concebidas y serenamente desarrolladas.

> (the theatrical architecture of 'The Mystic' is solid, preserving approriate proportions, which give the work that harmony which is characteristic of well conceived and serenely developed artistic creations.)

Nonetheless, there is a reasonable amount of detail on acting, directing and, more particularly, stage design, even if some of this also contains hyperbole. Borràs, as actor and director, is praised unreservedly: the reviewer calls him 'gloria de la escena española' (the great figure of the Spanish stage) – not 'Catalan stage', it will be noticed. Rusiñol, says the reviewer, could not have wished for a better actor: 'sobrio, justo de expresión siempre y hallando acentos y arranques de eminentísimo actor' (sober, always using the appropriate expression and finding the accents and the energy of a most eminent actor). He also praises Vilomara, the stage designer, in the only review which gives some idea of what the play might have looked like on stage. He describes how, when the curtain goes up, the audience applauds the fresh, pleasant room,[41] which communicates with a gallery lit up by the sun through arches decorated with flowers. The back of the stage depicts a blue sky and centre stage is the belfry with the two bells which typify parish life in a poor mountain village. This is clearly the set for the opening scenes, and the reviewer laments that a lack of time or money has not allowed adequate stage scenery in the later acts.

The hyperbole is even more in evidence in Carlos Juñer Vidal's review for *El Liberal*. In his exaggerated view, *El místic* is a great play by one of the greatest men the world has ever seen.[42] In contrast to Pomés, Juñer Vidal considers Ramon to be a typical mystic, reminding us, no less, of Dante, Ovid, Homer, Petrarch and St John of the Cross. However, the tone of the review changes in the final paragraphs, and contains a curiously veiled, even threatening allusion:

el éxito no satisfizo a todos por igual; pues mientras el público batía palmas, había en la sala algunos descontentadizos. Y tenga en cuenta Rusiñol, que algunos de esos mismos son los que entraron en el escenario y le felicitaron calurosamente . . .

(the success did not satisfy everyone equally; while the audience was clapping, there were some unhappy people in the auditorium. And Rusiñol should bear in mind that they are the same people who greeted him warmly when they entered . . .)

It is unclear who these allegedly two-faced and potentially dangerous individuals are, but there seems to be a hidden agenda here. Like the *La Publicidad* reviewer, M. y G. in *La Ilustració Catalana* believes that *El místic* contains some of the most solid material Rusiñol has written, but it is a play that leaves one ultimately dissatisfied. M. y G. is another critic who thinks that the final act is less convincing than the others and finds the weakest scenes those which precede the death of the protagonist, who

dexa de ser l'home tot esperit, tot misticisme, tot anar a Deu y al pròxim, pera convertirse en un enamorat *manqué* de la seva malhaurada cosina, en quals brassos mor.[43]

(the man ceases being all spirit, all mysticism, all going to God and his neighbour, and becomes instead his unfortunate cousin's lover *manqué*, and dies in her arms.)

One leaves the theatre, claims M. y G., unhappy at the wasted talents of the author, who is led by 'l'afany d'acontentar a la *galería* ab fochs d'artifici y pel desviament y la falta de llògica ab que se succehexen els fets' (the desire to keep the gallery happy with fireworks and by the loss of direction and the lack of logic with which the events unfold).

El Correo Catalán does not seem to have reviewed the play, but announces it – in Catalan – together with the following request: 'Avís important. – Se prega á las senyoras treures el sombrero durant la representació, y als senyors no fumar en la sala d'espectacles'[44] (Important notice – Ladies are requested to remove their hats during the performance, and gentlemen not to smoke in the theatre). Clearly, the social niceties were more important for this newspaper than the play itself.

Iglésies, Els Vells

Author: Ignasi Iglésies
Title: *Els vells*
Madrid premiere: Within Enric Borràs's Catalan season at the Teatro de la Comedia in May–June 1904; as a single listing at the Teatro de la Comedia in March 1905 by the Enric Borràs Company
Barcelona premiere: February 1903 at the Teatre Romea by the Romea's resident company headed by Borràs
Plot outline: The play deals with the suffering of textile workers in their sixties and seventies whose enforced retirement leaves them facing poverty. The alternatives facing the workers and their families are stark: in the absence of proper retirement provision, they either fight to retain their jobs or will have to turn to the poor house and charity to survive. One particular old couple, Joan and Úrsula, proud but embittered by their situation, try to persaude other workers and their families to resist, while some of these have a more selfish attitude, and claim that the workers are powerless to resist their bosses. Engracieta, Joan and Úrsula's daughter, is to marry Agustí, the son of Xiulet, another factory worker who is despised by the old couple for his idleness. Agustí's attitude to work is very different from that of his future parents-in-law in that he believes that old people should not have to work, and that the State should provide for them. He is also against the idea of his wife working in the factory, considering that her place is in the home. The play contains a measure of harsh realism in its portrayal of the lot of the old people. However, it is also discursive, with an element of sentimentality and ultimately melodrama, as Joan dramatically drops dead of a heart attack at the end of the play.

For audiences in the Spanish capital, plays with a social message were held in high regard at the turn of the century. One of the most overtly social Catalan plays of the period, Ignasi Iglésies's *Els vells*, is considered by many to be the best play by a writer who was highly regarded in both Barcelona and Madrid,[45] and, if Poblet is to be believed, it contributed to the framing of a new retirement law.[46] This suggests the inpact made by a play which was almost universally praised by reviewers. The *La Vanguardia* reviewer of the Barcelona premiere considered it to be the best play ever seen on the

Figure 4. The actor Enric Borràs in the role of Joan in
Ignasi Iglésies's *Els Vells* at the Romea Theatre in
Barcelona, 6 February 1903.

Barcelona stage.[47] *El Diario de Barcelona* is equally enthusiastic, praising its modern theme, emotional qualities, well-drawn characters, simple style and natural but correct dialogue.[48] The paper also emphasizes the enthusiastic response from the Barcelona audience. Like Luis Morote, the *Diario* does not accord the same generous reception to *Juan José*, a work with an equally sharp social message. This could, of course, be a case of local bias, just as with the Madrid press's enthusiasm for *Juan José*, although, to be fair, they were also very positive about *Els vells*.

The reviewer of the traditionalist Catalan paper *La Renaixensa* reports that the audience has been most impressed by the play.[49] He feels that, because of Iglésies's love of life, there are elements of hope and optimism in a play which, in the hands of another playwright would have been merely depressing. Borràs is singled out for praise both as actor and director. P. del O. considers *Els vells* to be both a great work of literature and a great work of compassion[50]

He is ecstatic about it, beginning his review with the following words: 'Al últim ha surtit un drama catalá, un verdader drama dels que son gloria de una literatura' (At last we have a Catalan play, a real play which covers a literature with glory), and later calling it a masterpiece. For him it is a fresh, young play, and he recalls how Iglésies and Rusiñol are perceived in Madrid as new and exciting authors. He views it as both very Catalan and universal. Some of his language is full of racial stereotyping: 'perque es sá, y fort, y te ánima, sanch, nervis, ossos y una admirable musculatura [. . .] son ayre castissament catalá' (for it is wholesome and strong, it has soul, blood, bones and marvellous muscles [. . .] its pure Catalan feel). His views on foreign influences on Catalan drama seem to run totally contrary to those of the *modernistes*, which is probably what one would expect from the organ of the traditionalist Renaixença movement. He criticizes Iglésies for a tendency to be influenced by foreign ideas in his previous plays, including symbolism and theatre of ideas. Pointing to the two main trends in European theatre of the late nineteenth century, he uses the language of the soil, a familiar one in conservative Catalan nationalist discourse of the period:

ni 'l teatro de ideas, ni 'l teatro simbolista li han sigut indiferents, y ab perill de perjudicar sas qualitats nativas de observador penetrant del ánima del nostre poble, algun cop s'ha empenyat en plantar aqueixas llavors forasteras, que no troban sahó favorable pera germinar en el terrer de Catalunya.

(he has been open to the theatre of ideas and symbolist theatre, and has on occasions endangered his natural qualities as a penetrating observer of the soul of our people by insisting on planting those foreign seeds, which do not find sufficiently fertile soil to germinate here in Catalonia.)

Els vells, on the other hand, deals with a purely Catalan subject: '[els] nostres honrats traballadors' (our honourable workers). P. del O.'s blinkered views are best exemplified in his claim that 'Per fin ha tingut la sort de trobar un assumpto tot nostre, tot de casa' (He has finally been lucky enough to find a topic that is exclusively ours, exclusively home-grown). This demonstrates an ignorance of the wider literary scene one would not normally associate with Catalonia: it was as if Zola and Hauptmann had never existed.

A more enlightened review than P. del O.'s is Ramon Perés's report on recent Barcelona premieres in his theatre section of the Madrid-based journal *La Lectura*. Perés considers *Els vells* to have definitively set Catalan theatre on the path to modernity.[51] He describes audience reaction to the play in Barcelona:

> *Els vells* es un drama sencillísimo y casi vulgar, si se quiere; pero que deja honda huella en el cerebro y en el corazón. El público barcelonés asiste a su representación sinceramente emocionado, con lágrimas en los ojos, o bien con grata sonrisa en los labios'.

('The Old Folks' is a very simple, almost vulgar play, but one which leaves a deep impression in one's mind and heart. Barcelona audiences are genuinely moved by it, and have tears in their eyes or a very pleasant smile on their lips.)

Perés ends his article by expressing the hope that *Els vells* will soon be translated into Spanish, so that the whole of Spain may see this modern play and be Europeanized theatrically:

> Drama de luchas, como se ve, de piedad humana, de poesía humilde y honda, es *Els vells* de Iglesias. Yo espero que se traduzca pronto al castellano, como muchos desean, y que recorra triunfalmente otros teatros, además del catalán, siendo viva muestra de la aptitud que un dramaturgo joven, a quien desde hoy llama ya eminente toda Cataluña, posee para darnos ese drama verdaderamente moderno a que aspiramos, muy propio, muy nuestro, y universal a la vez. Con obras así, y no con vanas palabras, ni entreteniéndonos en la estúpida labor de matar todo lo bueno y nuevo, para mantener en alto lo malo y caduco, es como hay que *europeizar* a España. Lo demás son bizantismos de pueblo que se ensimisma en la contemplación de su propia nada. (p. 439)

(Iglésies's 'The Old Folk' is a drama of struggle, of human mercy, of deep, humble poetry. I hope it will soon be translated into Spanish, as many people wish, and will triumphantly tour other theatres apart from Catalan ones as a living demonstration of how a young dramatist who from now on will be highly regarded in the whole of Catalonia is able to give us this really modern play to which we all aspire, something that is very much our own but is at the same time universal. Spain must be 'Europeanized' with plays like this, and not with empty words nor by wasting our time destroying everything new and good and maintaining what is bad and out-of-date. The rest is no more than the pointlessness of a people who turn in on themselves and contemplate their own nothingness.)

This need to 'Europeanize' Spain was, as was observed in Chapter 1, very much a concern of both the Catalan *modernistes* and the 1898 Generation of Spanish writers. Oddly, Iglésies never became a European playwright in the sense that Guimerà, for instance, did. Perhaps Perés was overstating the international appeal of a play that, in a Europe accustomed to playwrights of the quality of Ibsen, Zola and Hauptmann, might seem rather tame.

As has been demonstrated, the play was known and appreciated in Madrid from the original version put on by Borràs. Luis Morote expressed a common perception from turn-of-the-century Madrid when he wrote that *Els vells* was the kind of modern play that was badly needed in Spain. His view is that contemporary Catalan theatre is much more modern than its Castilian counterpart.[52] In a country in which taste has been corrupted by plays à la Echegaray, Morote believed that it would take time for work of the quality of *Els vells* to be appreciated. Unlike Bustillo, who found *Juan José* superior to Guimerà, Morote contrasts the natural dialogue of *Els vells* with that of Dicenta's play. The blame, according to Morote, may be attributed to an audience which he considers has been 'perverted' by Echegaray, adding:

Si le quitáis a *Juan José* los discursos soberbios, admirables, elocuentes, pero al fin irreales, absurdos, imposibles, ¿qué queda que merezca la pena de aplaudirse y de entusiasmar? (p. 107)

(If you take away from *Juan José* the proud, impressive, eloquent but ultimately unreal, absurd, impossible speeches, what is left that is worthy of applause and enthusiasm?)

According to Morote, there is a stark contrast between Catalan and Spanish theatre. The former has been well received in Madrid, especially by the younger spectators, because it represents a refreshing change from a theatre dominated by Echegaray and Dicenta (p. 109).

The Madrid press was equally enthusiastic about the Spanish translation of the play, which was performed by Borràs in his first season at the Comedia. J.A. praises Iglésies for leading Catalan theatre out of an unspecified 'false tendency', and for bringing 'real life' to the stage.[53] The critic finds the play less successful than when it was performed in Catalan the previous year, although the fact that it was in Spanish translation allowed the audience to understand it more fully. J.A. describes the emotion felt by the audience; both author and principal actor had to come out on stage at the conclusion of each act, and they received extraordinarily loud and prolonged applause at the end of the play. Miquis, too, emphasizes that the play was appreciated by the audience.[54] He declares that, at the risk of repeating what he said in his reviews of Borràs's Catalan season the previous summer, *Els vells* is the best modern Catalan play and that Borràs's greatness is more in evidence in this than anywhere else. Miquis praises Iglésies's realistic portrayal of the old worker, but, being Miquis, is critical of a number of aspects. He finds the translation (like Borràs's hands!) too polished, and the language – except for a few moments in Act 3 – more academic than 'real life'. Despite eulogizing Borràs's performance, he considers the rest of the cast to be no more than adequate and two of them to be completely unsuited to the genre.

Gual, El geni de la comèdia

Author: Adrià Gual
Title: *El geni de la comèdia*
Madrid premiere: April 1912 at the Teatro de la Princesa
Barcelona premiere: May 1912 at the Teatre Principal
Plot outline: *El geni de la comèdia* is an illustrated three-part history of Western theatre from the classical period to the Renaissance. The first lecture-performance was divided into three parts and consisted of a general introduction to comedy, a specific study of Greek comedy, including staging, ending with a performance of excerpts from *The Frogs* and from another Aristophanes play, *The Birds*, complete with commentaries by the Scholiast. The second session covered Latin and medieval theatre, and included a lecture on comic theatre of the Middle Ages, a performance in which clowns and troubadors participated, fragments from *The Dance of Death* by the rabbi Don Sem Job, and a section on the *commedia dell'arte*, which incorporated Gual's own short farce *Arlequí vividor*. The final session was dedicated to the Renaissance, with a lecture covering England, France, Italy and Spain. Spain was presented as the major country of this period, its theatre being illustrated by the performance of one act of *Paso segundo de los ladrones* by Lope de Rueda, the father of Golden Age Spanish

theatre. The final section of the show was dedicated to Molière, with excerpts from *Le Malade imaginaire*. Most of Gual's text had been translated for the occasion, with designs by Catalan and Madrid-based stage designers working together, and music which had been specially composed for the show. The influence of symbolist or poetic theatre, with its blend of sound and visual effects to complement the effect of the words, is quite clear.

If Iglésies typified the 'social' strand of *modernisme*, then, in many ways, Adrià Gual encapsulates the 'art-for-art's sake' side of this movement. Elegance and splendour were concepts associated with Gual's series of lecture-performances which took place at Madrid's Princesa Theatre on three separate days in April 1912,[55] and which was repeated at Barcelona's Principal Theatre in May of the same year. It clearly fitted well into the ethos of the Princesa, which, as was observed in Chapter 1, had been splendidly refurbished three years earlier and was a beacon, under María Guerrero, of poetic theatre. The Gual shows were an appropriate production for the Princesa, and one critic viewed them as an important landmark in the development of stage design in Madrid: 'no es difícil ver la novedad que supone, en primer lugar, el abandono de la representación realista'[56] (it is not hard to see what the abandonment of realist representation meant).

The Madrid venture received warm approval from press and audiences alike, although the ambition and novelty of the enterprise were lauded rather more than the end result. Miquis, for instance, describes Gual's initiatives as 'noble'.[57] But his review is generally quite critical – for him Gual's explanation of Greek comedy sounded too modern and he detected one or two errors in the costumes. He criticizes the cuts made in *The Birds*, although he understands the time constraints which necessitated these. He is also unhappy about the constant and over-solemn interventions of the Scholiast, which did not allow a sufficiently joyful atmosphere to be achieved. Miquis also feels that an open-air performance would have been fitting, possibly under the archway of the Fine Arts Museum, to accompany the exhibition being held there. However, the critic ends on a positive note, affirming that on certain occasions good intentions are sufficient.

It should be noted that this is an intelligent, quality-based review, with no mention of Spanishness or Catalanness. Miquis's review of

Figure 5. Adrià Gual's *El geni de la comèdia* at the Princesa Theatre in Madrid, April 1912.

Gual's second lecture-performance is also concerned with artistic issues. His main objection this time is that Gual uses too many foreign examples to illustrate his points. This he considers to be true of the cycle as a whole but especially noticeable in the second lecture (on medieval comic theatre) since Spain was the world leader in this type of drama, which makes its neglect by Gual unforgivable.[58] Another fault Miquis finds with both lectures is that there is too much talk and not enough action.

In his review of the third and final spectacle Miquis comments on the sizeable audiences attracted to the Princesa, and he calls on Gual and Díaz de Mendoza to undertake similar ventures in the future, but to be more ambitious. Once one has convinced the audience, writes Miquis, anything is possible.[59] Again, however, Miquis considers that Gual used too many foreign examples, but that there was more action this time. He also criticizes the fact that the theatre of Lope de Rueda was exemplified only in the Corral de la Pacheca: there was no documentation on this *corral*, says Miquis, so any creation is bound to be a matter of personal whim. This is yet another example of Miquis showing (off?) his knowledge of theatre history, and of the exacting nature of his demands. However, once more, he ends the review by praising Gual's initiative and by stressing just how positive the attitude of the audiences has been.

Gual comments on audience reaction to the shows in his memoirs. He reports that, although they turned up in numbers, they were unfamiliar with this type of spectacle and not on the same wavelength as its creator. Gual describes how the audience received the show in silence, which he took to mean lack of approval.[60] However, Díaz de Mendoza assured him that their mere presence demonstrated their appreciation, and tried to convince him that he had them in his pocket.

García de Cuadrado confirms the audiences's appreciation of Gual's enthusiasm and quality, while once more highlighting the fact that the show was minority taste:

> La personalidad literaria de Adrián Gual posee un justo relieve en las letras catalanas. Ante todo, Gual es un entusiasta, un espíritu que vive siempre en la plenitud de una romántica exaltación artística, un enamorado de toda manifestación dramática y que desea hacerla revivir ante un público que será siempre de elegidos. Como autor dramático, Adrián Gual ha escrito obras verdaderamente magistrales. Alguna de ellas ha salido del círculo estrecho de una ciudad española, para pasear

en triunfo por Europa. Adrián Gual sabe lo que valen y lo que significan los aplausos de París, que escuchó no hace mucho en el teatro Antoine.[61]

(Adrià Gual is deservedly well known in Catalan letters. Above all, Gual is an enthusiast, a spirit who lives permanently in the fullness of a romantic artistic exaltation, a lover of any kind of dramatic manifestation whose desire is to bring it alive before an audience which will always be select. As a dramatist, Gual has written truly masterly works. Some of them have moved out of the narrow circles of a Spanish city [presumably Barcelona] and marched in triumph through Europe. Adrià Gual knows the value of Parisian applause, which he heard not long ago at Antoine's theatre.)

For García de Candamo, Gual has managed to bring to life the dead literature of books, which bears out the view that his achievement was to put into practice on the stage ideas which for others had remained as theory. This is yet another critic who emphasizes how his efforts were warmly applauded by the select audience which filled the Princesa. In his review of the final performance, García de Candamo adds that the fact that a banquet was to be offered in Gual's honour in Madrid, to be attended by leading literati and artists, was proof of the esteem in which he was held there.[62]

Other favourable reviews of the Gual season appeared in *El Heraldo de Madrid* and *El Liberal*. La Almiranta praises Gual as a talented and a modest writer. He could possibly be criticized for representing Greek comedy through just one playwright (Aristophanes), but the reviewer asks which other Greek playwrights have stood the test of time. La Almiranta also praises Díaz de Mendoza for the generosity he has shown towards Gual.[63] Arimón recognizes Gual's 'vasta erudición, su exquisito buen gusto, su lucidez intelectual'[64] (vast erudition, his exquisite good taste, his intellectual lucidity). According to him, the theatre was full, and he commented: 'cómo el público madrileño ha respondido a tan laudable inciativa, lo demuestra el brillantísimo aspecto que ofrecía la sala' (the brilliant appearance of the theatre shows how the Madrid public has responded to this laudable initiative). For Arimón the most interesting parts of the first show were the excerpts from the play. The conditions in the theatre did not allow the original comedy to be reproduced faithfully, with the result that the fragments did not produce a great impression on the audience. Despite this, the scenery, costumes and accessories were magnificent and Gual was to be greatly applauded for his efforts, as were Guerrero and Díaz de Mendoza for making the series possible.

Arimón (who signs as J.A. this time) comments on the brilliance of Gual's lecture on Latin, medieval and early Renaissance theatre which constituted the first half of the second performance. He does criticize Gual for covering too wide a time span and for trying to be too authentic in his creation of the periods, confusing the audience somewhat. Nonetheless, they offered him enthusiastic applause, and he received numerous curtain calls at the end.[65]

In his review of the final spectacle, Arimón (J.A.) praises both Gual and Díaz de Mendoza for placing artistic above economic interest in mounting the series. He is delighted with Gual for dedicating 'entusiastas palabritas de admiración al glorioso teatro castellano'[66] (enthusiastic words of admiration to the glorious theatre of Spain). Not only is this an example of a revival of Spanish nationalism in theatre criticism, but we have the curious case of the enthusiasm for Spanish Golden Age drama being demonstrated by Adrià Gual, probably the individual who did most to develop Catalan theatre at the turn of the century and to establish Barcelona as a distinctive theatre centre.

The *ABC* reviews were almost completely without criticism. The reviewer claims that the theatre was not very full for the first performance, but was for the other two. According to this critic, it was Gual's own *Arlequí vividor* which best pleased the audience. He sums up the general view of Madrid critics that the Gual season represented an exciting new departure for the theatre in Madrid in general and the Princesa in particular.[67] The final *ABC* review is perhaps the most laudatory of them all:

> Ha sido algo inusitado y fascinante . . . En la memoria de todos quedará, lleno de prestigio, el recuerdo suave, plácido y risueño de estas nobles tardes entregadas al arte y a la cultura.[68]

> (This has been something new and fascinating . . . The gentle, placid and cheerful memory of these noble and dignified evenings devoted to art and culture will remain with us all.)

The reviewer comments on the austerity of the third show, adding that Gual could have gone for something lavish, brilliant and multicoloured with which to finish the spectacle, but that he did not take the easy option. The reviewer considers Gual's lack of showiness to be worthy of praise. The nationalistic strain which emerged from the third *El Liberal* review is even stronger here. Having praised the three great theatre cultures of the sixteenth and seventeenth centuries – namely those of England, France and Spain – Gual, declares the reviewer,

> terminó cantando a nuestra comedia, con verdadera unción, párrafos hermosos y floridos, que le valieron aplausos entusiastas. La emoción palpitaba en aquella voz fina, de suspirante acento poético, que iba exhumando esta gloria imperecedora de la raza.

> (ended by praising our theatre in beautiful, ornate words, words which earned him enthusiastic applause. That refined voice, with its gently poetic tone, trembled with emotion as it exhumed the everlasting gloria of the race.)

The key word is 'race': clearly the Spanish nation, as exemplified in its greatest period historically and theatrically speaking and as captured by a Catalan! The presence of nationalist sentiment in both Spanish and Catalan theatre criticism of the 1910s is evident, but the fact that Madrid-based critics could not see the irony of their praise for a Catalan as promoter of Spanish theatre tradition seems to be the result of cultural imperialism.

Such critics were used to Madrid's position as the leading theatre city in the Iberian Peninsula, and by now were also accustomed to seeing Catalan plays in their city before they had been premiered in Barcelona. As with *Terra baixa*, *El geni de la comèdia* was performed in Barcelona – at the Principal Theatre in May 1912 – one month after its Madrid premiere. There was one change in the excerpts performed, the Lope de Rueda play being replaced by a Lope de Vega text. Like their Madrid counterparts, a number of the Barcelona papers highlight the elite and select nature of the audiences (*El Diario de Barcelona*, *La Publicidad*, *El Teatre Català*). Despite this, the Madrid success with press and public was not repeated in Barcelona, as Gual recounts frankly in his memoirs, although without offering an explanation:

> L'èxit de Barcelona no va correspondre al de Madrid, i, per bé que no va succeir res desagradable, la cosa va transcórrer sense una gran compenetració, tant per part dels intèrprets com per part del públic, i

amb una manca absoluta d'afecció i assentiment de la banda de la premsa, a part que els resultats econòmics, lluny d'alleugerir l'estat de les meves finances, varen venir potser i tot a agreujar-lo.[69]

(The play was not so successful in Barcelona as it had been in Madrid. Nothing unpleasant happened, but there was no great rapport between audience and performers, coupled with a complete lack of warmth and approval by the press. In addition, the economic results, far from alleviating my financial problems, may even have made them worse.)

This could be another example of a Catalan theatre practitioner being more appreciated in Madrid than in Barcelona, although, in this case, it is the artist himself who highlights the contrast.

Nevertheless, the conservative *El Diario de Barcelona* is fulsome in its praise of *El geni de la comèdia*, although its emphasis is on social elegance rather than dramatic quality:

No se entusiasmaron en balde la crítica y el público ilustrado de Madrid al conocer la obra ciclo-histórica del señor Gual [. . .] La numerosa y selecta concurrencia agregada anoche [. . .].[70]

(Not for nothing did Madrid's critics and distinguished public get excited when they saw Señor Gual's historical cycle [. . .] The large and select gathering of yesterday evening [. . .].)

The adjectives 'distinguished' and 'select' suggests that the cultured middle-class audience who would attend such a show in both cities were united by their social class rather than divided by a language. However, in its review of the second Gual session, *El Diario de Barcelona* hints at a rivalry which had caused a certain bitterness in Catalan circles but which was not mentioned in the Madrid reviews, namely the possibility that Benavente had plagiarized *Arlequí vividor* (Harlequin the Freeloader[71]) in *Los intereses creados* (*The Bonds of Interest*).[72]

The underlying rivalry between Catalonia and Castile is pinpointed in a preview of the Barcelona series in *L'Esquella de la Torratxa*:

L'abonament a les tres sessions que sobre 'El geni de la comedia' organisa en Gual, diuen que comensa a esser nodrit, cosa que convindria moltissim, puig de lo contrari els castellans hauran demostrat tenir més curiositat y més gust per les coses de teatre que nosaltres.[73]

(They say that tickets are beginning to be sold for the three sessions that Senyor Gual is organizing on 'The Genius of Comedy'. This is just as well because, if not, the Castilians will have shown that they are more interested in the theatre than we are.)

This paper's later review uses words like 'discretion' to describe the show, and writes of Gual's portrayal of 'la victoria dels nostres comediografs en aquella època'[74] (the triumph of our comedy writers at that time), where 'our' presumably refers to Spain. However, *L'Esquella*'s view is that the audience, although polite, was neither convinced nor enthusiastic, and that they are not yet sufficiently educated for Gual's 'spiritual filigrees'.[75] Gual's own view – quoted above – backs this up, and surely questions whether Barcelona really was more receptive than Madrid to experimental theatre. However, it is doubtful whether one can describe *El geni de la comèdia* in these terms, since it seems to have been a rather conventional review of sections of the European theatrical tradition which emphasizes its enduring quality.

Although the Barcelona newspapers generally approve of Gual's initiative, they are more critical of the outcome than their Madrid colleagues. One defect which a number of Barcelona critics commented on was the presentational aspect. An otherwise favourable review of the first two sessions in *L'Esquella* is critical of this aspect: 'El detall que deixa més que desitjar es la presentació; les dues sessions han patit del mateix mal: presentació migrada y fins inapropiada, en alguns casos.'[76] (The detail which leaves most to be desired is the presentation. The two sessions have suffered from the same problem: insufficient and even inappropriate presentation in some cases.) Rodríguez Codolá, writing in *La Vanguardia*, criticizes the set among other things, and sharply comments that if a show is presented as something out of the ordinary, then this it what it should be.[77] *La Publicidad*'s review, although descriptive rather than critical, also disapproves of the set: 'Los trajes eran superiores y más apropiados que el decorado' (The costumes were better and more appropriate than the set). The reviewer claims that it had already been used for *A Midsummer Night's Dream*.

El Teatre Català, having emphasized the select nature of the audience in its review of the first Gual performance, censures the actors for not having rehearsed their parts sufficiently in the first session,[78] and for their representation of medieval theatre during the second show.[79] The review of the third session is even more critical, and specific blame is placed on the management of the Principal, the theatre in which the performances took place:

> Ni la presentació, ni l'interpretació, ni res, responien a lo que en Gual ens deia poc abans. Allò era tristíssim, aborrit, incoherent. La direcció del Principal sembla que hagi tingut interès en que l'acció contradís les paraules de l'ilustre disertant.[80]

(Neither the presentation nor the interpretation, nothing in fact, corresponded to what Gual was saying a short time ago. This was pathetic, boring, incoherent. It seems that the management of the Principal was interested in contradicting the words of the illustrious lecturer.)

The criticism of the Principal is expanded later in the review:

> Acabades les sessions d'*El geni de la Comèdia*, siguins permès recordar un solt publicat en aquestes columnes en el qual ens dolíem de que aquest espectacle hagués de demanar-se al Principal, aont tant segur era que no hi hauría, pera aquesta important manifestació d'art, el respecte que's mereixía. Desgraciadament, i contra lo que nosaltres hauríem desitjat, els fets ens han vingut a donar la raó. Ni l'empresa ni la direcció han sabut sobreposar-se a lo que sembla llei d'aquella casa – o de totes les cases aont el senyor franqueza [*sic*] governa – i les ilustracions que en Gual ha intercalat en la seva notable disertació han estat posades en escena com s'hi posaría una comedia en un acte que s'estrenés per compromís.

(Now that the 'Genius of Comedy' sessions are over, let us recall a piece published in these columns in which we lamented the fact that the Principal should be asked to mount this spectacle, since we were sure that they would not show this important artistic manifestation the respect it deserved. Unfortunately, we have been proved right. Neither the company nor the management have been able to overcome what seems to be the norm in that theatre – and indeed of all the theatres which are controlled by Senyor Franqueza[81] – and the illustrations which Gual used for his excellent lecture were staged as if they were any old one-act play they were contracted to put on.)

The specific agenda of this publication – the development of a Catalan national theatre – must be borne in mind as criticism of an individual play or show is always set within this wider perspective.

This chapter has demonstrated how popular the leading turn-of-the-century Catalan playwrights, actors and directors were in Madrid. Indeed, there is some evidence that certain plays were more favourably received in Madrid than they were in Barcelona. The last decade of the nineteenth century and – more specifically – the first decade of the twentieth – represent the high point of Madrid's interest in Catalan playwrights.

It seems that the promotion of Catalan drama in Madrid had more to do with the efforts of a few individuals than with the city's theatrical establishment. Chief among these individuals were Rusiñol, Gual and Borràs. Rusiñol was the ambassador *par excellence*, while Borràs was a pivotal figure not only in exposing the Madrid public to new Catalan playwrights but also in cultivating a certain style of acting there. Chapter 2 demonstrated that, well into the 1920s, Gual was still held up in Madrid as an example of how the Spanish theatre could and should be reformed, and also that there was a continuing interest in Barcelona's theatre activity in the Spanish capital's press. Despite Benavente's apparent encouragement, there was little or no interest in Gual's plays (I cannot find any reference to any performance in the Spanish capital), but his work as a director and educator continued to be respected and admired there. With the Escola Catalana d'Art Dramàtic (Catalan School of Dramatic Art, or ECAD) he performed Guimerà at a theatre festival for schoolchildren in Madrid in 1924. He continued to keep abreast of new developments in the theatre almost to the end of his life. In 1929, for example, ECAD organized the Third International Theatre Congress in Barcelona, sponsored by the Société Universelle du Théâtre, exposing the Barcelona public to Brecht and Piscator and complete with a lecture by Gual entitled 'Hacia un teatro nuevo' (Towards a New Theatre). Although he is often viewed as a dramatist, as with Martínez Sierra, Gual's real influence is as a director and facilitator.

By the 1920s, the dramatists who were in vogue in Barcelona did not excite the same interest in Madrid as Guimerà, Rusiñol and Iglésies had. A case in point is Josep M. de Sagarra, who did not attain anything like the popularity in Madrid that he did in Barcelona, which is also true of lesser known Catalan playwrights like Carles Soldevila and Josep Millàs-Raurell. A glance at the Madrid listings in the 1920s and 1930s will confirm that the old favourites like Guimerà and Rusiñol were performed more often than Sagarra.[82] The emphasis had shifted to Spanish playwrights, including highly popular ones like the Álvarez Quintero brothers, Muñoz Seca or Benavente, and to Martínez Sierra, who drew the same kind of audience as Gual. In intellectual circles, the dramatists who aroused most interest were the remnants of the 1898 Generation like Azorín and Unamuno and, by the 1930s, the new generation of Casona, Alberti and García Lorca.

Reception of Spanish Theatre in Barcelona and Madrid

Dicenta, Juan José

Author: Joaquín Dicenta
Title: *Juan José*
Madrid premiere: October 1895 at the Teatro de la Comedia by Emilio Mario
Barcelona premiere: June–July 1896 at the Teatre Líric by Emilio Mario
Plot outline: Like Iglésies's *Els vells*, *Juan José* deals with the suffering of a group of factory workers at the hands of their ruthless boss. The play is set in the working-class suburbs of Madrid, and was revolutionary in its portrayal of the urban proletariat, complete with their dialect. However, to a greater extent than *Els vells*, *Juan José* is a not altogether felicitous mixture of harsh realism and melodrama. The exploitation of the workers is evoked vividly, but also with down-to-earth humour. Nevertheless, Juan José hates his employer, the young man-about-town Paco, partly because of the way he feels exploited by him but more especially for the latter's designs on his common-law wife, Rosa. It is through the treatment of this love triangle that the element of melodrama comes more and more to the fore as the play progresses. Juan José is dismissed by his boss following a row between the two over Paco's interest in Rosa. In desperation, Juan José steals to survive, and ends up in prison. While he is there Rosa, who has become increasingly attracted to Paco's wealthy lifestyle, goes to live with him. Juan José manages to escape from prison, discovers the truth and kills both Rosa and Paco.

Having considered in Chapter 5 how specific Catalan plays and authors were viewed in Barcelona and Madrid, the focus of attention now shifts to Spanish plays, as I compare their reception in both cities. Barcelona often had the chance to view plays which Madrid-based companies brought to their city as part of their provincial spring tours. However, this did not mean that the Barcelona performances were of secondary importance to Madrid-based companies and, as this chapter will demonstrate, leading Spanish playwrights of the early twentieth century attached considerable weight to the Barcelona premiere of their plays. In certain cases, as in a number of García Lorca plays, these were also the Spanish premiere. The present chapter will consider representative works ranging from the social naturalistic to the symbolic modes. The first of these is Joaquín Dicenta's *Juan José*, premiered at the Teatro de la Comedia in Madrid in 1895, and destined to become the second-most performed Spanish play.[1] As Chapter 2 illustrated, Dicenta (1863–1917) was the Spanish translator of Rusiñol's *El místic* and an admirer of the Catalan playwright. He was a leading socialist, and editor of the socialist newspaper *El País* and the weekly journal of the Germinal group, whose name derives from Zola's novel. This group were fervent admirers of Zola's socialist and positivist views, and their naturalism is strongly influenced by the works of the French author. Dicenta's most bitter exposure of social justice is *Daniel* (1907), a play that lacks the Romantic element of *Juan José*. Although the working classes were beginning to be represented on the Madrid stage, Dicenta's presentation of the harsh world of the Madrid proletariat represented a relatively new departure.[2] Ironically, however, the theatre in which it was premiered, the Comedia, was one of Madrid's most traditional houses, so *Juan José* was performed by the middle class for the middle class.

Audiences and critics were divided on whether *Juan José* was a thesis play or not:

> *Juan José* no es socialista, ni anarquista, ni nada que se le parezca. Es sencillamente un enamorado que roba y mata, no por necesidad y por anhelos de desquite social, sino por amor.[3]

> ('Juan José' is not socialist, nor Anarchist, nor any such thing. He is no more than a man in love who robs and kills, not out of necessity or a desire for social revenge, but for love.)

Some of the audience were obviously convinced that the opposite was true: according to Urrecha, a socialist orator appeared in the foyer to preach his views to the audience, who applauded him. The police arrested a man following a heated exchange between spectators at the end of Act 1, and each interval was punctuated by similarly passionate discussions. Such episodes illustrate that the theatre was not only an important social institution in turn-of-the-century Spain but was also a barometer of the state of an increasingly agitated nation. As Gies has shown, the young writers of the 1898 Generation appreciated the play's social content,[4] while the Madrid press generally enthused over the premiere. Urrecha's view is that it is not a thesis play, but simply 'good' drama, which demonstrates that it is possible to create an excellent play about humble people without resorting to elegant drawing rooms or employing rhetorical or lyrical language and to create something new out of a well-worn formula.[5] Urrecha considers that Dicenta was taking a risk by presenting on stage violent scenes set in the tavern or in Madrid's Modelo Prison in an unfamiliar linguistic register, but 'el peligro desapareció en las primeras escenas, y el lenguaje pareció hasta familiar en los oídos del público' (the danger disappeared in the opening scenes and the language even seemed familiar to the audience's ears). Urrecha is impressed by the play's naturalism:

> el primer acto – la taberna– es de lo mejor expuesto que se ha llevado al teatro; la presentación naturalísima de las figuras se hace con arte y sobriedad; nada sobra y nada falta.
>
> (the first act – the tavern – is one of the best things to have been put on in the theatre; the highly natural presentation of the figures is achieved with skill and sobriety; not too little, not too much.)

He considers that all the characters are created with affection and care, although the main protagonist is the most upright and vigorously drawn. He praises the actors, especially Emilio Thuillier, one of the leading Spanish actors of the late nineteenth and early twentieth centuries, who 'interpretó admirablemente el Juan José, con pasión y arranque de gran artista' (played Juan José superbly, with the passion and energy of a great artist). His final view is that *Juan José* is a play which is very well planned, constructed and written.

El A. Pirracas (*sic*) was also fulsome in his praise in *La Correspondencia de España*, beginning his review thus: '*Juan José* es una obra hermosísima'[6] ('Juan José' is a very beautiful play). The reviewer sees it as slice-of-life naturalism, and the harsh evocation of the prison he judges true to life. He is another critic who views *Juan José* as a very human drama, written in a sober and simple language. He takes issue with those who maintain that such plays have no place in a theatre like the Comedia. His view is that what is not licit in the theatre is 'la mentira artificiosa y las imposiciones del capricho' (contrived artifice and the imposition of whim). Audiences nowadays expect natural dialogue, and 'action, passion and truth', which is exactly what they get with *Juan José*.

Summing up the 1895–6 season, Salvador Canals emphasizes that it was a huge, noisy success with Madrid audiences.[7] Without preaching, writes Canals, it is a revolutionary play (p. 149), while its harsh facts speak louder than words. Canals does not consider the play to be a melodrama, disagreeing with some interval comments he heard on the subject. Melodramas, writes Canals, must contain some supernatural intervention to reward good and punish evil. In the Dicenta play everything

> se produce por recuros natuarles, a flor de tierra, por la fuerza misma de las pasiones y de las circunstancias (p. 152).
>
> (happens through natural resources, close to the soil, through the very power of the passions and the circumstances.)

Rather than a 'drama vertiginoso, [. . .] es drama de cuadros' (dizzy drama, [. . .] it is a play about local customs), which contains moments of passion (p. 153).[8] Its characters are solid and well-drawn (p. 153), and Juan José is one of Thuiller's best creations.

A more dispassionate view of the play is given by a French contemporary, Henry Lyonnet. For this critic, the play is too simplistic in its portrayal of social class. Lyonnet seems to fall into the trap of racial stereotyping when, commenting on the play's depiction of the honour theme, he concludes: 'Mais que voulez-vous faire dans un pays de soleil où l'on est tenté par tempérament à tout exagérer et à voir des génies partout'[9] (But what do you expect in a sunny country where one is temperamentally tempted to exaggerate everything and to see geniuses everywhere). He is sharp but somewhat cruel in his assertion that Madrid's enthusiasm for the play is due to the lack of opportunities its audiences have had to see the working classes portrayed on stage. According to Lyonnet, this is a reflection of just how far Spanish theatre lags behind that of the rest of Europe: 'ce théâtre espagnol qui retarde d'un bon quart de siècle sur le mouvement dramatique contemporain'[10] (that Spanish theatre which is a good quarter of a century behind the contemporary scene).

Be that as it may, *Juan José* was equally popular with what one might have imagined would have been a less receptive Barcelona audience and with some of their newspaper critics when it was taken to the Líric Theatre of Barcelona as part of Emilio Mario's June–July 1896 touring season. According to *La Publicidad*, 'el público distinguido que llenaba casi el teatro, aplaudió y celebró el discutido "Juan José"'[11] (the distinguished audience which almost filled the theatre applauded and celebrated the controversial 'Juan José'). The adjective 'controversial' is revealing in that it is indicative of the wider process of the transfer of plays from Madrid to Barcelona. The Barcelona public knew all about an individual play before it reached their city, and, as Chapter 5 demonstrated, this was even the case with Guimerà's *Terra baixa*, since the time lapse between the Madrid and the Barcelona premieres would have allowed people in the Catalan capital time to read it before seeing it on stage, thus removing its sense of novelty and excitement.

In a fuller review the following day, *La Publicidad* reports the play was a real success and that the applause it received was justified. They consider Act 1 to be especially

> hermoso, lleno de vida y de color, de estructura dramática casi perfecta, desarrollándose las escenas con naturalidad y lógica . . . Es un cuadro tomado del natural, con figuras vivas que impresionan de un modo extraordinario.[12]

> (beautiful, full of life and colour. Its dramatic structure is almost perfect, and the scenes develop naturally and logically . . . It is a picture of real life, with living figures who make an extraordinary impression.)

However, this reviewer regards the other acts as inferior, especially the third, in which Juan José becomes a character from melodrama: '*Juan José* es un romántico, no es un obrero ni como un obrero se expresa; es el tipo menos verdad del drama, el más falso y menos observado' (Juan José is a romantic, he is not a worker, nor does he express himself like a worker; he is the least realistic of the characters, the most false and the least carefully observed). Rosa is the most convincing character, while the go-between Isidra is good too. The most discerning members of the audience in artistic questions found that *Juan José* does not fulfil the criteria which are necessary for it to be considered a modern play, lacking as it does a sociological purpose or a social moral (p. 3). The reviewer agrees with this viewpoint, but believes that Dicenta is to be congratulated for getting away from the rhetoric which blights contemporary Spanish drama (no mention is made of Catalan drama.)

Writing in *La Vanguardia*, P. highlights the success of the play with the Barcelona audience, the actors and the author being given many curtain calls.[13] Unlike the *La Publicidad* reviewer, P. finds Rosa defective, a feature that became more noticeable the longer the play went on. He particularly approves of the serious ending of Act 1. There were some touches in Act 2 which make us fear for the play's literary success, while he concurs with his counterpart in *La Publicidad* that Act 3 falls totally into melodrama. He generally approves of the acting, although he criticizes Thuiller to an extent. He finds Juan José's down-to-earth friend Andrés particularly good, despite being unable to remember the name of the actor who played the part.

A less balanced view of the play and a very different picture of the audience's reaction to it emerges from the conservative *Diario de Barcelona*. They consider it to be prosaic and vulgar and not to be to the taste of the distinguished Líric audience.[14] Their reviewer shows none of the sympathy towards the play which emanates from the Madrid-based critics, including the Catalan Salvador Canals. Whether the comments on audience reaction are reliable, or simply a reflection of the paper's conservative bias, is unclear, but the picture of a suave, refined audience, not wishing to be disturbed by Dicenta's melodramatic social questionings, was to be reflected in the Barcelona edition of *El Liberal*'s account of audience reaction to the very different *Los intereses creados* in 1908.[15]

Despite these negative comments, the broad public and critical reaction to *Juan José* was similar in Madrid and Barcelona. However, there were two specific elements which coloured response in the Catalan capital: a sense of grievance that it had taken so long for the play to be brought there, and the fact that there was a strong Anarchist presence in the city. Moreover, the Barcelona reviewers engaged in a fuller discussion than their Madrid counterparts of the moral implications of the play. P. in *La Vanguardia* is characteristic in complaining that Barcelona audiences have been the last ones in Spain to see *Juan José*, while P. del O. in *L'Esquella de la Torratxa* also makes the point that Barcelona has been forced to wait for *Juan José* despite the demand there for it to be played the previous winter. But this reviewer highlights another problem, which has to do with the perceived social content of the play and the social unrest in Barcelona. Following the Anarchist bombing of the Liceu Theatre in 1893 and of the Corpus Christi procession in Canvis Nous which just preceded the Barcelona premiere of *Juan José*, people were reluctant to attend the theatre. Furthermore, it was possible that the play could be interpreted as Anarchist propaganda at this particularly sensitive time, although P. del O., echoing some of his Madrid counterparts, believes this would be unfair, seeing it rather as the tale of a man avenging himself against the bounder who stole his woman.[16]

P. del O. is the commentator who is most concerned with the moral issues thrown up by the play. He remarks that for some critics it is immoral as the two couples are not married, but mocks such prudery, declaring

> y visca la moral de aquests Tartufos que aparentan curarho tot colocant en las estátuas una fullas de parra, que si per alguna cosa serveixen, es sols per excitar encare mes l'imaginació dels que las contemplan. (p. 386)

> (and long live the moral values of those Tartuffes who pretend to solve everything by placing fig leaves on statues, which serve only further to excite the imagination of those who contemplate them.)

He adds that Dicenta could have married off Andrés and his common-law wife Toñuela, and the former could then have lectured Juan José about marriage rather than extolling the virtues of alcohol to him. P. del O. attacks those who insist that the theatre should contain a Christian moral message and, in a passage heavy with the irony that typifies *L'Esquella*, makes a plea for moralizing to be limited to the Church, and for the theatre to dedicate itself to art:

> Hi ha en aquest mon qui vol que s'acumuli en las iglesias tota la pompa externa convertintlas en verdaders teatros, y en cambi no passan per menos sino perque en los teatros hi senyorejin las austeritats de la moral mes exigent, propias de las iglesias. Siguém justos y diguém: – Cada cosa al seu lloch. A la Iglesia la moral; al teatro l'art. (p. 386)

(There are those who want our churches to be filled with outward show, converting them into real theatres, and at the same time insist on austere morals in our theatres, making them more like churches. Let's be fair and say: 'Everything in its proper place. Morals in church and art in the theatre'.)

Specifically, the type of art to which P. del O. refers is, as in *Juan José*, inspired by life's struggles and human passions – 'l'art sugestiu; l'art de *Juan José*' (suggestive art, the art of 'Juan José'). He praises the play's flesh-and-blood characters, the vigorous, colourful language which comes directly from the common people and is always more real than the language of any Academy dictionary. He then makes a comparison with Fedra, a married woman who falls in love with her husband's son, and asks if there is anything more repugnant than incest. And yet, he claims, *Fedra* is a universal play.

This suggestion that the play possesses resonances wider than the purely Madrid context is something the Madrid critics do not really mention, but is taken up by another Barcelona Catalan-language reviewer.[17] He does not consider it necessary to have been born in Madrid to appreciate the world which Dicenta paints so admirably. The passion of the play is universal, and it sometimes produces so much emotion in audiences that they remain silent so as not to miss a single word. For this reviewer the acting is excellent, and there is no weak scene. Like P. del O he appreciates it for its superior artistic qualities (p. 3561). This appreciation from Barcelona of what one might have thought of as a quintessentially Madrid play is interesting and suggests Barcelona's openness to what was perceived as quality work from wherever it may have emanated. Another leading Spanish playwright who was highly valued in Barcelona, at least during his early career, is Jacinto Benavente, the author of the next play whose reception will be considered, the highly popular and enduring *Los intereses creados*.

Benavente, Los intereses creados

Benavente (1866–1954) was an innovator in the Spanish theatre, at least during his early years, while at the same time managing to become the most popular living Spanish dramatist of his day. Along with Pérez Galdós, he was the first to introduce a more natural style of speaking onto the Spanish stage. As well as this limited form of naturalism, Benavente cultivated poetic theatre, for example in *Teatro fantástico* (1892), while his Children's Theatre (1909–10) was, as was observed in Chapter 1, part of the development of an alternative theatre culture in Madrid. As with Gual, commentators on Benavente's theatre liked to see him as a Europeanizing element.[18] Benavente was an individualist, and often a prickly character, but urbane, detached and sceptical. He was undoubtedly one of the major figures in Spanish theatrical life at the turn of the century, although lack of serious competition in Spanish-language drama sometimes led critics to overvalue his importance. Writing in 1909, Manuel Bueno believes he has few equals in Spain or abroad, and has not been fully appreciated because of the uncultured nature of his homeland. He comments on:

> esas novedades de técnica que nadie ha superado en España ni fuera de España. Aspira a ponerse a tono con Europa, a recoger modos de pensar y aptitudes morales que de fronteras allá se oyen y se ven con asentimiento o con urbana sorpresa, y que aquí, por nuestra ineducación espiritual, suenan a osadías y [. . .] blasfemias.[19]

> (these technical novelties which no one has bettered in Spain or outside. His aim is to keep up with Europe, to absorb ways of thinking and moral talents which are heard and seen there with agreement or with urbane surprise and which here, because of our lack of spiritual education, are taken as temerity and [. . .] blasphemy.)

Author: Jacinto Benavente
Title: *Los intereses creados*
Madrid premiere: December 1907 at the Teatro Lara
Barcelona premiere: January 1908 at the Eldorado
Plot outline: The play draws on the *commedia dell'arte* tradition both for its intrigue and for its characters. These include well-known figures like Harlequin, the Captain, the Doctor, Pantaloon and Pulcinella. Arlequín is a poet who lives in the past and impotently laments that his talents as a poet are no longer appreciated by society. He has lost his role as scheming servant, this having been taken over by Crispín. The other *commedia* characters fulfil more or less their traditional roles. The Captain is a blustering *matamoros*, the Doctor is pretentious and shows off his learning at

every opportunity, Pantalón is extremely mercenary, while Polichinela is a powerful figure in society who is not averse to using violence to achieve his goals. The plot revolves around Crispín's scheming to get Polichinela to agree to the marriage of his daughter Silvia to Crispín's master, the penniless noble Leandro. Like a skilful puppet-master, Crispín expertly manipulates the greed and stupidity of the other characters so that their 'bonds of interest' demand that the marriage take place.

The reviewers of the premiere at Madrid's Lara Theatre of Benavente's best-known play, *Los intereses creados* (*The Bonds of Interest*), were equally ecstatic. García de Candamo wrote:

> Pocas veces se ha visto en el teatro contemporáneo obra que responda tan fielmente a un concepto personal de la vida. Entre Banville y Benavente no hay que afirmar cuál es el verdadero artista.[20]

> (Seldom has there been a contemporary play which responds so faithfully to a personal concept of life. There is no need to say who is the true artist, Banville or Benavente.)

He calls it a work of artistic perfection and makes comparisons with Shakespeare, Musset and Heine. For the *El Heraldo de Madrid* reviewer the play is 'de lo más exquisito que puede pedirse'[21] (the most exquisite thing one could ask for) – he sees something in it for all tastes and, like García de Candamo, praises the quality of the acting. He sees Crispín as one of the most interesting characters in contemporary Spanish theatre.

Writing in the Madrid edition of *El Liberal*, J. Arimón considers Benavente to be the most varied of the contemporary Spanish dramatists, since he has written successfully in all the main categories of drama. For Arimón, *Los intereses* is a moving, poetic play. The end of the second act 'es un encanto de suprema hermosura, que arrebató de entusiasmo a todo el auditorio'[22] (a charming, supremely beautiful work, which captivated the whole audience). He is also thrilled with the quality of the language: '¡Qué diálogo tan brillante, tan castizo y de tan singular pureza castellana!' (What a brilliant dialogue, so purely Spanish!). Arimón also points out the enthusiasm of the audience, who interrupted the performance with their applause several times. The *ABC* reviewer also highlights just how attractive the audience found the play, in a sentence whose sentiments would not have found favour with the likes of García Lorca: 'El público, supremo tribunal para todas estas causas, ha concedido a Benavente su predilección y otorga a sus estrenos la categoría de solemnidades.'[23] (The audience, which is the supreme judge of these things, has granted Benavente their favours and confers on his premieres the category of ceremonies).

As far as the reception of the play in Barcelona is concerned, there is an important contrast between the Spanish- and Catalan-language newspapers. With the exception of M. Rodríguez Codolá in *La Vanguardia*, whose analysis is dedicated to the play's literary qualities rather than the production,[24] the Spanish-language newspapers praise its elegance and sophistication, which were appreciated by an equally elegant and sophisticated audience. The Barcelona edition of *El Liberal*, for instance, declares that they knew the play would be a success because of its quality, and that the Barcelona public would not, as some people had predicted, take revenge for the way the Madrid critics had berated Rusiñol's *La mare* when it was performed at the Teatro de la Princesa.[25] The *El Liberal* reviewer specifies the type of theatre *Los intereses* was being played in, as he praises the cultured, sophisticated and unbiased nature of Barcelona audiences, whom he considered to be intelligent and discerning:

> El teatro Eldorado estaba brillantísimo. En la platea y en los palcos tenía numerosa representación la mejor sociedad barcelonesa, la crítica, el periodismo y el arte. Pocas veces habría sido juzgado un autor por público más inteligente y selecto.
> No es el público de Barcelona un público inocente que se deje arrastrar por la historia brillante de un autor ilustre. Culto, estudioso, sin pasiones de ninguna especie y rindiendo culto únicamente a la expresión de lo bello en todas sus formas, juzga inexorable, aplaudiendo lo bueno y rechazando lo malo cuando no llena sus aficiones. Por eso anteanoche el público no se entregó, rompiendo en un aplauso entusiasta, hasta el final del primer acto.[26]

(The Eldorado looked splendid. The elite of Barcelona society, theatre criticism, journalism and art was well represented in the stalls and boxes. An author has rarely been judged by a more intelligent or select audience.

The Barcelona public is not the sort of innocent audience which allows itself to be taken in by the brilliant history of a famous author. Cultured, studious, without passion of any sort and paying homage only to the expression of beauty in all its forms, it judges unyieldingly, applauding quality and rejecting inferior material when it is not to its taste. That is why last night's audience did not succumb, breaking into applause only at the end of the first act.)

The *Diario de Barcelona* reviewer too emphasizes the quality of the play, considering that, as a satire, it probably has no equal in contemporary Spanish literature, and declares that it was one of the biggest successes in the history of the theatre in Barcelona.[27]

While fully recognizing the play's qualities, the review in *L'Esquella de la Torratxa* is much less fawning than the others considered so far. This is to be expected from a satirical journal like *L'Esquella*, and indeed the Catalan-language press in general is more detached and ironic, and on occasions sarcastic, than the Madrid press or the Barcelona-based Spanish-language newspapers:

> Un bon 'tanto' s'ha guanyat l'empresa ab *Los interses creados* d'en Benavente, que s'ha quedat quasi tot sol pera mantenir lo que vint o treinta anys enrera ne deyan l'alta comedia a l'escena castellana. Potser el pes es massa feixuch per un home, y ja's veu que s'ha de ajupir de tant en tant; pero, no se li pot negar que's refá de las caygudas ab obras enginyosas y elegants. *Los interses creados* es una trobaIla de construcció, molt mes meritoria avuy que se'n fan tant pocas d'obras ben teixidas. Es afrancesada, aixó sí. En Benavente no hi pot fer mes. Agafa ara mateix personatjes de llinatje literari tant castellá com el criat murri y el senyor *bizarro* y sens'un clau, els barreja ab las vellas máscaras italianas ... y li surt una pessa francesa. De Moliére a Banville, passant − y parantse − en Beaumarchais, tot l'esperit satírich de la comedia francesa s'infiltra en la comedia de'n Benavente. No es pas una copia, no; fins se pot concedir que no es una imitació. Es un cas d'adaptació espontánia, que té molt sovint voladas d'originalitat.[28]

(The company has made a bit of money with Benavente's *The Bonds of Interest*, which is the only play to maintain the tradition of what twenty or thirty years ago was known on the Spanish stage as drawing-room drama. Perhaps the burden is too heavy for one man, and he has to bend occasionally; but it cannot be denied that he has recovered from his falls with clever, elegant plays. *The Bonds of Interest* is a very well constructed play, much more praiseworthy today when so few well woven plays are written. It is Frenchified, that's true. That's Benavente's style. He has taken characters from a very Spanish line, such as the cunning servant and the penniless gentleman, he mixes them with the ancient Italian masked characters . . . and out comes a French play! From Molière to Banville, pausing at Beaumarchais, the satirical spirit of French comedy permeates Benavente's work. It's not a copy, one could even concede that it's not an imitation. It's a case of spontaneous adaptation with many original touches.)

However, Barcelona was not always so welcoming to Benavente as it had been on the occasion of the premiere of *Los intereses creados*. In a 1924 article in *L'Esquella de la Torratxa* entitled 'Hostes vindran que de casa els treurem' (Guests will come and we'll throw them out),[29] Paradox describes how Benavente has been abused and reviled in Barcelona by Catalans and Castilians alike.[30] Much water had passed under the bridge since the premiere of *Los intereses creados* in the city. Catalan nationalism had developed and positions hardened. There was the feeling in some quarters that Benavente had treated Gual badly, and had plagiarized his work. Many intellectuals not only in Catalonia but in Spain as a whole were unhappy with Benavente's pro-German stance during the Great War. Whatever the reasons, there was a lot of hostility in Barcelona by the 1920s. Paradox forcefully criticizes it, but attributes it not to envy, Francophile revenge for his pro-German stance during the Great War or to any other logical reasons, but because an irrational anti-Benavente attitude had taken root rather like a flu epidemic.[31] Paradox describes the pursuit of the dramatist in terms of Christ's persecution. Benavente did his best, he reports, but hardly had he raised his head to cry 'Visca Catalunya!' (Long live Catalonia!) than he was assailed again by Catalan and Castilian speakers: the latter called him a coward and the former a joker. All this seems a long way from what one was reading in 1908 after the premiere in Barcelona of *Los intereses*.

Further hostility had been generated in Barcelona when Benavente was awarded the Nobel Prize in 1922. The Lliga newspaper *La Veu de Catalunya* took a dim view, declaring:

En Benavente, rebut al Teatre castellà com a un innovador, en els temps que va significar una tendència rectificadora dels corrents representats per l'Echegaray, ha acabat essent una valor completament nul.la. Les seves obres dramàtiques no són obres de teatre.
     [. . .] Ara bé; si afegiu a això que el pessimisme d'En Benavente no és sinó el reflectiment exacte de l'esperit de la seva societat, haureu de

convenir en què la seva valor de dramaturg encara disminueix més. En aquest cas, resta reduït al simple copiador d'una realitat.[32]

(Benavente was hailed as an innovator in the Spanish theatre in the days when his work acted as a corrective to that of Echegaray. Now, however, his value is nil. His dramatic works are not real plays. [. . .] If you add to that the fact that Benavente's pessimism is no more than an exact reflection of his society, you will have to agree that his value as a playwright diminishes still further. In this case, he is reduced to a simple imitator of reality.)

This article criticizes not only Benavente himself but by implication Spanish theatre as a whole, as that was the only context which would allow Benavente to be viewed as an innovator. However, by this time, it was not only the Catalan-language press which was attacking Benavente. Later that same year *Tribuna* was highly critical of the playwright. The author of the article in question pointedly remarks that Benavente has not visited Barcelona since 1905 and reopens old wounds regarding the the non-performance of Gual in Madrid:

Bienvenido sea Don Jacinto, si es que desea visitarnos. No faltarán empresas ni compañías que organicen funciones teatrales en su honor. Todos los actores deben contribuir a este homenaje. Y no estará de más dar a conocer a Benavente, en castellano, alguna obra catalana que no pudo ser dada a conocer en Madrid por largos y enojosos motivos.
  Alternando con los dramas y comedias de Don Jacinto, bien se podría dar a conocer, por si acaso no lo conoce, el aplaudido autor de 'La Malquerida', la traducción castellana que el malogrado Luis Morote hizo del famoso drama de Adrián Gual, 'Misterio de dolor'.
  Acaso, después de asistir a la representación, el autor de 'La Malquerida' prohijara el drama de Gual y lo patrocinara a fin de que el público madrileño trabara conocimiento con la obra catalana, que a pesar de haber mandado pintar el decorado, el matrimonio Guerrero-Díaz de Mendoza no se atrevió, −¿por qué razón? − a estrenarla en el teatro de la Princesa.[33]

(Don Jacinto will be welcome if he wishes to visit us. There will be plenty of companies who will organise theatre festivals in his honour. Every actor must contribute to the homage. And it wouldn't be a bad idea to make him familiar (in Spanish) with one of those Catalan plays which could not be performed in Madrid for long-standing and tedious reasons.

Don Jacinto's plays could alternate with the unfortunate Luis Morote's Spanish translation of Adrià Gual's famous play 'Mystery of Grief', just in case the much admired author of *The Passion Flower* doesn't know it.[34]

Maybe, after attending the performance, the author of *The Passion Flower* will adopt Gual's work and sponsor it in order that Madrid audiences may get to know the Catalan play which, despite already having the set painted, Guerrero and Díaz de Mendoza did not dare, for some unknown reason, to put on at the Princesa.)

By the 1920s, therefore, Barcelona seems to have taken a dislike to Benavente, but then so had intellectuals in the rest of the country, in complete contrast to his continuing popularity with audiences. After the Spanish Civil War, Benavente retained his great popular appeal, despite (or perhaps even because of) the fact that he was firmly identified with the values of the Franco regime. As protest against the regime grew in the 1960s and 1970s, he was rejected for his association with a conservative, outmoded theatrical past. It is only more recently that he has come to be seen once more as an innovator, and his contacts with and reception in early twentieth-century Barcelona are an important element of his theatrical development.

Galdos, Marianela

Another of the innovators in the Spanish theatre at the turn of the century, Benito Pérez Galdós, seems to have been held in much higher regard in Barcelona than Benavente was by the end of the Great War. He did, however, provoke a negative reaction amongst the city's conservative press because of his well-known left-of-centre views and his involvement in politics. For example, the conservative *Diario de Barcelona*, reviewing a 1904 production of *El abuelo* by the Guerrero/Díaz de Mendoza Company at the Novetats, claims that 'Galdós no puede substraerse a la manía de defender o atacar doctrinas mientras hace arte'[35] (Galdós cannot help attacking or defending doctrines while creating art). Even this newspaper, however, approved of *Marianela*, and shared the appreciation demonstrated by their Madrid counterparts of the play and of Margarita Xirgu as the leading actress.[36]

Author: Benito Pérez Galdós
Title: *Marianela*
Madrid premiere: October 1916 at the Teatro de la Princesa by the Margarita Xirgu Company
Barcelona premiere: April 1917 at the Teatre Novetats by the Margarita Xirgu Company
Plot outline: In a mining village in the north of Spain, Marianela, a plain, sixteen-year-old orphan, acts as a guide to Pablo, who has been blind since birth. Dr Teodoro Golfín, an ophthalmic surgeon who has just returned to the village, successfully operates on Pablo, giving him sight for the first time in his life. Marianela, who has enjoyed an idealized, spiritual relationship with the young man, does not want him to realize how ugly she is. The first person he sees is the beautiful Florentina, with whom he falls in love. When he sees Marianela he is shocked by her ugliness. Having feared this reaction, Marianela had earlier tried to commit suicide like her late mother. Pablo's expression of revulsion when he sees her is now too much for her, and she dies of grief.

Marianela was an adaptation for the stage by the Álvarez Quintero brothers of an early Pérez Galdós novel which had been published in 1877, and received its stage premiere at the Princesa Theatre in Madrid in October 1916.[37] It contains themes such as the physical and moral implications of blindness, and the idealism/reality, science/spirituality dichotomies which were prominent in his early novels. However, it lacks the depth and sharpness one associates with Pérez Galdós's great works, and its Romanticism is to the fore in this adaptation by the Álvarez Quintero brothers. Pérez Galdós himself was warm in his praise of the adaptation. The Álvarez Quinteros were prolific and popular playwrights noted for their sentimental plots and folksy evocation of Spanish life, particularly in their native region of Andalusia. In an interview with *ABC*, Pérez Galdós explains why he did not adapt the novel for the stage himself: he had tried, he says, as had Valle-Inclán, but had found it too difficult, adding: 'estos Quinteros son unos diablos'[38] (those Quinteros are amazing). It is perhaps surprising that an actress who was noted for her choice of challenging female roles should have agreed to play Marianela, but, in the sense that it poignantly portrays a young woman's tragedy, it reflects the sort of play she performed throughout her career.

In some ways, *Marianela* was Xirgu's breakthrough play, her first really major popular success in the Spanish, as opposed to the Catalan, language. According to her biographer Antonina Rodrigo, following the dress rehearsal of *Marianela* on 16 October 1916, which Pérez Galdós attended, the author

> abrazó a la actriz emocionado, mientras le dedicaba encendidos elogios, llegando en su entusiasmo, a decir que su creación de *Marianela* era mejor que la suya. Esta interpretación consagró a la Xirgu de forma arrolladora, en la escena castellana, como actriz indiscutible. Acabada la temporada en Madrid, la Xirgu y Pérez Galdós presentaron *Marianela* en Barcelona y en provincias.[39]

> (overcome by emotion, he embraced the actress as he sang her praises. Such was his fervour that he even went as far as to say that Xirgu's *Marianela* was better than his own. This performance ensured in a resounding fashion Xirgu's place as an undisputed actress in Spanish theatre. Following the Madrid season, Xirgu and Pérez Galdós presented *Marianela* in Barcelona and the provinces.)

The Madrid press generally waxed lyrical. A number of critics felt as if they had been taken back to their youth and their reviews contain a good deal of nostalgia for the novel. Even the normally severe Miquis was not exempt from the nostalgia. He criticized those who said that Pérez Galdós was old-fashioned and out of date, and considered it to be a charming play, with vital, authentic characters, full of passion and sensitivity, and lacking the sober harshness of Pérez Galdós's usual portrayal of contemporary Madrid.[40] According to Miquis, the Álvarez Quinteros had captured the whole novel in their adaptation. He concluded by suggesting that Pérez Galdós's *œuvre* be looked at afresh and viewed as new and contemporary. He approved of the acting, but, curiously, made no mention of names.

Like Miquis, the *ABC* reviewer praised the faithfulness of the adaptation. The nostalgia and emotion of the occasion seem to have got the better of reviewer's critical judgement as he called *Marianela* Pérez Galdós's best work. This time Xirgu is mentioned by name, in glowing terms: 'El trabajo de la actriz catalana fue sencillamente asombroso' (The performance of the Catalan actress was, quite simply, astonishing), adding that Marianela was her best-ever role.

There was also praise for the rest of the cast and for the stage designer. The reviewer observes that the theatre was full, and that the audience was wildly enthusiastic. There was a huge ovation at the end of each act, and murmurs of approval at other points. At the end, Pérez Galdós and the Álvarez Quinteros took numerous curtain calls to thunderous applause.

El Liberal devoted a lot of space to the premiere. Antonio Zozoya, the Director of the Teatro Español, wrote a long piece on Pérez Galdós, mentioning that the author was now frail and blind, but that forty years previously the novel had moved a whole generation, previously accustomed to cold, mediocre literature. Employing gushing prose, Zozoya analyses the character of Marianela, emphasizing her purity. The play is reviewed by Pedro de Répide, and there is an interview with Pérez Galdós by a critic writing under the pseudonym of El Caballero del Verde Gabán (The Gentleman in the Green Overcoat).[41]

Nostalgia was also in abundant supply in Bernardo García de Candamo's *El Mundo* review. For him, the premiere was a night of emotion and an unforgettable spectacle. As with other reviewers, the novel brought back childhood memories. He found the appearance of Pérez Galdós on stage especially moving: 'viejo y venerable, conmovido y lloroso' (old and venerable, emotional and in tears). García de Candamo goes into considerable detail about the plot, and waxes eloquent about Xirgu.[42] Although she is constantly referred to in the reviews as the Catalan actress, as far as I can ascertain, this seems to have been merely descriptive with no socio-political subtext.[43] One further point worth making is that Marianela is a frail waif, in stark contrast to Salomé or García Lorca's tragic heroines, which highlights Xirgu's ability to play a wide variety of dramatic roles.

Marianela was just about the only Pérez Galdós play that the conservative *Diario de Barcelona* seemed to like. When it received its Barcelona premiere at the Novetats in April 1917, the newspaper wrote approvingly:

> La compañía de Margarita Xirgu, que estuvo en funciones desde el 7 de abril hasta el 3 de mayo, debutó con el estreno de *Marianela*, la bellísima novela de Pérez Galdós escenificada por los hermanos Álvarez Quintero. En ella la señora Xirgu alcanzó la altura de las grandes actrices, siendo también notable el trabajo de los restantes intérpretes.[44]

Figure 6. Margarita Xirgu playing the lead role in Pérez Galdós's *Marianela* at the Novetats Theatre in Barcelona, June 1918.

(Margarita Xirgu's company began their 3 April–7 May season with the premiere of *Marianela*, Pérez Galdós's beautiful novel, adapted for the stage by the Álvarez Quintero brothers. Señora Xirgu reached the heights achieved by great actresses, and the performances by the rest of the cast were very good too.)

There is a long review in *La Vanguardia*, praising the adaptation as an example of the dexterity of the Álvarez Quinteros.[45] The critic of *El Liberal*, writing under the pseudonym Vital, agrees with the Madrid critics that *Marianela* has maintained its freshness and continues to move the present younger generation as it did that of his parents.[46] He graphically evokes the audience's tense concentration on the action:

El público siguió el desarrollo de la idea generatriz con una ansiedad y un interés inmenso. Un ruido, una tosecilla indiscreta, hacía reclamar el silencio [. . .] un silencio completo, un silencio solemne, denunciador de una emoción profunda, esperaba las frases, los gestos de los actores para saborear en ellos la maravilla de la pluma galdosiana, honra de España y orgullo legítimo de todos los españoles,[47]

(The audience followed the development of the main idea with anxiety and great interest. Any noise, any indiscreet cough brought cries of 'silence!' [. . .] a total silence, a solemn silence, which betrayed a deep emotion, greeted the actors' words and gestures to savour in them the wonder of the Galdós pen, honour of Spain and justifiable pride of all Spaniards,)

among whom the Catalans are clearly to be counted. The reviewer's emotion overflows as he describes how Pérez Galdós, old in body but young in spirit, went on stage at the end of the play to receive his ovation. All aspects of the performance are praised – Xirgu and the rest of the cast, as well as the staging. At least as far as this reviewer is concerned, the Madrid nostalgia has been transferred to Barcelona.

Pérez Galdós's presence at the Barcelona premiere demonstrates the regard in which he held the native city of his leading actress. It also gave the city's press a chance to interview him. In *El Día Gráfico*, Diego Montaner discusses with him such issues as the Álvarez Quinteros' adaptation of the novel, Margarita Xirgu, Catalan theatre and politics, Spanish republicanism, protests in the theatre and his future projects.[48] With great discretion, Pérez Galdós refrains from expressing any views about politics, including nationalism, since he has now retired from active political life and is not au fait with the latest developments.[49] As was seen earlier, he is full of admiration for the Álvarez Quinteros, both generally and for their adaptation of *Marianela*, while he can only admire Xirgu's performance as Nela. He thinks highly of several contemporary Catalan dramatists, including his fellow Canarian Guimerà, as well as Rusiñol and Iglésies, while he considers the greatest Catalan to be the Republican politician Pi i Margall. As for the future of Catalan theatre, Pérez Galdós believes that it lacks a sufficiently wide audience base, and that it needs to be translated more in order to gain wider acceptance and more frequent performances in the centre of Spain and in the other Spanish regions.[50]

Pérez Galdós's interest in and knowledge of the Barcelona theatre scene is typical of the respect it commanded in Madrid, although, as Chapter 5 demonstrated, the most popular Catalan dramatists continued to be those who had made their mark earlier in the century. The man most responsible for putting Spain in touch with the new European trends, the director Cipriano de Rivas Cherif, viewed Gual as an innovator, even in the 1920s, and Barcelona was still regarded as a centre of theatrical innovation. However, as far as dramatic literature was concerned, the real innovations were coming from playwrights writing in Spanish or, to be more precise, a Galician and an Andalusian. The 1920s saw the beginnings of García Lorca as a dramatist and the emergence of Valle-Inclán's *esperpentos*, although Valle-Inclán's continued to be minority theatre throughout his lifetime, being performed mainly at the small private theatres which were discussed in Chapter 1. Valle-Inclán acquired a certain following in Barcelona as in Madrid, and the Barcelona public sympathized with him, since they saw him as an intellectual opposed to the Primo de Rivera dictatorship. The Barcelona premiere in 1925 of Valle's version of the Salomé legend, *La cabeza del Bautista*, was especially significant. It had been premiered in Madrid in 1924, but it was not until it was first performed in Barcelona that the great Sicilian actress Mimí Aguglia, who had been in Spain as early as 1907 and who had returned to Madrid in 1924 to perform Spanish works, actually played the main role. Valle-Inclán himself attended the Barcelona premiere, having missed the first Madrid performance.[51]

Barcelona proved decisive in making the Spanish theatre scene of the Second Republic one of the most exciting in Europe through the actress Margarita Xirgu and the stage designers Manuel Fontanals and Sigfrido Burmann. Valle-Inclán's relationship with Xirgu was sometimes stormy, but her performance in *Divinas palabras* (*Divine Words*) is considered to be a key factor in the critical success of what is one of the best plays of the period, despite its being a commercial flop.[52]

García Lorca, Yerma

Author: Federico García Lorca
Title: *Yerma*
Madrid premiere: 29 December 1934 at the Teatro Español by the Margarita Xirgu Company
Barcelona premiere: 17 September 1935 at the Teatre Barcelona by the Margarita Xirgu Company
Plot outline: *Yerma* is set in a small rural village and is the poetic evocation of the frustration endured by a childless married woman, whose name indicates her barren state. She is an isolated individual, misunderstood by society. She becomes ever more alienated from her husband, and ever more tormented by her awareness of just how different her barrenness makes her from the other women who live in her community, and even to nature itself. She goes to increasingly extreme lengths to try to conceive, including attending a kind of a pagan fertility ritual in the form of a pilgrimage to the countryside. All these efforts are in vain, and her traditional sense of honour precludes unfaithfulness as a possible solution, which make her suspicious husband's fears doubly cruel. Her final act is to strangle her husband on stage, declaring that she has killed her own child.

Xirgu's role in *Yerma*, one of García Lorca's best-known and most enduring plays, confirmed the status of both of them as leading theatre figures, and Fontanals's stage designs for the production further enhanced his reputation. It was not the first time – nor would it be the last – that Xirgu and García Lorca had collaborated on a production. They had worked together on *Mariana Pineda* (Spanish premiere at the Goya in Barcelona in June 1927; Madrid premiere at the Fontalba in October 1927), for which another famous Catalan, Salvador Dalí designed the set. In an essay on Enric Borràs, the famous Catalan actor Adolfo Marsillach looks back on the García Lorca–Xirgu collaborations as a golden age of Spanish theatre, and admires her for her boldness in putting on the work of young playwrights. According to Marsillach, this is a phenomenon that has never been repeated:

> Desde el final de la guerra civil hasta acá no ha habido ninguna actriz ni ningún actor – y me incluyo – que se haya arriesgado a estrenar consecuentemente a autores jóvenes y desconocidos como lo fueron en su época Valle-Inclán, Alberti o García Lorca.[53]

> (Since the end of the Civil War, no actor or actress – myself included – has dared to premiere out of principle such unknown young authors as Valle-Inclán, Alberti and García Lorca were in their day.)

The fact that such an important collaborative production as *Mariana Pineda* should be premiered in Barcelona before Madrid is testimony to the importance attached to the Catalan capital by major Spanish playwrights, as well as to the continued drawing power of Spanish-language theatre there. As far as *Yerma* is concerned, the opinion of Dougherty and Vilches is that Xirgu was masterful in the role of Yerma,[54] while one of the leading Spanish theatre critics of the period, Enrique Díez-Canedo, wrote in *La Voz*:

> Su compenetración con el personaje, al que ha dado todo su sentir, sin regatearle emoción ni esfuerzo, es tal, que raya en lo más alto del arte. Todo en ella, desde los sordos acordes iniciales hasta los arrebatos del desenlace, funde expresión y belleza en un ademán, en una palabra. He aquí la actriz que sabe llegar a todas las cumbres. Nadie irá a descubrirla ahora. Mas conviene que lo recuerden los que la han visto en sus interpretaciones menores y tienen casi olvidada la reacción de su sensibilidad ante las obras realmente grandes, así las de sentido realista como las de pura concepción poética. Para la gran actriz española fueron los aplausos y las aclamaciones, que la saludaban como la más fiel intérprete y colaboradora del poeta dramático.[55]

> (Her empathy with the character, to which she has given herself completely, sparing no emotion or effort, is such that it borders on the highest level of art. Everything in her, from the muffled initial chords to

the fits of anger at the end, blends expression and beauty in a gesture, in a word. This is the actress who has reached all the heights. No one needs to discover her now. This should be remembered by those who have seen her in minor roles and who have almost forgotten the reaction of their sensibilities before the really great works, be they realist or poetic. The applause and the acclamation were aimed at the great Spanish actress, as they greeted her as the most faithful exponent of and collaborator in the dramatic poem.)

Here Díez-Canedo lauds Xirgu's ability to perform to a high standard plays in a variety of genres. It is curious that questions of her identity, in this case her Spanishness, should be present even in a review of this sort, which is all about her artistic quality. Her Catalanness has been subsumed into an identity of the 'Greater Spain' as she has become a figure to be admired by the whole of the country. As Chapter 3 demonstrated, Xirgu herself was happy with this association.

Contemporary critics also praised the quality of the stage designs of Fontanals:

Los decorados realizados por Manuel Fontanals − seis escenarios − supieron captar el carácter simbólico de los espacios dramáticos donde se desarrollaba la acción.[56]

(Manuel Fontanals's designs − six sets − succeeded in capturing the symbolic character of the dramatic spaces in which the action unfolds.)

Díez-Canedo wrote of the 'magnífico decorado de Fontanals. De una plástica sin minucias, está realizado en grande, como severo fondo español. Fontanals participó, con justicia, de los aplausos.'[57] (Fontanals's magnificent designs. The set is realized on a grand scale, with few details, conveying a harsh Spanish background. Fontanals rightly shared in the applause.) The play was premiered in Madrid on 29 December 1934, where it received over 100 consecutive performances, while it ran in Barcelona's Barcelona Theatre from 17 September to 20 October 1935. Many leading figures from the worlds of theatre and the arts attended what turned out to be one of the most polemical ever productions in either city. People either loved or hated it.[58] Reaction to the play depended, in a way never seen in the modern Spanish theatre, on individual political views.

The reception of *Yerma* encapsulates the deep divisions that were tearing Spain apart in the years leading up to the Civil War, as it was loved by radical progressives and hated by Catholic conservatives. The leading Spanish left-wing politician, Manuel Azaña, Rivas Cherif's brother-in-law, had just been released from prison where he had spent some two months not for any specific crime but for allegedly supporting the declaration of an independent Catalan state and for wishing to participate in the setting up of a provisional republican government in Catalonia. Xirgu defied the anti-Azaña campaign by offering her house in Badalona (near Barcelona) to his wife and to the politician himself once he was released. This action added to the anti-Xirgu feelings which were prevalent in right-wing circles following her performance of *Fermín Galán* in 1931. So *Yerma* was politicized not only in terms of Spain as a whole, but specifically in the context of the growing independence demands in Catalonia.

Some of the right-wing reviews of the Madrid premiere were vituperative, the following outburst by José de la Cueva being typical: 'No cabe nada más soez, grosero y bajo que el lenguaje que el señor García Lorca emplea; se ha contaminado el poeta y enfangado su pluma.'[59] (The language employed by Señor García Lorca is the most coarse, vulgar and common imaginable. The poet has contaminated himself, and sullied his pen.) The assertion by Vilches and Dougherty that in Barcelona as in Madrid *Yerma* was a great success with public and critics alike[60] was probably truer of the former city than the latter. The Barcelona press was glowing in its praise. For instance, *El Popular* considers it to be the best play in Barcelona, and describes Xirgu as their noble and illustrious fellow countrywoman.[61] In their edition of the following day, the newspaper claims that the premiere of *Yerma* has been an unprecedented event in Barcelona's theatre history. It is the last but one week of the Xirgu season, but, despite great demand, she is unable to extend it.[62] Xirgu also comes in for special praise in *La Vanguardia*, where the reviewer María-Luz Morales goes as far as to claim that ' "Yerma" es Margarita Xirgu' (*Yerma* is Margarita Xirgu), adding: 'Singularísimo talento de esta actriz, que ha sabido – y ha podido – elevarse sobre sí misma y sobre su fama'[63] (Most singular talent of this actress, who has managed to rise above herself and her fame). Likewise, *La Veu de Catalunya* announced the premiere of *Yerma* on 29 September 1935 in the following terms: 'Inimitable creació de

Margarida Xirgu'[64] (Inimitable creation by Margarita Xirgu). This identification of the play with the actress rather than with the playwright highlights her importance as well as the continuing drawing power and influence of the leading actor/actress in Spain. Pérez Galdós's comment following the dress rehearsal of *Marianela* that Xirgu's Marianela was better than his own will be recalled. Xirgu's ability to make specific female parts very firmly her own reflects the way in which Borràs was identified in the popular mind with certain characters, most notably Manelic. It also reflects the way in which the diva/star system still survived in Spain, even with such a theatrical revolutionary as Xirgu, and suggests that the major stars travelled better to Madrid than workaday actors.

The most polemical note in the Barcelona press reviews was struck by *L'Esquella de la Torratxa*. They had no quarrel with the quality of the play: on the contrary, for them it is precisely plays like *Yerma* which they wish were written for the Catalan theatre.[65] Their target is the conservative press in Barcelona, which the paper accuses of double standards on two counts. In the first place, claims the reviewer, the press has not criticized *Yerma* with the same rigour as they employ with Catalan plays. As usual, *L'Esquella* links its point with the language question, and claims that, if *Yerma* had been written in Catalan by a Catalan playwright, it would not have been premiered. The second charge of hypocrisy concerns the attitude of the conservative press towards whether the theatre should simply aim to entertain or whether it should deal with moral questions, and, once more, these issues are linked with Catalanism:

> Assegurem igualment que un equivalent de 'Yerma' en català hauria fet cridar la major part dels crítics dels diaris de Barcelona, que haurien tocat a ravatada en pro de la moral. També hauria sortit allò que el teatre ha d'ésser 'divertit, amè, amable, i ha de fer riure'.

> (We can also assure our readers that an equivalent of *Yerma* in Catalan would have caused most of the Barcelona critics to bleat about morals and about the theatre having to be entertaining, pleasant and nice.)

The reviewer also asserts that it would not have been performed in Castile were it not for Xirgu's great enthusiasm. According to *L'Esquella*, she is one of the few committed actresses around.

In another article earlier the same month, *L'Esquella* had forcefully claimed that it it was Xirgu who had done more than anyone else for

Castilian theatre by, among other things, performing uncommercial authors, and risking putting on Valle-Inclán's experimental plays, Unamuno's version of *Medea* and facilitating García Lorca's success.[66] The article consists of a series of rhetorical questions, culminating in a forceful and bitter declaration that it is the Catalan actress who has made the triumph of Spanish dramatists possible, and that she is the only worthwhile factor in contemporary Spanish theatre:

> ¿Qui ens fa parlar a nosaltres amb plaer del teatre de Castella? Margarida Xirgu.
>
> ¿Qui ha acollit obertament autors nous castellans de la ponderació i l'equilibri poètic d'en Casona? Margarida Xirgu, la catalana Margarida Xirgu.
>
> I que oblidin, els que ho vulguin oblidar per mesquinesa política, que Margarida Xirgu és l'únic puntal ferm del teatre castellà actual.

> (Who makes us speak with pleasure of the theatre of Castile? Margarita Xirgu.
>
> Who has welcomed with open arms the new Castilian writers as poised and with the poetic balance of Casona? Margarita Xirgu, the Catalan Margarita Xirgu.
>
> And as for those who wish for reasons of political meanness to forget that Margarita Xirgu is the only strong point in contemporary Castilian theatre, well, let them forget.)

The exaggerated final claim once more reveals the extent to which political considerations intrude into discussions on the theatre in the polarized Spain of the mid-1930s.

As well as *Yerma*, two other García Lorca plays were performed in Barcelona by Xirgu in the mid-1930s: *Bodas de sangre* (which had originally been premiered by Josefina Díaz de Artigas with designs by Manuel Fontanals and under García Lorca's direction at the Beatriz Theatre in Madrid in 1933) and *Doña Rosita la soltera.* Aguilera and Aznar's view is that

> el éxito fue rotundo y tanto la prensa barcelonesa como la madrileña, que peregrinó a la capital catalana con motivo del estreno de la obra del autor granadino, recogieron por extenso los ecos de un triunfo sin paliativos.

> (The play was a resounding success with the Barcelona and Madrid critics. The latter travelled to the Catalan capital for the premiere and recorded extensively the echoes of an unqualified triumph.)

As with *Mariana Pineda*, the Madrid critics travelled to Barcelona when they considered a premiere there to be of national importance. Aguilera and Aznar quote a Catalan critic of the play, Lluis Capdevila, who highlights the perfection of the production, and bestows the following high praise on the director: 'Cebrià Rivas Cherif és aquest excellent director únic. En el teatre castellà no n'hi ha cap que l'iguali. En el català tampoc.'[67] (Cipriano de Rivas Cherif is that excellent, unique director. There is no one to touch him in Spanish theatre. Nor in Catalan theatre.)

The fact that *Mariana Pineda* and *Doña Rosita* received their Spanish premieres in Barcelona is especially significant, as it highlights the enduring importance of the city as a theatre centre. Significantly, one of the key Spanish plays of the twentieth century, Valle-Inclán's *Divinas palabras*, was premiered there by Xirgu, and Barcelona maintained a special significance for García Lorca in particular. Even today, some of the pre-Civil War legacy remains, with Barcelona viewed as the city of experimentation and Madrid as the more staid theatrical landscape. Xirgu's continuing links with her native city are evident, although, as was observed in Chapter 3, her performances were exclusively in the Spanish language. Whereas at the turn of the century Catalan theatre was grabbing the headlines in Madrid, by the 1930s it was Spanish theatre which was making a deep impression in Barcelona, although this was channelled through Catalonia's biggest international figure: Margarita Xirgu.[68]

Conclusion: Collaborators, *Ma Non Troppo*

Turn-of-the-century Barcelona was one of the most exciting yet turbulent cities in Europe. It was highly receptive to the new European movements in art and literature, and it is hard to over-emphasize the importance of Catalan *modernisme* in the penetration of these movements not only into Catalonia but into Spain as a whole. The outburst of creativity in literature and, more strikingly, painting, architecture and the decorative arts had a knock-on effect on all branches of the theatre in Barcelona. The period saw the emergence of a new group of playwrights and stage designers of a high quality, while Adrià Gual's work at the Íntim placed him at the level of such innovative practitioners as Antoine, Lugné-Poë, Craig, Copeau and Meyerhold. Like them, he was constantly engaged on an artistic quest to discover how the theatre worked, a seminal figure who opened the way for others, including Margarita Xirgu. Although Gual's work has until recently been scandalously neglected, at least outside Catalonia, we are now beginning to understand his true importance, and to see him as the theatrical revolutionary he was, on a par with with Xirgu and Rivas Cherif. (It has to be said, however, that Gual's own plays are far less significant and ground-breaking than his work as a director.) Gual's more far-sighted Spanish contemporaries did recognize his worth, and indeed, the Barcelona theatre generally was greatly admired in Madrid, where the leading Catalan playwrights, designers, actors and actresses were much in demand.

Correspondingly, many of the Spanish playwrights of the period, including Pérez Galdós, Valle-Inclán and García Lorca, attached great importance to the Barcelona premieres of their works, as evidenced by their attendance at a number of the major ones. Indeed, our study has demonstrated that it was a fallacy to think that Valle-Inclán and García Lorca were working in a vacuum: there was a vibrant theatrical scene in Madrid and Barcelona, in which Catalan practitioners played a vital role. The turn of the century was the period of maximum interest in the Barcelona theatre as far as Madrid was concerned. Catalan playwrights were popular with critics and audiences alike, while Enric Borràs and Margarita Xirgu acquired widespread popularity and respect amongst Madrid theatre-goers. Guimerà made the initial impact in the Spanish capital, and he was followed by the newer generation of dramatists which included Rusiñol and Iglésies. The most significant event was Enric Borràs's short Catalan season in the spring of 1904, both because it consisted of plays performed in the original Catalan at a time when so-called regional theatre was viewed from the Spanish capital as of secondary importance, and also because it opened the way for the permanent move to Madrid of Borràs and Xirgu. They were followed by Fontanals, who, along with Sigfrido Burmann, was arguably the most influential stage designer in Spain during the 1920s and 1930s.

If Barcelona theatre practitioners were a novelty as far as Madrid was concerned, and an escape route from the rut in which Spanish theatre was stuck, Barcelona's contact with Madrid-based theatre was more routine. Resident companies like that of María Guerrero and Fernando Díaz de Mendoza made frequent appearances in Barcelona, mainly as part of their spring and summer tours. These were generally well attended and received by public and most critics, particularly where hits like Benavente's *Los intereses creados* were concerned. However, at least until the arrival of Valle-Inclán and García Lorca, they were hardly considered to be of a quality to rival European contemporaries.

Contacts between Barcelona- and Madrid-based practitioners between the 1890s and the 1930s were frequent. The motives were artistic as well as commercial, and involved directors, actors and actresses, and stage designers, as well as dramatists. On the whole, the joint ventures were based on mutual respect, although, as in the case of Guimerà's collaboration with Guerrero and Díaz de Mendoza and more generally between Benavente and the Catalans, the links occasionally dissolved into bad feeling. The Catalans were possibly better able to negotiate the relationships than some of the Madrid-based practitioners. Some of the collaborative ventures were decisive in the development of Spanish-language theatre, particularly the productions involving Valle-Inclán and García Lorca as authors, Xirgu as actress, Fontanals and Burmann as stage designers, and Rivas Cherif as director and *animateur*.

Along with Borràs, Xirgu was probably the best-known Catalan theatrical figure in Madrid. Both found fame in the Spanish capital, as well as in the Spanish provinces and, more significantly, in Spanish America. Indeed, the long period of exile which Xirgu spent in that continent is one of the most important yet under-studied phases of her long theatrical career. Both Borràs and, more especially, Xirgu continued to be the acting models to be followed until well after the Civil War. The roots of so much that happened in the theatre during the post-Franco years belong to the period 1892–1936. The Civil War frustrated attempts to build on it, but the legacy of those years is scattered across Latin America and Europe, where pracitioners like Xirgu and Alberti settled. Xirgu especially functioned as a powerful oppositional force under Franco, a symbol of what had been lost. Rivas Cherif was imprisoned, but defiantly carried on his theatre work in prisons, including a remarkable production with fellow-prisoners of Calderón's *El alcalde de Zalamea* (*The Mayor of Zalamea*).

One question which has concerned us in this study is the extent to which Xirgu and Borràs were Castilianized. Reviews of their early work in Madrid make it clear that, as far as the quality of their spoken Spanish and accent are concerned, Xirgu was much more noticeably Catalan than Borràs. However, with the passing of the years, she became fully associated with a Spanish and foreign repertoire, and left behind her Catalan past. She was without doubt the most important Spanish actress of her era, and on a par with the great foreign actresses like Bernhardt, Duse and Aguglia. She felt a strong affinity with the Second Spanish Republic, and fully participated in its cultural and social projects. Borràs, on the other hand, became identified with political conservatism and with a more traditional style of acting. Ironically, he never abandoned his Catalan repertoire and returned frequently to Barcelona. Nonetheless, he broadly stuck to the tried and trusted hits of the early years of the century, and was not involved in any real attempts to renew the Barcelona stage in his later career.

As far as the reception of Borràs and Xirgu in Madrid is concerned, they were appreciated in much the same way as their contemporaries in the field of dramatic literature. Reviewers generally concentrated on issues of quality, in which they were usually full of praise for the Catalans who performed or were performed in their city. However, when questions of Catalanness were raised, reviewers were much less sympathetic. Borràs and Xirgu were viewed as essentially Spanish performers, rather as Guimerà was considered as a Spanish dramatist. Their Catalan identity was erased, as they were subsumed into the broad area of Spanish theatre which was, of course, centred in Madrid. Enthusiasm for the talents of Catalan theatre practitioners was mixed with rejection of any manifestation of Catalan identity in the Barcelona theatre. Catalonia was a part of Spain, albeit with its own cultural traditions. There were also smug claims that Borràs for one was better appreciated in Madrid than he was in his native Barcelona.

Attitudes to Borràs and Xirgu in Barcelona varied according to whether the newspaper in question was written in the Catalan or the Spanish language. The (majority) Spanish-language press usually wrote favourably about them, but sections of the Catalan-language press were more hostile. This was particularly true of *El Teatre Català*, which was linked with attempts to establish a specifically Catalan theatre in Barcelona at a time of a growing Catalan consciousness and the development of specifically Catalan civic and political institutions. These attempts were doomed to failure – in part because of a lack of tradition and a critical audience mass. Some of the defenders of Catalan-language theatre felt that Xirgu had betrayed their cause by leaving for Madrid and abandoning Catalan for Spanish theatre.

The Spanish-language offering in Barcelona was extensive, and the demand from Barcelona audiences for Catalan theatre was perhaps not sufficiently extensive to support a national theatre or similar enterprise. There was also fierce competition from the music-hall, vaudeville and cabaret, particularly in the area around the Paral.lel, while the cinema developed earlier in Barcelona than it did in Madrid, posing yet another threat to the conventional theatres. There was a perception that Catalan theatre was somehow boring and less exciting than other forms of entertainment on offer. The Romea was the main centre of Catalan drama during the late nineteenth and early twentieth centuries, but even this theatre offered plays in Spanish rather than in Catalan between 1911 and 1917.

In this context, it is small wonder that those who were attempting to establish an identifiably Catalan theatre should be frustrated by what they saw as the desertion of stars like Xirgu. It also hurt that Catalan plays of the quality and the renown of Guimerà's *Terra baixa* should be premiered in Madrid rather than in Barcelona, and the Catalans felt slighted when there was a delay in bringing big Spanish hits to Barcelona. This happened with *Juan José* and more generally with Benavente, and Barcelona was annoyed when it was ignored by Spanish writers. It felt itself to be at the forefront of the European avant-garde in the wider artistic sense, a feeling recognized by such major theatre figures as Genet, who was there in 1933, and Piscator. García Lorca, too, felt a special affinity with Barcelona, premiering *Mariana Pineda* and *Doña Rosita la soltera* there, in an implicit recognition that the city was more open to experimentation than Madrid. It also highlights the fact that there was in Barcelona a sizeable and influential audience for Spanish-language theatre.

Indeed, Barcelona was always regarded by Madrid as a city where experimentation was possible – in the theatre as much as in the other arts. This is a view that prevailed throughout the period covered by the present study. At the turn of the century, Catalan playwrights were in vogue in Madrid, where their plays were greeted as new and modern both for their content and for their dramatic form. However, later in the period there was relatively little interest in younger Catalan playwrights, although Guimerà, Rusiñol and Iglésies continued to be performed. This decline in interest perhaps suggests that the Madrid stage was in a healthier state by the 1920s than it had been earlier in the century – at least as far as the presence of quality playwrights was concerned.

Finally, my study has demonstrated that relations between the theatre worlds of Madrid and Barcelona were complex, and went right to the heart of questions of national and regional identity. Madrid's possibly unconscious dismissal of 'regional' theatre fails to take account of the serious attempts in Barcelona to establish a specifically Catalan theatre, an attempt that was doomed to enjoy only limited success because of the continued domination of the Spanish language in many of Barcelona's theatres. Moreover, in asserting that the likes of Guimerà and Borràs were essentially Spanish, certain critics seem to have ignored the fact that they were in reality working in another, foreign language. However, Guimerà was not a Catalan by birth, and Borràs was an accomplished speaker of Spanish with hardly a trace of a Catalan accent. What this study has shown is that it would be a mistake to view Madrid as the sole or even the principal theatre centre in Spain. Its traditions and structures would suggest that it was the main centre, but if one's definition of theatre includes amateur theatre, and embraces designers, directors, actors/actresses and dramatists as well as buildings, then Barcelona's claims to equality with Madrid are compelling. Barcelona's struggle to forge a non-Spanish, specifically Catalan identity during the early years of the twentieth century goes side by side with and sometimes runs counter to its internationalism and permeability to other theatre cultures, including Spanish. In this sense, the theatre was a microcosm of culture in the broader sense, and of society at large.

It would be a long time before the desire for a national theatre in Barcelona would be satisfied. The frustration that the successes of the turn of the century failed to crystallize into distinctly Catalan theatrical structures was as nothing compared to the fate that the Catalan theatre shared with the rest of Catalan society during the Franco regime. It was not until after the re-establishment of democracy in the late 1970s that a programme of promotion of Catalan theatre in Barcelona was undertaken, culminating in the establishment of the coveted Catalan National Theatre in 1997. This is in stark contrast to the situation in Madrid, where the Spanish National Theatre had been established in the early years of the Franco regime, but relaunched according to the French model of national theatres in 1978 under the directorship of Adolfo Marsillach (significantly another Catalan). There are still collaborative ventures between Barcelona- and Madrid-based practitioners and Catalan playwrights, directors, actors and actresses still perform regularly in Madrid and other Spanish cities, but they are no longer forced to go there in order to seek audiences and attention. These days, their home is most definitely Barcelona.

Notes

Foreword

[1] A interesting recent debate on the Madrid–Catalonia question was the one published in *El País* between the President of the Comunidad de Madrid, Alberto Ruiz-Gallardón, and the Socialist leader of the opposition in the Catalan Parliament and former Mayor of Barcelona, Pasqual Maragall: 'Madrid y Cataluña, frente a frente', *El País. Domingo* (13 May 2001), 1 and 3–4.

Chapter 1 : Setting the Scene

[1] G. G. Brown, *A Literary History of Spain: The Twentieth Century* (London and New York: Ernest Benn and Barnes & Noble, 1972), 110. Geoffrey Ribbans makes a similar point, although he makes it more cautiously: 'The twentieth century brings also a certain renovation to the theatre, but it never attains the same level as poetry or the novel' ('Spanish Literature after 1700', in P. E. Russell (ed.), *Spain: A Companion to Spanish Studies* (London: Methuen, 1973), 381–428 (p. 414). Ribbans is, of course, referring to dramatic literature rather than to the theatre in a wider sense.

[2] Jesús Rubio Jiménez, 'La renovación teatral en el cambio de siglo: 1880–1914', in Miguel Medina (ed.), *Teatro y pensamiento en la regeneración del 98* (Madrid: Resad, 1998), 207–41 (p. 213).

[3] José-Carlos Mainer, *La Edad de Plata (1902–1939)*, 3rd edn (Madrid: Cátedra, 1983), 165.

[4] The work of María Francisca Vilches and Dru Dougherty, together with the team of researchers at the Consejo Superior de Investigaciones Científicas (CSIC) in Madrid, has been ground-breaking in this area. Their project covers 1900–36, and to date the period 1918–36 has produced two exhaustive studies: Dru Dougherty and María Francisca Vilches de Frutos, *La escena madrileña entre*

1918 y 1926: Análisis y documentación (Madrid: Fundamentos, 1990); and María Francisca Vilches de Frutos and Dru Dougherty, *La escena madrileña entre 1926 y 1931: Un lustro de transición* (Madrid: Fundamentos, 1997). For a sharp, succinct and highly readable introduction to the Spanish theatre of the late nineteenth and early twentieth centuries, see Dru Dougherty, 'Theatre and Culture, 1868–1936', in David T. Gies (ed.), *The Cambridge Companion to Modern Spanish Culture* (Cambridge: CUP, 1999), 211–21.

5   See, for example, Jesús Rubio Jiménez, 'La renovación teatral', 217–18.

6   A recent special number of *ADE Teatro* is a case in point (*Teatro de la España del siglo XX, i 1900–1939, ADE Teatro*, 77 (1999)). Another especially noteworthy study, in terms of its quality and exhaustive analysis, is Aguilera and Aznar's study of the influential Spanish director Cipriano de Rivas Cherif: Juan Aguilera Sastre and Manuel Aznar Soler, *Cipriano de Rivas Cherif y el teatro español de su época (1891–1967)*, Teoría y Práctica del Teatro, 16 (Madrid: Publicaciones de la Asociación de Directores de Escena de España, 1999).

7   For example, there are articles on Santiago Rusiñol and Adrià Gual and one on the Theatre Institute of Barcelona, as well as sections of more general studies devoted to Catalan theatre in the recent special number of *ADE Teatro*. Naturally, there is more critical material on Catalan theatre published in Barcelona, mainly in the Catalan language, where the contributions of Xavier Fàbregas and Enric Gallén stand out.

8   See, for example, two articles by Gwynne Edwards on performances of García Lorca: '*Bodas de sangre* in Performance', *ALEC*, 22 (1997), 469–91; and '*Yerma* on Stage', *ALEC*, 24 (1999), 433–51.

9   The English term 'Catalonia' is rendered in Catalan as 'Catalunya' and in Spanish as 'Cataluña'. All three forms appear in this study.

10 Francisco Ruiz Ramón, *Historia del teatro español siglo XX*, 6th edn (Madrid: Cátedra, 1984), 12.

11 The convention for referencing English translations of titles is as follows: where an English translation of the original title exists, this is quoted in italics after the first reference to the title; where none exists to my knowledge, my own translation of the Catalan or Spanish original is given in roman after the first reference to the title, or, in the case of other foreign titles, the original title only is given. Where roman is used to indicate a title within my own translation of a critical citation, single quotation marks are used to indicate that we are dealing with a title. Where the English translation is, or would be, the same as the original, no translation is given. A valuable, if by now

outdated, source of reference for translations of Spanish titles is Robert S. Rudder (ed.), *The Literature of Spain in English Translation* (New York: Frederick Ungar, 1975).

[12] A recent scholarly edition of *Realidad* is Benito Pérez Galdós, *The Theatre of Galdós: Realidad*, ed. Lisa Pauline Condé (Lewiston and Lampeter: The Edwin Mellen Press, 1993). For Pérez Galdós's relationship with contemporary Spanish actresses, see Lisa Pauline Condé, 'Galdós and his Leading Ladies', *BHS* (Liverpool), 75 (1998), 79–91.

[13] A very useful collection of essays on the social and urban development, architecture and cultural and intellectual life of Barcelona in the period under discussion here is Alejandro Sánchez (ed.), *Barcelona 1888–1929* (Madrid: Alianza, 1994).

[14] Raymond Carr, *Spain 1808–1975*, 2nd edn (Oxford: Clarendon Press, 1982), 552. Carr's critique of Catalan nationalism within the wider Spanish context is a concise, sharp and readable analysis of the issue.

[15] On the contrast between Catalan and Basque nationalism see Daniele Conversi, *The Basques, the Catalans and Spain: Alternative Routes to Nationalist Mobilisation* (London: Hunt & Co., 1997).

[16] For the divergence of critical opinion on the subject, see Alejandro Sánchez Suárez, 'Del regionalismo al nacionalismo', in *La Restauración (1874–1902)*, which is vol. x of Antonio Domínguez Ortiz (ed.), *Historia de España*, 12 vols (Barcelona: Planeta, 1990), 459–97 (p. 464). See also the Epilogue to Joan-Lluís Marfany, *La cultura del catalanisme* (Barcelona: Empúries, 1995), 379–85.

[17] Joseph Harrison, *An Economic History of Modern Spain* (Manchester: MUP, 1978), 95.

[18] Carr describes 'the mass suffering at the base of urban life' as characteristic of the labour world of Europe in the late nineteenth century (*Spain*, 438).

[19] For further details, see, for example, Harrison, *Economic History*, 117–21.

[20] Colonel Francesc Macià (1859–1933), Catalan nationalist leader, who declared for a Catalan state in 1931, but who later accepted autonomy through the Generalitat, or autonomous parliament.

[21] Raymond Carr explains the leftward movement of Catalan nationalism thus: 'Simplicity in politics means violence, and it was violence which this quiet man (i.e. Macià) brought to Catalan youth and to Catalan intellectuals weary of the realism of the Lliga. It was the alarm inspired by the separatist violence of the younger Catalan nationalists that turned the older politicians of the Lliga into reluctant backers of an army *coup* in 1923. They paid for this folly with the electoral defeat of the Lliga in 1931. Catalanism had finally

deserted its conservative origins and flowed into the rising torrents of the left' (Carr, *Spain*, 555–6).

22 'Política y moral en el teatro comercial a principios del siglo XX', in María Francisca Vilches de Frutos and Dru Dougherty (eds), *Teatro, sociedad y política en la España del siglo XX*, special monographic number of *Boletín de la Fundación García Lorca*, 19–20 (1996), 27–47 (p. 42).

23 Michael Ugarte, *Madrid 1900: The Capital as Cradle of Literature and Culture* (University Park, PA: Pennsylvania State University Press, 1996), 36.

24 Carr, *Spain*, 375. The war Carr refers to is the Great War.

25 Ibid., 415–16.

26 Lily Litvak, *Transformación industrial y literatura en España (1895–1905)* (Madrid: Taurus, 1980), 73.

27 P. Bohigas Tarragó, *Compañías dramáticas extranjeras en Barcelona*, Investigaciones, 2, Nov. 1946 (Barcelona: Diputación Provincial and Instituto del Teatro, 1946), 81–2.

28 *Modernisme* is sometimes translated as 'modernism', although it is in many ways closer to art nouveau than to the English term 'modernism'. The best study in English of *modernisme* and other artistic movements in the context of the history of Barcelona is Robert Hughes, *Barcelona* (New York: Vintage Books, 1993).

29 The characteristics of *noucentisme* are neatly summed up by Balcells: '*Noucentisme* was the cultural movement which began to take the place of Modernism from 1906 onwards. It was to some extent opposed to the most vital and Romantic aspects of the latter movement. Both, however, were closely linked to the construction of Catalonia as a European society and to its overall modernization. The standardization of the Catalan language, a certain neo-classicism, and the desire for order and practical achievements within the framework of the Mancomunitat were the main characteristics of *noucentisme*, whose influence on Catalonia was little affected by new avant-garde trends' (Albert Balcells, *Catalan Nationalism Past and Present*, trans. Jacqueline Hall (London: Macmillan, 1996), 82n.).

30 Fèlix Fanés, 'The First Image – Dalí and his Critics: 1919 to 1929', in Michael Raeburn (ed.), *Salvador Dalí: The Early Years* (London: South Bank Centre, 1994), 90–6 (p. 92).

31 For further details see Xavier Fàbregas, *Història del teatre català* (Barcelona: Millà, 1978), 143–4. Enric Gallén links the building of theatres in Barcelona in the late nineteenth century to the development of its image as a new, modern city and with the exodus of the wealthy sectors of society from the inner city to the suburbs: 'La imatge de la Barcelona moderna, la de la *ciutat nova*, s'anà

consolidant en l'última dècada del segle XIX alhora que, en expandir-se com a urbs, integrava alguns dels vells municipis i viles de l'entorn, l'any 1897. L'èxode, a més, gradual i progressiu de les classes benestants de la *ciutat vella* cap a l'Eixample es produí, mentre s'anà configurant un nou mapa ciutadà de les sales d'esbarjo i d'espectacles.' (The image of modern Barcelona, of the *new city*, was consolidated during the final decade of the nineteenth century while some of the old outlying areas became incorporated into the exponding city around 1897. Moreover, the steadily increasing exodus of the well-off classes from the old city to the Eixample coincided with the configuration of a new city map of entertainment palaces.) (Enric Gallén, 'El teatre', in M. de Riquer, A. Comas and J. Molas (eds), *Història de la literatura catalana*, 11 vols (Barcelona: Ariel, 1980–8), viii, 379–449. Valentín García Plata makes a similar point in 'Primeras teorías españolas de la puesta en escena: Adrià Gual', *ALEC*, 21 (1996), 291–312 (pp. 293–4).

[32] *ABC* (24 November 1909), 9–10.

[33] *El arte dramático en el resurgir de Cataluña* (Barcelona: Minerva, [1917?]), 401–3.

[34] The word 'levado' does not actually exist in Spanish. This appears to be a false cognate, based on the Catalan 'llevat' which means 'yeast'.

[35] 'The publication in 1895 of Enric Prat de la Riba and Pere Muntanyola's *Compendi de Doctrina Catalanista* (*Compendium of Catalanist Doctrine*), a type of catechism of Catalanism of which over 100,000 copies were printed, contributed to the diffusion of the definition of Catalonia as a nation, though it continued to use the term "fatherland".' Balcells, *Catalan Nationalism*, 41.

[36] In 1897 the Catalanists incurred the wrath of the Spanish government by sending a message of solidarity to the King of Greece over the conflict in Crete, which was ruled by the Turks. One Catalan playwright who dealt with Catalan nationalism in the context of national liberation in a wider European context was Josep Burgas, in such plays as *Jordi Erin* (1906) and *Els segadors de Polònia* (The Reapers of Poland) (1912); for further details see Fàbregas, *Historia*, 246–7.

[37] For further details, ibid., 214–15.

[38] P, 'Comentario de la semana. Se crea un Teatro Nacional en Cataluña', *El Debate* (28 Jan. 1934), 'Suplemento extraordinario', 8. Although some Barcelona theatres closed down during the first years of the century, others were opened, including the Polioroma (1914), the Goya (1915) and the Barcelona (1923). However, these mostly performed plays by contemporary Spanish rather than Catalan authors; for further details see Enric Gallén, 'El teatre', in *Història de la literatura catalana*, ix, 413–62 (pp. 413–16).

39 Jesús Rubio Jiménez, 'La renovación teatral', 215. On theatre and the 1898 crisis see Derek Gagen, '¿El santo o la esfinge? El teatro ante la crisis de 1898', *Rilce*, 15 (1999), 253–66.

40 Serge Salaün and Claire-Nicole Robin, 'Arts et spectacles: Tradition et renouveau', in Carlos Serrano and Serge Salaün (eds), *1900 en Espagne* (Bordeaux: Presses Universitaires de Bordeaux, 1988), 105–28 (p. 106).

41 Information from ibid., 108.

42 For details, see María Pilar Espín Templado, *El teatro por horas en Madrid (1870–1910)* (Madrid: Instituto de Estudios Madrileños and Fundación Jacinto e Inocencio Guerrero, 1995), 72–3.

43 'Contrariamente al favor que los Teatros por horas gozaron siempre por parte del público, su aparición, desde el primero de ellos en el café teatro El Recreo en 1869, fue siempre unida a una amplia campaña de prensa negativa y demoledora . . . En resumen, los Teatros por horas, según la crítica instituida, eran la vergüenza y el baldón del arte teatral del momento, el síntoma inequívovo de la definitiva decadencia en que se encontraba el arte dramático español.' (In contrast to the support that the Theatres enjoyed with the general public, following their first appearance at the café theatre El Recreo in 1869, they were always the subject of a broad press campaign that was negative and destructive. In short, according to the established critics, these satirical one-act plays were the embarrassment and disgrace of contemporary theatrical art, an unmistakable symptom of the terminal decadence of Spanish dramatic art.) (Espín Templado, *El teatro por horas*, 78–9). A full-length study in English of the *teatro por horas* phenomenon is Nancy Membrez, 'The "teatro por horas": History, dynamics and comprehensive bibliography of a Madrid industry, 1867–1922 ('género chico', 'género ínfimo' and Early Cinema)' (unpublished doctoral thesis, University of of California at Santa Barbara, 1987). On the *zarzuela* and musical theatre in Spain see Andrés Amorós (ed.), *La zarzuela de cerca*, Colección Austral (Madrid: Espasa Calpe, 1987); Manuel Lagos, 'El otro teatro. El teatro musical en Madrid (1900–1939): Ópera, zarzuela y revista', in *Teatro de la España del siglo XX, i 1900–1939*, special number of *ADE Teatro*, 77 (1999), 264–73; and Ángel Montesinos, 'Últimas décadas del teatro musical en España: La zarzuela', ibid., 274–8. A general study of *género chico* is José Deleito y Piñuela, *Origen y apogeo del género chico* (Madrid: Revista de Occidente, 1949). For a view that the *género chico* was a kind of cultural pact between the bourgeoisie and the lower classes, see Serge Salaün, 'El "género chico" o los mecanismos de un pacto cultural', in Equipo de Investigación sobre el Teatro Español (ed.), *El teatro menor en España a partir del siglo XVI* (Madrid: CSIC, 1983), 251–61.

44   On the tradition of the Catalan *sainet*, see Fàbregas, *Historia*, ch. 7.
45   These last two *zarzuelas* originated in Madrid and were especially popular there. *El Santo de la Isidra* in particular is viewed as perhaps *the* archetypal Madrid *zarzuela*, and its success in Barcelona illustrates that nationalism or regionalism were less prominent when it came to popular entertainment.
46   *Almanaque del Diario de Barcelona* (1899), 92. For convenience, most of the reviews appearing in *El Diario de Barcelona* have been consulted in the *Almanaque*. The newspaper articles and reviews which are quoted or referred to in this study, and referenced in footnotes, will not be cited in the Bibliography.
47   Serge Salaün, 'El Paralelo barcelonés (1894–1936)', *ALEC*, 21 (1996), 329–49 (p. 336).
48   See Fàbregas, *Historia*, 143–4. In Jordi Coca's words: 'Des del punt de vista teatral el fet més remarcable a la ciutat [. . .] era la nova situació creada per l'expansió dels teatres cap a l'Eixample i pel floriment en el Paral.lel d'un conjunt de barraques i sales dedicades als espectacles frívols.' (From the point of view of the theatre, the most remarkable feature of the city [. . .] was the new situation created by the expansion of the theatres towards the Eixample and by the flourishing in the Paral.lel of a series of booths and halls dedicated to frivolous spectacles.) Carles Batlle, Isidre Bravo and Jordi Coca (eds), *Adrià Gual: Mitja vida de modernisme* (Barcelona: Diputació de Barcelona, 1992), 30.
49   Fàbregas, *Historia*, 145.
50   This is a reference to the famous novel, later published in play form, *L'auca del senyor Esteve*, by Santiago Rusiñol, which parodied a respectable shopkeeper and his family, and treated a familiar Rusiñol theme of the incompatibility between the artist and the bourgeois.
51   This theatrical form is described by one critic as a 'degeneración de un híbrido teatral cuyos elementos mayores proceden del juguete cómico y del melodrama cómico' (degeneration of a theatrical hybrid whose major elements derive from light comic theatre and comic melodrama). Ruiz Ramón, *Historia*, 58.
52   Dru Dougherty, 'Espectáculo y pequeño burguesía: El público de Pedro Muñoz Seca', *Hispanística XX*, 15 (1997), 71–8 (p. 78). The article is a particularly interesting study of the class composition of Muñoz Seca's audiences. On the popularity of Muñoz Seca, see Dru Dougherty and María Francisca Vilches de Frutos, *La escena madrileña entre 1918 y 1926*, 78, *passim*.
53   According to Joan Abellán, Iglésies 'llegó a ser estrenado por Lugné-Poë en su Théâtre Livre' (was premiered by Lugné-Poë in his Théâtre Livre): 'La literatura dramática catalana 1900–1939: Trabajos de

amor perdidos', *Teatro de la España del siglo XX*, i *1900–1939*, 67–74 (p. 69).

54   'La Vitaliana al Paralelo', *El Poble Català* (30 May 1907), 1.

55   A family who performed pantomime in turn-of-the-century Barcelona, where they arrived from Marseille.

56   This is a derogatory name applied to erotic revues.

57   Iglésies's crusade was not limited to this one article. A 1912 speech of his, which was reported in the press, continues the theme of the need to Catalanify and dignify the Paral.lel (*La Escena Catalana* (22 June 1912), 3–5).

58   Francesc Curet's views will be recalled here: see above. On the theatre's place in proletarian culture in Spain during the 1930s, see Christopher H. Cobb, *La cultura y el pueblo: España 1930–1939*, Historia/Papel, 451 (Barcelona: Laia, 1980), 58–67. On the Spanish Civil War period, see Jim McCarthy, *Political Theatre during the Spanish Civil War* (Cardiff: University of Wales Press, 1999); and Robert Marrast, *El teatre durant la Guerra Civil Espanyola*, Monografies de Teatre, 8 (Barcelona: Institut del Teatre and Edicions 62, 1978).

59   Iglésies's *Els vells* and Dicenta's *Juan José* will be considered in Chapters 5 and 6 respectively.

60   On the impact of naturalism on social theatre, see Lily Litvak de Pérez de la Dehesa, 'Naturalismo y teatro social en Cataluña', *Comparative Literature Studies* (Maryland) (1969), 279–302.

61   In Catalan, her name is spelt 'Margarida' or 'Marguerida'; in this book, I use 'Margarita' as the name by which she was internationally known. The difficulty of rendering in meaningful English a word or concept which does not have the same import in the English-speaking world as it does in Spain is highlighted in the word 'castellano'. As well as denoting an inhabitant of the region of Castile, the word also means 'the Spanish language'. Where it indicates the language, I normally render 'castellano' as 'Spanish', except where it is specifically linked with Castile.

62   His role as a critic, particularly of Ibsen and Zola, will be considered briefly in Chapter 4.

63   This will be be dealt with in Chapter 5. Such a stance is typical of Catalan *modernisme*, for instance in Raimon Casellas's *Els sots feréstecs* (The Savage Hollows) (1901). Within Spain, a similar view of the countryside is given by Benavente in plays such as *La malquerida* (*The Passion Flower*) (1913), which owes much to Adrià Gual's *Misteri de dolor* (Mystery of Grief) (1904). An excellent introduction to Rusiñol's theatre is Enric Gallén, 'Santiago Rusiñol', in *Història de la literatura catalana*, viii, 449–80.

[64] Julio Enrique Checa Puerta, *Los teatros de Gregorio Martínez Sierra* (Madrid: Fundación Universitaria Española, 1998), 24. On the question of audience opinion, a colourful view is expressed in a publication called the *Enciclopedia del Año (1899)*: 'pero es indudable que empresarios y actores han hecho frente a no pocas dificultades motivadas por la actitud del público; porque es éste, según reza una frase muy conocida, "turbulento como el oleaje del mar en día de tormenta, y voluble como mujer coqueta"' (but it is undeniable that impressarios and actors have faced a significant number of difficulties caused by the attitude of audiences; but, according to a well-known phrase, audiences are 'as turbulent as the ocean swell on a stormy day, and as fickle as a flirtatious woman'). R. Ruiz Benítez de Lugo, *La Enciclopedia del Año (1899)* (Madrid: Est Tip Sucesores de Rivadeneyra, 1900), 46.

[65] Joan Abellán, 'La literatura dramática catalana 1900–1939: Trabajos de amor perdidos', *Teatro de la España del siglo XX*, i. *1900–1939*, 70.

[66] *El reino interior*, trans. Vicente Martín Pindado (Madrid: Encuentro, 1986), 362.

[67] Salaün, 'Política y moral', 33–4.

[68] Jesús Rubio Jiménez, 'Los nuevos horizontes de la literatura dramática de 1900 a 1920', in *Teatro de la España del siglo XX*, i. *1900–1939*, 16–26 (p. 16).

[69] Miquis is described by Martín Rodríguez as 'conocido campeón del Naturalismo desde principios de siglo' (a well-known champion of naturalism from the beginning of the century). Mariano Martín Rodríguez, *El teatro francés en Madrid (1918–1936)* (Boulder, CO: Society of Spanish and Spanish-American Studies, 1999), 444. See also Jesús Rubio Jiménez, 'Anselmo González, "Alejandro Miquis"', in *Teatro de la España del siglo XX*, i. *1900–1939*, special number of *ADE Teatro*, 77 (1999), 288. Cristina Santolaria is in no doubt about the quality of Miquis and other critics of his generation: 'Fue la suya en realidad una generación de grandes críticos teatrales. Para hoy quisiéramos en nuestros diarios un elenco semejante. Asistían cada día a los teatros y seguían con pasión las novedades europeas, sólo la desmemoria posterior explica que de muchos de ellos nuestras historias del teatro de este siglo no recojan ni sus nombres. Alejandro Miquis fue uno de ellos y leyéndolo se constata que ese aislamiento y el retraso del teatro español en nuestro siglo es una gran mentira; gentes como Miquis conocían por donde debía ir la renovación teatral. Cosa bien distinta es que el sistema de producción teatral comercial fuera impermeable a sus propuestas, que hallaron eco, sin embargo, en pequeñas agrupaciones.' (His was in truth a generation

of great theatre critics. How good it would be to have such a quality breed in today's newspapers. They went to the theatre every day, and followed passionately the latest European trends. It is only subsequent amnesia which accounts for the fact that our theatre histories do not even mention the names of many of them. Alejandro Miquis was one such critic; when one reads his reviews, one realizes that the isolation and backwardness of twentieth-century Spanish theatre is a lie. People like Miquis knew the direction that reform of the theatre had to take, although it is quite another matter that the system of commercial production remained impervious to his proposals, which did find an echo in small groups.) 'Enrique Díez-Canedo o el ejercicio de una crítica erudita y honrada', in *Teatro de la España del siglo XX*, i. *1900–1939*, 289. Other articles on theatre criticism in the press are Raquel Asún, 'A la inmensa mayoría: La crítica literaria de Eduardo Gómez de Barquero, *Andrenio*', *Boletín de la Biblioteca de Menéndez y Pelayo*, 56–7 (1980–1), 295–360; and Juan Miguel Godoy Marquet, '*Comedias y comediantes. Revista quincenal (1909–1912)*: Al servicio de un teatro español de calidad', *ALEC*, 18 (1993), 503–15.

70 In practical terms, according to Checa, this meant that 'se iban incorporando con muy pocos años de diferencia los avances técnicos y estéticos introducidos en otros países durante los últimos años del siglo XIX' (technical and aesthetic advances which had been introduced in other countries during the final years of the nineteenth century were incorporated within a short period of time). Checa Puerta, *Los teatros*, 25.

71 On the Teatro de Arte group, see Dru Doughtery, 'Una iniciativa de reforma teatral: el grupo "Teatro de Arte" (1908–1911)', in Pedro Peira *et al.* (eds), *Homenaje a Alonso Zamora Vicente*, 5 vols (Madrid: Castalia, 1994), iv. 177–92.

72 García Lorca's first play, *El maleficio de la mariposa* (*The Butterfly's Evil Spell*) – a box-office and critical flop – was performed at the Eslava.

73 See, for example, Aguilera Sastre and Aznar Soler, *Cipriano de Rivas Cherif*, 173–4.

74 Ramón Pérez de Ayala, 'Las máscaras. La reteatralización', *España*, 44 (25 Nov. 1915). The article is cited in Jesús Rubio Jiménez, *El teatro poético en España: Del modernismo a las vanguardias* (Murcia: Universidad de Murcia, 1993), 66–7. For an analysis of Pérez de Ayala's ideas on the theatre see Jesús Rubio Jiménez, 'Ramón Pérez de Ayala y el teatro: Entre Momo y Talía', *España Contemporánea*, 1 (1988), 27–53.

75 For an analysis of links between symbolist and avant-garde theatre see Frantisek Deak, *Symbolist Theater: The Formation of an Avant-Garde* (Baltimore and London: Johns Hopkins University Press, 1993).

[76] Martín Rodríguez, *El teatro francés*, 450.

[77] For further details, see Chapter 2.

[78] See John London, 'Twentieth-century Spanish stage design', in *Spanish Theatre, 1920–1995: Strategies in Protest and Imagination* (3), *Contemporary Theatre Review*, 7/3 (1998), 25–56 (p. 26).

[79] For details, see *Cuatro siglos de teatro en Madrid* (Catalogue produced for Madrid as European City of Culture in 1992) (Madrid: Apsel, 1992), 89–94.

[80] García Plata's view is that Gual's theatre never really evolved to integrate the new ideas that emerged in the early twentieth century ('Primeras teorías', 307).

[81] For Gual's interest in El Mirlo Blanco, see Gloria Rey Faraldos, 'Pío Baroja y "El Mirlo Blanco" ', *Revista de Literatura*, 47/ 93 (Jan.–June 1985), 117–27 (p. 119).

[82] The 1930s saw the growth of agit-prop theatre in Spain, culminating in the so-called *teatro de urgencia* during the Spanish Civil War. An invaluable study of this phenomenon is McCarthy, *Political Theatre during the Spanish Civil War*.

[83] See Jordi Coca, introduction to *Adrià Gual: Mitja vida de modernisme*, 13–37 (p. 32).

[84] R. Ruiz Benítez de Lugo, *La Enciclopedia del Año (1899)*, 38.

[85] 'Los nuevos horizontes de la literatura dramática de 1900 a 1920', 22. On the Teatro de Arte, see Dru Dougherty, 'Una iniciativa de reforma teatral'.

[86] 'Los nuevos horizontes de la literatura dramática de 1900 a 1920', 23.

[87] 'Los teatros íntimos y experimentales en Barcelona y Madrid (1900–1936)', in *Teatro de la España del siglo XX, i. 1900–1939*, 117–26.

[88] 'Propósitos incumplidos del Teatro Íntimo en Madrid, con otros atisbos de esperanza', *Teatrón*, 1 (Oct. 1926), 2. Quoted in Aguilera Sastre and Aznar Soler, *Cipriano de Rivas Cherif*, 50.

Chapter 2: Building the Bridges between Madrid and Barcelona

[1] 'Frederic Soler: Su aparición en escena', *El Diario del Teatro* (4 Jan. 1895), 1. 1894 also saw the premiere of Benavente's first play, *El nido ajeno* (The Other Man's Nest), which is generally credited with introducing naturalistic discourse into the Spanish theatre.

[2] Salvador Canals, 'Santiago Rusiñol: El modernismo en España', *El Diario del Teatro* (14 Jan. 1894), 1–2 (references taken from p. 1).

3   On anticlericalism in the Restoration, see Raymond Carr, *Spain 1808–1975*, 2nd edn (Oxford: Clarendon Press, 1982), 466.

4   Joan Martori, *La projecció d'Àngel Guimerà a Madrid (1891–1924)*, Textos i Estudis de Cultura Catalana, 46 (Barcelona: Curial Edicions Catalanes and Publicacions de l'Abadia de Montserrat, 1995), 275.

5   Margarida Casacuberta, *Santiago Rusiñol: Vida, literatura i mite* (Barcelona: Curial and Publicacions de l'Abadia de Montserrat, 1997), 274.

6   *La Lectura*, 1 (1903), 433–9.

7   Perés's review of the play is discussed in Chapter 5.

8   Albert Bensoussan, 'José Yxart 1852–1895, Théâtre et critique à Barcelone', 2 vols (Université de Lille III; Atelier National de Reproduction de Thèses, 1982), i. 582.

9   'Adrià Gual, además de ser el primer director de escena en el pleno sentido de la expresión que aparece en España, constituye un permanente punto de referencia por su labor escénica y pedagógica para todos los intentos que se producirán en las dos décadas siguientes' (Adrià Gual, beside being the leading director in Spain in the full sense of that word, is, because of his stage and pedagogic work, a permanent reference point for any new project in the following two decades.) Juan Antonio Hormigón, 'Teatro español del siglo XX', in *Teatro de la España del siglo XX*, i. *1900–1939*, special number of *ADE Teatro*, 77 (1999), 5–13 (p. 9). Another article in the same publication makes the point that Gual has remained neglected for many years, despite being recognized as a leading thetrical figure in his day: 'La figura de Adrià Gual en la mayoría de las ocasiones ha quedado semioculta, sino completamente olvidada, cuando no discutida, a pesar de que algunos de los principales hombres del teatro catalán le han rendido tributo como uno de los grandes hombres del teatro y de la cultura en Cataluña.' (The figure of Adrià Gual has remained half hidden on most occasions, is not completely forgotten or undiscussed, despite the fact that some of the leading Catalan theatre practitioners have paid tribute to him as one of the great men of Catalan theatre and culture.) Enric Ciurans, 'Adrià Gual y el Teatro Catalán', in *Teatro de la España del siglo XX*, i. *1900–1939*, 204–7 (p. 204).

10   Joaquín Montaner, '*ABC* en Barcelona: El ejemplo del Teatre Íntim, a D. Gregorio Martínez Sierra', *ABC* (16 May 1917), 8.

11   Chapter 4 will consider examples of these.

12   *El Heraldo de Madrid* (18 April 1925), 5.

13   Ibid. (16 May 1925), 5, contained a review of Schoenberg's *Pierrot Lunaire* at the Wagnerian Palau de la Música Catalana, which was designed by the *modernista* architect Doménech i Montaner in 1908. According to the reviewer, the audience at the Palau, the weight of

tradition weighing heavily on their shoulders, rejected what they felt was the lack of seriousness of the Schoenberg piece. On the Palau de la Música, see Robert Hughes, *Barcelona* (New York: Vintage Books, 1993), 456–63.

[14] S. Canals, *El año teatral (1895–96)* (Madrid: Establecimiento Tipográfico de el Nacional, 1896), 108–9.

[15] For the political affiliations of this and other Catalan newspapers and journals of the period, see Albert Balcells, *Catalan Nationalism Past and Present*, trans. Jacqueline Hall (London: Macmillan, 1996), 40, 44, 50 and 57.

[16] *La Veu de Catalunya* (16 May 1897), 165–6.

[17] Quoted in Vance R. Holloway, 'La crítica teatral en *ABC*, 1918–1936', in *American University Studies*, Series 2, *Romance Languages and Literatures*, 181 (New York: Peter Laing), 1991 (pp. 111–12). According to Holloway, José Alsina expressed his admiration for the Catalans in the theatre page of *ABC*.

[18] For his review of Atenea's production of Ibsen's *John Gabriel Borkmann*, see Chapter 4.

[19] E. Estévez-Ortega, *Nuevo escenario* (Barcelona: Lux, 1928), 37.

[20] As well as a journalist, José Escofet was an occasional playwright, writing mainly farces.

[21] José Escofet, 'El teatro y el "cine"', *La Voz* (17 December 1926), 1.

[22] For details on Muñoz Seca's *astracanes*, see Chapter 1.

[23] There was a major debate on Spain on whether the cinema represented a threat or a challenge for the theatre. See Dru Dougherty, '¿Pantalla o escenario?', which is chapter 6 of 'Talía convulsa: La crisis teatral de los años 20', in Robert Lima and Dru Dougherty, *2 ensayos sobre teatro español de los 20*, ed. César Oliva (Murcia: Universidad de Murcia, 1984), 119–24. On the cinema and its effect on the theatre in Spain, see Nancy Membrez, ' "Llévame al cine, mamá": The cinematograph in Spain 1896–1920', in Ben Lawton and Anthony Julian Tamburri (eds), *Romance Languages Annual 1989* (West Lafayette, IN: Purdue Research Foundation, 1990), 540–7.

[24] The early cinemas in Barcelona and Madrid were improvised sheds or building basements, and were especially numerous in working-class neighbourhoods: 'By 1910 Barcelona had over 100 cinemas and according to one estimate 160 in 1914. There were also a large number of larger, more luxurious cinemas, located in the center of the city . . . Some of these had over 1,000 seats and one had 3,000.' Adrian Shubert, *A Social History of Modern Spain* (London: Routledge, 1992), 200.

[25] Adolfo Marsillach, 'El teatro en Barcelona', *ABC* (16 March 1933), 3. One particular Spanish designer/director, the remarkable Enrique Rambal, borrowed some of cinema's more spectacular effects and used

them in the theatre. On Rambal's contribution to the Spanish theatre, see the following two articles by Maria M. Delgado: 'Enrique Rambal: The Forgotten Auteur of Spanish Popular Theatre', *Spanish Theatre 1920–1995: Strategies in Protest and Imagination* (3), *Contemporary Theatre Review*, 7/3 (1998), 67–92; and *Erasure and Inscription on the Twentieth-Century Spanish Stage: The Popular Theatre of Enrique Rambal*, Papers in Spanish and Latin American Theatre History, 8 (London: Department of Hispanic Studies, Queen Mary and Westfield College, University of London, 2001).

26 Adolfo Marsillach, 'El teatro en Barcelona', 3.

27 For details on this composer, see Chapter 3.

28 For the ERC and Macià, see Chapter 1. It should be noted that the grave accent does not exist in Spanish as it does in Catalan. Hence, 'Macià' is spelt 'Maciá' in Spanish, 'Borràs' becomes 'Borrás', 'Guimerà' becomes 'Guimerá', etc.

29 A detailed and splendidly-illustrated history of the Romea Theatre is Enric Gallén (ed.), *Romea, 125 anys* (Barcelona: Generalitat de Catalunya, 1989).

30 His survey in the 6 September 1933 edn of the paper contained a highly favourable review of Margarita Xirgu's famous production (with Enric Borràs) of Unamuno's adaptation of Seneca's *Medea* (6 Sept. 1933), 6–7.

31 Manuel Bueno, *Teatro español contemporáneo* (Madrid: Biblioteca Renacimiento, 1909), 61.

32 Martori, *La projecció d'Àngel Guimerà*, 272.

33 Ibid., 126–7.

34 He declared that he would put a *barretina* on his children and learn Catalan himself.

35 *La projecció d'Àngel Guimerà*, 140.

36 Ibid., 137. *La filla del mar* is set in a small Catalan fishing village whose inhabitants display intolerance towards both Pere Màrtir, the local don Juan who has returned from the Americas, and the young woman Àgata, who has lived among them ever since as a little girl she was washed up as the sole survivor of a shipwrecked Arab boat. She has been baptized a Christian, having been adopted by the parents of Mariona, one of the village girls, and has been cared for by Mariona's uncle, Cinquenes, since the death of the parents. However, Àgata is never really accepted as an equal member of the community. She is not like other women, and is the only female to go fishing with the men. Above all, she is considered to be unattractive and incapable of sexual love, and the community is therefore surprised when Pere Màrtir falls for her. Pere Màrtir's latest flame is Mariona, but Cinquenes does not approve of the match between his niece and the village rake. Mariona

suggests Pere pretend to court the unattractive Àgata in order to avert suspicion, little suspecting that Pere will find true love for the first time in his life and be reformed in the process. Pere, who continues to see Mariona by secretly entering her house at night, resolves to split up with her and marry Àgata, but in the dark he mistakes the latter for the former on the night he resolves to break the news to Mariona. Àgata is furious at what she considers Pere's unfaithfulness, but is persuaded by him of his good intentions and gives him another chance. She subsequently sees him in what she believes to be an embrace with Mariona, and, not realizing that he is desperately trying to break free from Mariona's clutches, is finally convinced of his unfaithfulness. She stabs him in the back with a fishing spear. Pere's declaration of love for Àgata as he lies dying makes her realize her mistake too late. She flings herself into the sea, her suicide being a desperate attempt to escape from the intolerant village and return to her parents, who were lost at sea when their boat was wrecked. For a study of a 1990s production of the play see David George, 'A young lad in the arms of an old man: Sergi Belbel directs Àngel Guimerà's *La filla del mar* (*The Daughter of the Sea*)', in *Spanish Theatre 1920–1995: Strategies in Protest and Imagination* (3), *Contemporary Theatre Review*, 7/4 (1998), 45–64.

[37] Balcells, *Catalan Nationalism*, 40–1.

[38] See Martori, *La projecció d'Àngel Guimerà*, chapters 6 and 7.

[39] J. Francos Rodríguez, *El teatro en España, 1909*, Año II (Madrid: Imprenta de Bernardo Rodríguez, 1910), 148–9.

[40] Ibid., 149.

[41] Ibid.

[42] Ibid., 158.

[43] Martori describes how these views did, of course, affect the perception of Guimerà in Madrid: 'La crítica empezó a mezclar la lectura de la literatura dramática de Guimerà con diferentes elementos que denotaban los prejuicios hacia el regionalismo. Hablar del teatro de Guimerà comportaba tomar parte en el debate existente entre una concepción centralista del Estado español y las reivindicaciones del catalanismo literario.' (The critics began [in the 1890s] to mix the reading of Guimerà's dramatic works with different elements which betrayed the prejudices towards regionalism. To speak of Guimerà's theatre implied taking part in the current debate between a centralist concept of the Spanish state and the defence of literary Catalanism.) Joan Martori, 'Guimerà en Madrid', *ALEC*, 21 (1996), 313–27 (p. 315).

[44] Andrés González Blanco, *Los dramaturgos españoles contemporáneos*, 1a serie (Valencia: Cervantes, 1917), 245.

[45] Martori, 'Guimerà en Madrid', 324.

[46] Ibid.

[47] El Caballero Audaz (pseud. of José María Carretero Novillo), *Lo que sé por mí (Confesiones del siglo)*, cuarta serie (Madrid: V. H. de Sanz Editores, 1917).

[48] See María Àngels Heras, 'Una relectura del modernisme català. Santiago Rusiñol: Desde el dialogisme intercultural a la construcció d'una identitat nacional' (unpublished doctoral thesis, University of Nottingham, 2000).

[49] Jesús Rubio Jiménez, ' "Llibertat!" de Santiago Rusiñol, o de cómo negros e intelectuales son hermanos', in *Santiago Rusiñol, Llibertat!/¡Libertad!*, Serie Literatura Dramática, 28 (Madrid and Barcelona: Publicaciones de la Asociación de Directores de España and Institut del Teatre de la Diputació de Barcelona, 2000), 15–42 (p. 16).

[50] However, in order to put his work into perspective, it is useful to note the views of Spain's most important theatre innovator, the director and playwright Cipriano Rivas Cherif. While he appreciated the value of Martínez Sierra's work in the Spanish context, in the words of Juan Aguilera and Manuel Aznar, 'Rivas Cherif expresa un menosprecio sistemático por el trabajo escénico de Martínez Sierra al valorarlo comparativamente con el de otros directores y puestas en escena europeos.' (Rivas Cherif expresses a systematic contempt for the work of Martínez Sierra when compared with other European directors.) Juan Aguilera Sastre and Manuel Aznar Soler, *Cipriano de Rivas Cherif y el teatro español de su época (1891–1967)*, Teoría y Práctica del Teatro, 16 (Madrid: Publicaciones de la Asociación de Directores de Escena de España, 1999), 47. Rivas was particularly critical of Martínez Sierra's production of Manuel de Falla's *The Three-Cornered Hat* at the Eslava, which he compared unfavourably with the Diaghilev version he had seen in Paris.

[51] She thought very highly of Rusiñol, and in the following passage evokes his love for life, and what one might call his moderate hedonism: 'Cuando evoco la arrogante figura de Santiago Rusiñol paréceme su persona la encarnación más perfecta, casi el símbolo de la felicidad. ¡Cómo amaba la vida y hasta qué punto poseyó la indomable voluntad de sacar de ella y de saborear en ella la mayor suma de placer normal y razonable! Hedonista absoluto, maestro en el vagar y en el divagar, supo medir el paso y moderar su anhelo sin restarle belleza, pero sin permitirle traspasar el límite que separa el ensueño del desvarío. El mero hecho de vivir fue para él manantial de inagotable gozo.' (When I evoke the dashing figure of Santiago Rusiñol, his person seems to me to be the most perfect incarnation, almost the symbol of happiness. How he loved life and how he possessed the indomitable spirit needed to get out of it and to savour in it the maximum amount of normal and reasonable pleasure! An absolute hedonist, he was a master wanderer

and raconteur, he knew how to measure his step and moderate his desire without taking any beauty away from it, but without allowing it to cross the boundary which separates fantasy from delirium. The mere fact of living was for him a source of endless pleasure.) María Martínez Sierra, *Gregorio y yo* (Mexico: Biografías Gandesa, 1953), 50. See also her charming evocation of Rusiñol's refined love of food and drink, linked with his generosity, on pp. 54–5. On María Martínez Sierra see Susan Kirkpatrick, 'The "Feminine Element": *Fin-de-siècle* Spain, modernity, and the woman writer', in Joseph Harrison and Alan Hoyle (eds), *Spain's 1898 Crisis: Regenerationism, Modernism, Post-Colonialism* (Manchester: MUP, 2000), 146–55 (pp. 149–54). See also Alda Blanco, introduction to M. Martínez Sierra, *Una mujer por caminos de España* (Madrid: Castalia and Instituto de la Mujer, 1989), 7–40, for details of her life as a feminist and socialist.

[52] *Gregorio y yo*, 58.

[53] Ibid., 60–1.

[54] Rosario Pino (1870–1933) was one of the leading Spanish actresses of her era and was associated with the move away from Echegarayan theatre initiated by Benavente. She developed her own individual style of acting, abandoning the affected sentimentality which dominated the Spanish stage in the late nineteenth century.

[55] If *El místic* was generally successful in Madrid and Barcelona, the same could not be said for *La mare* (The Mother). In this case, politics seem to have entered into the equation, as even the affable and charismatic bridge-builder Rusiñol fell victim to the tensions and rivalry which lay beneath the surface: for details see Casacuberta, *Santiago Rusiñol*, 472–3. According to Casacuberta, the Spanish translation of *La mare* had only a very short run in Madrid (at the Teatro de la Princesa) due to the small size of the audiences, something which happened very rarely to Rusiñol (p. 473). Casacuberta also examines the reaction in Barcelona to Madrid's rejection of *La mare*, and she quotes (p. 475) from an article in *La Tribuna* which demanded that 'retiren de los carteles todas estas mamarrachadas del género ínfimo, que los autores madrileños exportan a provincias, contra los cuales nos hemos rebelado' (all those awful semi-pornographic pieces which Madrid-based authors export to the provinces and against which we have rebelled should be removed from the listings).

[56] The reception of this play in Madrid and Barcelona is discussed in Chapter 6.

[57] The content of the play will be analysed in more detail in Chapter 5.

[58] Jaume Melendres, 'Notas del revisor', in Santiago Rusiñol, *Llibertat!/ ¡Libertad!*, 43–6.

[59] *Epistolari Adrià Gual*, vi. 3 (document 14043 in register). Collection held at the Institut del Teatre in Barcelona.

[60] He is presumably referring to the Borràs's season at Madrid's Comedia Theatre in May–June 1904 (see Chapter 4).

[61] Benavente's quarrelsome character was well known in Spanish theatre circles.

[62] Benavente's handwriting is unclear at this point.

[63] *Epistolari Adrià Gual*, i. 3 (document 11888 in register). Collection held at the Institut del Teatre in Barcelona.

[64] However, lest we think that all was sweetness and light between Gual and Benavente, it should be pointed out that there has always been a certain bitterness in Catalan circles regarding alleged plagiarism. Benavente was accused of basing *La malquerida* on Gual's *Misteri de dolor*.

[65] See Adrià Gual, *Mitja vida de teatre* (Barcelona: Aedos, 1960), 257.

[66] Ibid., 156.

[67] Carles Batlle, Isidre Bravo and Jordi Coca (eds), *Adrià Gual: Mitja vida de modernisme* (Barcelona: Diputació de Barcelona, 1992), 119.

[68] Un Crítico Incipiente, 'Hacia un teatro nuevo', *La Pluma*, 35 (April 1923), 330. Quoted in Aguilera Sastre and Aznar Soler, *Cipriano de Rivas Cherif*, 48.

[69] Ibid.

[70] Enric Gallén, 'La reanudación del "Teatre Íntim" de Adrià Gual', in Dru Dougherty and María Francisca Vilches de Frutos (eds), *El teatro en España entre la tradición y la vanguardia (1918–1939)* (Madrid: Tabapress, 1992), 165–73.

[71] Aguilera Sastre and Aznar Soler, *Cipriano de Rivas Cherif*, 173.

[72] A general study of the Eslava is Carlos Reyero Hermosilla, *Gregorio Martínez Sierra y su teatro de arte*, Serie Universitaria, 142 (Madrid: Fundación Juan March, 1980).

[73] Julio Enrique Checa Puerta, *Los teatros de Gregorio Martínez Sierra* (Madrid: Fundación Universitaria Española, 1998), 161–7.

[74] According to Vila San-Juan, another Spanish dramatist who admired Borràs was Benavente: 'Enrique Borràs conoce a Jacinto Benavente desde que fue por primera vez a Madrid con su discutido Teatro Catalán. Don Jacinto simpatiza con Enrique desde el primer momento, y luego va acercándose a él, visitándole en su camerino de la Comedia. En una de esas temporadas Borràs interpreta *El nido ajeno*, y don Jacinto le abraza entusiasmado, fructificando una amistad [. . .] que no se rompe más que con la muerte del genial dramaturgo.' (Enric Borràs had known Benavente since his first visit to Madrid with his controversial Catalan Theatre. Don Jacinto [Benavente] got on well with Enric from the outset, then got closer to him, visiting him in his dressing room at the Comedia. During one of those seasons Borràs performed *The Other Man's Nest*, and don Jacinto embraced him with

enthusiasm. Thus a friendship came to fruition, [. . .] which was to end only with the death of the great dramatist.) P. Vila San-Juan, *Memorias de Enrique Borrás* (Barcelona: AHR, 1956), 73–4.

[75]   Checa Puerta, *Los teatros*, 410. Page references to other letters are taken from this book and are given in parentheses after the relevant quotation.

[76]   Two studies on Spanish stage design of the early twentieth century highlight the superiority of Barcelona over Madrid in this area. Cossío attributes it to the political situation of the two centres, claiming that the inflexible, unchanging nature of stage design in Madrid reflected the rigid nature of Restoration politics in Spain. She claims that stage design in Barcelona was on a par with that in other European countries (Ana María Arias de Cossío, *Dos siglos de escenografía en Madrid* (Madrid: Mondadori, 1991), 297); Panadero Martínez links it to the presence of *modernisme* and *noucentisme* in the Catalan capital (María Panadero Martínez, 'La pintura de teatro en España (1900–1950)' (unpublished dissertation within the doctorate programme 'Arte del siglo XX', University of Madrid, 1997), 13).

[77]   A case in point is Soler i Rovirosa: 'In the 1860s he worked for seven years in Paris and was made aware of the importance of lighting for audiences and actors. Following a trip to Germany in 1890, he gave a lecture in Barcelona three years later, defending the need to switch off the lights in the auditorium once a production had started.' John London, 'Twentieth-century Spanish stage design', in *Spanish Theatre 1920–1995: Strategies in Protest and Imagination (3)*, *Contemporary Theatre Review*, 7/3 (1998), 25–56 (p. 27). This latter practice was introduced by Adrià Gual.

[78]   See *Picasso y el teatro*, exhibition catalogue (Barcelona: Museu Picasso, 1996).

[79]   For details on Miró's work as a scene designer for the theatre and ballet see *Miró en escena*, exhibition catalogue, co-ordinated by Victòria Izquierdo Brichs (Barcelona: Fundació Joan Miró and Ajuntament de Barcelona, 1994).

[80]   Manuel Abril, 'Los pintores de Eslava', in Gregorio Martínez Sierra (ed.), *Un teatro de arte en España (1917–1925)* (Madrid: Ediciones de la Esfinge, 1926), 19–36 (p. 19). This book contains important articles by critics who were involved in or close to the Eslava, but its most noteworthy feature is the beautiful illustrations by the three designers, including sets and costumes. The book won the Grand Prix at the Exposition Internationale des Arts Decoratifs in Paris in 1925.

[81]   'Aunque de origen barcelonés y trabajador al principio de su carrera como decorador de interior en la línea del modernismo catalán junto a Puig i Cadafalch, fue nuevamente Martínez Sierra y su Teatro Eslava el que lo forme como un verdadero escenógrafo.' (Although he was

originally from Barcelona and worked at the beginning of his career as an interior designer in the *modernista* style with Puig i Cadafalch, it was once more Martínez Sierra and his Teatro Eslava which trained him as a true stage designer.) José Luis Plaza Chillón, *Escenografía y artes plásticas: El teatro de Federico García Lorca y puesta en escena* (Granada: Fundación Caja de Granada, 1998), 265–6).

82 Abril, 'Los pintores', 22. Rubio's view is that, given the backward and unadventurous nature of the commercial theatre in Spain, the illustrated edition was an alternative outlet for creative theatre practitioners, illustrators and designers who rejected both commercialism and naturalism. Jesús Rubio Jiménez, 'Ediciones teatrales modernistas y puesta en escena', *Revista de Literatura*, 53/105 (Jan.–June 1991), 103–50.

83 Abril, 'Los pintores', 22.

84 For further details on Burmann, see Ursula Beckers, 'La escenografía teatral de Sigfrido Burmann' (unpublished doctoral thesis, University of Madrid, 1992).

85 *ABC* (23 July 1980), 44.

86 The Burmann archive is now housed at the Institut del Teatre in Barcelona. Lest one be tempted to underestimate the importance of the three Eslava designers, it is worth noting that, according to Estévez-Ortega, Burmann, Fontanals and Barradas astonished Russian directors and a stage designer of the category of Bragaglia at the Exhibition of Decorative Arts in Monza (see Estévez-Ortega, *Nuevo escenario*, 34–5). For further details on the Eslava and the contribution of Fontanals, Burmann and Barradas to it see London, 'Twentieth-century Spanish stage design', 32–3. A detailed study of Catalan stage design is Isidre Bravo, *L'escenografía catalana* (Barcelona: Diputació de Barcelona, 1986).

87 Another Catalan dramatist who wrote exclusively in Spanish was Jacinto Grau, whose mother was from an Andalusian noble family. He was far less popular/populist than Marquina, was highly critical of the commercial theatre in Spain, and may be considered as a precursor of the avant-garde. His best-known play is *El señor de Pigmalión* (Mr Pygmalion) (1921), which contains a critique of what he saw as the defects of the commercial theatre to which the author presents a stylized alternative in the form of the popular puppet tradition. There are several well-known Catalan-born novelists whose language of literary expression is Spanish rather than Catalan in the post-Civil War period. These include the Goytisolos, Mendoza, Marsé and Vázquez Montalbán.

88 *El Imparcial* (24 June 1901), quoted in Pedro Ojeda, ' "España y yo somos así, señora": Eduardo Marquina en su contexto', in *Teatro de la España del siglo XX*, i. *1900–1939*, 47–8 (p. 48).

[89] 'Hablando con los autores', *España*, 19 (4 June 1915), 5–6.

[90] See Dru Dougherty, ' "Es un asco el teatro": Eduardo Marquina y el estreno de *Mariana Pineda* en Barcelona', in Antonio Monegal and José María Micó (eds), *Federico García Lorca i Catalunya* (Barcelona: Institut Universitari de Cultura and Universitat Pompeu Fabra and Diputació de Barcelona, 1999), 17–31 (p. 17).

[91] *Diario Universal* (20 Nov. 1923), 3.

[92] *El Mundo* (20 Nov. 1923), 1.

[93] *La Voz* (20 Nov. 1923), 2.

[94] *El Sol* (20 Nov. 1923), 2.

[95] *El Liberal* (20 Nov. 1923), 3.

[96] *ABC* (20 Nov. 1923), 27.

Chapter 3: From Barcelona to Madrid and Back Again

[1] This is the title of a play by the seventeenth-century Spanish playwright Rojas Zorrilla.

[2] *Quatre Gats*, 3 (23 Feb. 1899), 4. Amadeu Vives (1871–1932) was one of the founder members of the Orfeó Català. He was one of the most important composers of music for *zarzuelas*, but, in contrast to the majority of his fellow composers in this style, was steeped in the classical music tradition.

[3] *Pel i Ploma*, 6 (8 July 1899), 4.

[4] E. Conteras y Camargo, 'Crónica General', *El Teatro*, 44 (May 1904), pp. 1–4 (p. 4). All references to this article are from p. 4.

[5] For details on individual Madrid theatres, see Henry Lyonnet, *Le Théâtre en Espagne* (Paris: Paul Ollendorff, 1897); and Augusto Martínez Olmedilla, *Los teatros de Madrid (Anecdotario de la farándula madrileña)*, 2 vols (Madrid: no publ., 1947).

[6] Justino Ochoa, *Santiago Rusiñol: Su vida y su obra* (Madrid: Pueyo, n.d.), 112.

[7] Eduardo Zamacois, *Desde mi butaca (Apuntes para una psicología de nuestros actores)*, 2nd edn (Barcelona: Maucci, 1911), 43, 46–7.

[8] Enric Gallén, 'Margarita y Cataluña: La forja de una primera actriz', in *Margarita Xirgu: Crónica de una pasión*, special number of *Cuadernos El Público*, 36 (Oct. 1988), 6–13 (p. 7).

[9] José Montero Alonso, 'Historia gráfica de Margarita Xirgu', *Semana* (May 1969), 5–8 (p. 7) (this is an obituary).

[10] Carmen de Burgos (Colombine), *Confesiones de artistas*, 2 vols (Madrid: V. H. de Sanz Calleja, n.d.), i. 30.

[11] Ibid., 33–4.

12 Marisa Siguán, *La recepción de Ibsen y Hauptmann en el modernismo catalán* (Barcelona: PPV, 1990), 93.

13 *Diario de Barcelona* (26 April 1969), 4.

14 See the comments on cinema and theatre in Chapter 2.

15 'Quan el cinema s'imposa a Madrid el 1926, i es repeteix allà el fenomenon que Barcelona travessà ja el 1915, el flux d'actors agafa un sentit invers. I Enric Borràs i Margarida Xirgu tornaran, de manera alternada però regular, al conreu del teatre autòcton.' (When the cinema became established in Madrid in 1926, and the phenomenon which occurred in Barcelona in 1915 was repeated there, the flow of actors was reversed. And Enric Borràs and Margarita Xirgu returned to cultivate their native theatre on a regular basis, although they alternated it with their Madrid seasons.) Xavier Fàbregas, *Història del teatre català* (Barcelona: Millà, 1978), 216.

16 P. Vila San-Juan, *Memorias de Enrique Borrás* (Barcelona: AHR, 1956), 57–8. It is particularly ironic that an author who was writing during a regime that was hardly noted for its understanding of regionalism should make such comments.

17 See Dru Dougherty and María Francisca Vilches de Frutos, *La escena madrileña entre 1918 y 1926* (Madrid: Fundamentos, 1990), 452–3; and María Francisca Vilches de Frutos and Dru Dougherty, *La escena madrileña entre 1926 y 1931* (Madrid: Fundamentos, 1997), 560–1.

18 *El Sol* (5 Jan. 1926), 8. One should note that it was customary in the Spanish theatre of the period for the audience to applaud at several points in a play.

19 The main character of the play, and a part that Borràs made his own.

20 Vila San-Juan, *Memorias*, 80.

21 Ibid.

22 A study of Francoism's attempt at cultural genocide in Catalonia is Josep Benet, *L'intent franquista de genocidi contra Catalunya* (Barcelona: Publicacions de l'Abadia de Montserrat, 1995).

23 Spanish translation of *La festa del blat*.

24 Martínez Olmedilla, *Los teatros de Madrid*, ii. 228–9.

25 Martínez Olmedilla uses the Catalan peasant's hat or *barretina* to symbolize Catalonia. The *barretina* was usually referred to with scorn by Spanish centralists.

26 I have checked contemporary press reviews, but have not been able to find any reference to the banning of this play.

27 Josep Ma Poblet, *Enric Borràs*, Biografies Populars, 6 (Barcelona: Alcides, 1963), 33. The raising of the issue of Catalan identity, plus the fact that the book was written in Catalan, perhaps reflects the rather more open atmosphere of Spain in the early 1960s.

28 Ibid., 34.

[29] Ibid.

[30] *ABC* (5 Nov. 1957), 46. The source of the Sassone quotation is not given.

[31] Salvador Bonavía, 'Una conversa amb l'Enric Borràs', *El Teatre Català* (17 May 1913), 316–22 (p. 317). I have translated 'Teatre Català' as 'Catalan theatre'; however 'Teatre Català' with capital letters does also refer specifically to the company which was permanently installed at the Romea in Barcelona).

[32] Ibid., 317–18.

[33] 'Si en Borràs es quedés', *El Teatre Català* (17 May 1913), 323–4.

[34] 'Lletra oberta a l'eminent actor Enric Borràs', *El Teatre Català* (17 May 1913), 324–5.

[35] Prudencio Iglesias, *De mi museo* (Madrid: Imprenta Ibérica, 1909), 26.

[36] *La Renaixensa* (15 March 1903), mcmiii.

[37] 'Mentre Enric Borràs fou, en bona part, recuperat per a l'escena catalana, Margarida Xirgu, al seu torn, es convertí en els anys vint i trenta en una de les principals difusores i promotores del teatre espanyol i europeu més innovador.' (While Enric Borràs was largely recovered for the Catalan stage, during the 1920s and 1930s Margarita Xirgu became one of the people mainly responsible for the diffusion and promotion of the most innovative Spanish and European theatre.) Enric Gallén, 'El teatre', in M. de Riquer, A. Comas and J. Molas (eds), *Història de la literatura catalana*, 11 vols (Barcelona: Ariel, 1980–8), ix. 413–62 (p. 419).

[38] A weekly satirical magazine which ran from 1872 to 1939, *L'Esquella de la Torratxa* is described by Balcells as 'of popular, republican inspiration'. Albert Balcells, *Catalan Nationalism Past and Present*, trans. Jacqueline Hall (London: Macmillan, 1996), 26.

[39] *L'Esquella de la Torratxa* (29 February 1924), 122.

[40] Federico García Lorca, 'Charla sobre teatro', in *Obras completas*, 23rd edn, 3 vols (Madrid: Aguilar, 1989), iii. 458–61 (p. 459).

[41] Some of the appreciations are quoted in Antonina Rodrigo, *Margarita Xirgu: Actriz predilecta de García Lorca* (Barcelona: Plaza y Janés, 1980), 9–11.

[42] Ignacio Amestoy, 'Margarita Xirgu, maestra', in *Teatro de la España del siglo XX*, i. *1900–1939*, special number of *ADE Teatro*, 77 (1999), 240–3 (p. 242).

[43] See Domènec Guansé, 'Toda una vida', in *Margarita Xirgu: Crónica de una pasión*, special number of *Cuadernos El Público*, 36 (Oct. 1988), 29–63 (p. 42). This article is a translation by Antoni Lloret of Guansé's *Margarita Xirgu*, Biografies Populars, 11 (Barcelona: Aloides, 1963).

[44] *Almanaque del Diario de Barcelona* (1915), 104–5.

[45] *Almanaque del Diario de Barcelona* (1911), 85.

[46] *La Vanguardia* (30 May 1914), 15.

[47] *La Publicidad* (31 May 1914), 4.

[48] *El Día Gráfico* (31 May 1914), 8–9 (p. 8).

[49] Gabrielle-Charlotte Réjane (1856–1920) was a French actress and manager who specialized in boulevard comedy. She was known abroad, and played in London and New York. In 1906 she took over the Théâtre Nouveau in Paris, renaming it the Théâtre Réjane.

[50] Amichatis (pseudonym of Josep Amich i Bert) was a playwright as well as writing satirical pieces for *L'Esquella de la Torratxa*. He wrote mainly comic revues and was the most popular author in the theatres of the Paral.lel district. Curiously, the satirical vein associated with him is completely absent from his article on Xirgu.

[51] 'A propòsit del retorn de na Marguerida Xirgu', *El Teatre Català* (30 May 1914), 357–8.

[52] Adrià Gual claims that he was accused of being un-Catalan for his lecture performance series *El geni de la comèdia* in 1912, while the same elements who attacked him did not dare to censure the Orfeó Català choir who were playing in Madrid at the same time because of their sheer weight of numbers. *Mitja vida de teatre* (Barcelona: Aedos, 1960), 265. On the reception of *El geni de la comèdia* in Madrid and Barcelona see Chapter 5.

[53] *L'Esquella de la Torratxa* (29 May 1914), 360.

[54] Yacco played in both Barcelona and Madrid in 1902. For the reception of her and her company, see V. David Almazán Tomás, 'La actriz Sada Yacco: El descubrimiento del teatro japonés en España', *ALEC*, 23 (1998), 717–31.

[55] *L'Esquella de la Torratxa* (5 June 1914), 370–1. *L'Esquella* adopts a similar attitude towards the famous Catalan acting duo Pius Daví and Maria Vila in a much later article, *L'Esquella de la Torratxa* (28 Dec. 1935), 1714.

[56] *El Correo Catalán* (1 June 1914), 2.

[57] *L'Esquella de la Torratxa* (22 Nov. 1935), 1641.

[58] Sebastià Gasch, 'Margarida Xirgu', *Mirador*, 285 (19 July 1934), 5.

[59] *La Rambla de Catalunya* (14 Sept. 1935), 5.

[60] This is the Catalan version of the Spanish 'Señora', or 'Mrs'.

[61] Juan Aguilera Sastre and Manuel Aznar Soler, *Cipriano de Rivas Cherif y el teatro español de su época (1891–1967)*, Teoría y Práctica del Teatro, 16 (Madrid: Publicaciones de la Asociación de Directores de Escena de España, 1999), 167–8.

[62] Ibid., 174–5.

[63] Obituary by José Montero Alonso, *Semana*, May 1969, 52–3 (p. 52).

[64] *El Correo Catalán* (27 April 1969), 36.

Chapter 4: Foreign Theatre in Madrid and Barcelona

[1]   María Francisca Vilches de Frutos, prologue to Mariano Martín
      Rodríguez, *El teatro francés en Madrid (1918–1936)* (Boulder, CO:
      Society of Spanish and Spanish-American Studies, 1999), vii.

[2]   For an overview of the various types of foreign theatre which were
      performed in Madrid during the period 1918–31, see Dru Dougherty
      and María Francisca Vilches de Frutos, *La escena madrileña entre 1918
      y 1926: Análisis y documentación* (Madrid: Fundamentos, 1990), 41–6;
      and María Francisca Vilches de Frutos and Dru Dougherty, *La escena
      madrileña entre 1926 y 1931: Un lustro de transición* (Madrid:
      Fundamentos, 1997), 275–319.

[3]   I have been unable to discover any record of productions in Barcelona.
      Other influential foreign dramatists in Spain include Pirandello and
      O'Neill, on whose impact in Spain studies have already appeared. See
      Juan Gutiérrez Cuadrado, 'Crónica de una recepción: Pirandello en
      Madrid', *Cuadernos Hispanoamericanos*, 33 (1978), 347–86: despite
      the title, Gutiérrez Cuadrado deals fully with Pirandello's reception in
      Barcelona and Catalonia, comparing and contrasting it with its fate in
      Madrid; and Dru Dougherty and María Francisca Vilches de Frutos,
      'Eugene O'Neill in Madrid, 1918–1936', *The Eugene O'Neill Review*,
      17 (1993), 157–64.

[4]   Jesús Rubio Jiménez, 'Los nuevos horizontes de la literatura dramática
      de 1900 a 1920', in *Teatro de la España del siglo XX*, i. *1900–1939*,
      special number of *ADE Teatro*, 77 (1999), 16–26 (p. 18).

[5]   Lidia Bonzi and Loreto Busquets, *Compagnie teatrali italiane in Spagna
      (1885–1913)* (Roma: Bulzoni, 1991).

[6]   For instance, Unamuno felt that he learned much about foreign
      literature from Catalans: 'Puedo decir que es por catalanes por los que
      me relaciono *directamente* con el mundo externo.' (I can say that it is
      through Catalans that I have my *direct* contacts with the outside
      world.) Letter from Unamuno to Rusiñol in 1898, quoted in María
      Rusiñol, *Santiago Rusiñol vist per la seva filla*, 2nd edn (Barcelona:
      Aedos, 1955), 199. A particularly significant role in bringing foreign
      theatre to Barcelona was played by the impresario Josep Canals: for
      details, see Xavier Fàbregas, *Història del teatre català* (Barcelona:
      Millà, 1978), 220.

[7]   On the influence of Maeterlinck in Spain more generally see Mariano
      Martín Rodríguez, *El teatro francés en Madrid*, 131–8. See also, Rafael
      Pérez de la Dehesa, 'Maeterlinck en España', *Cuadernos Hispano-
      americanos*, 255 (1971), 572–81. One should also remember, however,
      that Benavente's *Teatro fantástico* was written in 1892; this collection of
      playlets was very much in the symbolist mode and quite different from

other plays in the naturalistic mode, such as *El nido ajeno*, which Benavente was writing at the same time.

8   Valentín García Plata, 'Primeras teorías españolas de la puesta en escena: Adrià Gual', *ALEC*, 21 (1996), 291–312 (p. 294).

9   One critic writes of 'la veneración por el teatro de Ibsen, que tuvo entre nosotros devotos fanáticos' (the veneration of Ibsen who had fanatical devotees among us). P. Bohigas Tarragó, *Compañías dramáticas extranjeras en Barcelona*, Investigaciones, 2, Nov. 1946 (Barcelona: Diputación Provincial and Instituto del Teatro, 1946), 82–3.

10   S. Canals, *El año teatral (1895–96)* (Madrid: Establecimiento Tipográfico de El Nacional, 1896), p. 124.

11   Albert Bensoussan, 'José Yxart 1852–1895: Théâtre et critique à Barcelone', 2 vols (Université de Lille III; Atelier National de Reproduction de Thèses, 1982), i. 539.

12   'El primer text on se serveix dels mètodes cientificistes és *Lo teatre català* (1878), en el qual, sobre una base dialèctica a la manera de Hegel i aplicant les teories determinades de Taine (raça, medi i moment històric), elabora una anàlisi diacrònica primer i sincrònica després del teatre en llengua catalana. De tota manera, *Lo teatre català* és el primer text a Catalunya en el qual es reclama "veritat, observació, naturalisme en lo modo d'estudiar i presentar els caràcters".' (The first text to use scientific methods is *Catalan Theatre* (1878). Using a dialectic base in the fashion of Hegel and applying Taine's determinist theories (race, environment and historical moment), [Yxart] develops first a diachronic and then a synchronic analysis of Catalan theatre. In any case, *Catalan Theatre* is the first text in Catalonia to insist on 'truth, observation, naturalism in the study and presentation of characters'.) Josep Yxart, *Àngel Guimerà*, ed. Rosa Cabré i Monné, Antologia Catalana, 76 (Barcelona: Edicions 62, 1974), 8–9.

13   José Yxart, *El arte escénico en España*, 2 vols (Barcelona: Imprenta de 'La Vanguardia', 1894), i. 149–50.

14   Ibid., 247.

15   Marisa Siguan, *La recepción de Ibsen y Hauptmann en el modernismo catalán*, Estudios de Literatura Española y Comparada (Barcelona: PPU, 1990), 113.

16   Review in *España*, 11 (9 April 1915), 3. An important study of Anarchist theatre in Spain is 'Teatro anarquista', which is ch. 7 of Lily Litvak, *Musa libertaria* (Barcelona: Bosch, 1981), 213–52.

17   A Catalan adaptation of the Zola novel by Eduard Vidal i Valenciano and Rossend Artús, entitled *La taverna*, was put on at the Tívoli in Barcelona in 1884. According to Fàbregas, the adaptation was probably instigated by the influential Catalan actor Antoni Tutau (for details, see Fàbregas, *Història*, 159). On the penetration of naturalism into Spain

and its subsequent influence see Martín Rodríguez, *El teatro francés en Madrid*, 104–31.

[18] *El Imparcial* (2 Dec. 1883), 3–4 (p. 4).

[19] *La Ilustració Catalana* (6 Dec. 1903), 344.

[20] *La Vanguardia* (2 Dec. 1903), 1.

[21] *La Veu de Catalunya* (2 Dec. 1903), 1–2.

[22] *L'Esquella de la Torratxa* (4 Dec. 1903), 774–5.

[23] On the reception of Ibsen in Madrid, see Jesús Rubio Jiménez, *Ideología y teatro en España: 1890–1900* (Zaragoza: Pórtico, 1982), 62–70. It is significant that Rubio refers to articles about Ibsen rather than actual productions.

[24] A study of this group is Andrew A. Anderson, 'Una iniciativa teatral: Ricardo Baeza y su compañía dramática "Atenea" (1919)', in John P. Gabriele (ed.), *De lo particular a lo universal: El teatro español del siglo XX y su contexto* (Frankfurt am Main: Vervuert Verlag, 1994), 29–40.

[25] *Diario Universal* (28 Sept. 1919), 1.

[26] *ABC* (28 Sept. 1919), 19.

[27] *El Liberal*, (28 Sept. 1919), 2.

[28] Eduardo Mignoni was one of the leading Spanish stage designers of the period.

[29] *ABC* (22 March 1928), n.p.

[30] Halfdan Gregersen, *Ibsen and Spain* (Cambridge, MA: Harvard University Press, 1936), 95.

[31] Translator's prologue to Henrik Ibsen, *Los espectros*, trans. Pompeyo Gener (Barcelona: Maucci, 1903), 5–11 (pp. 12–13). In 1894 Gener had translated the play into Catalan, with J. Casas-Carbó.

[32] *España*, 270 (3 July 1920), 13–15 (p. 13).

[33] For details of the reviews, see Enric Gallén, 'El teatre', in M. de Riquer, A. Comas and J. Molas (eds), *Història de la literatura catalana*, 11 vols (Barcelona: Ariel, 1980–8), ix. 413–62 (pp. 423–4).

[34] The profound effect which the Russian Ballet's performances in Barcelona in 1917 and 1918 had on the young Joan Miró is described by Isidre Bravo, in 'Un home de teatre anomenat Joan Miró', in *Miró en escena*, exhibition catalogue, co-ordinated by Victòria Izquierdo Brichs (Barcelona: Fundació Joan Miró and Ajuntament de Barcelona, 1994), 15–46 (p. 18). On the limited impact of Diaghilev and Picasso on Spanish drama, see V. G. de la Concha (ed.), *Época contemporánea (1914–1939)*, which is vol. vii of F. Rico (ed.), *Historia y crítica de la literatura española* (Barcelona: Crítica, 1984), 536. Alberti also mentions Diaghilev in Madrid in his autobiography: 'el ballet ruso de Diaghilev continuaba asombrando al mundo y removiendo a su paso los ámbitos artísticos' (Diaghilev's Ballets Russes continued to amaze the world and to stir up artistic circles in its wake). *La arboleda perdida*

(Barcelona: Seix Barral, 1975; repr.), 125. There are detailed comments on the diffusion of Cocteau in Spain in Andrew A. Anderson, 'Bewitched, bothered and bewildered: Spanish dramatists and surrealism, 1924–1936', in C. Brian Morris (ed.), *The Surrealist Adventure in Spain*, Ottawa Hispanic Studies, 6 (Ottawa: Dovehouse, 1991), 240–81, especially pp. 246, 259 and n. 5, 11, 27 and 105.

35 A fascinating essay on one such dancer is Ramón Pérez de Ayala, 'Pastora Imperio', in *Las máscaras*, Libro 2, in *Obras completas*, 4 vols (Madrid: Aguilar, 1966), iii. 285–90.

36 *La bailarina* was published in a separate volume of *Prometeo*, 24 (1910): no page numbers are printed. Jesús Rubio Jiménez rightly describes Gómez de la Serna's *pantomimas* as 'propuestas en las que plásticamente se revelara el lado misterioso e inquietante de la existencia' (proposals in which the mysterious and disturbing side of existence would be revealed through the plastic arts), adding that dance, intimately connected with mime theatre, 'se ofrece a Gómez de la Serna como una serie de signos cabalísticos producidos por los danzantes en la escena que descifra como espectador' (presents itself to Gómez de la Serna as a series of cabalistic signs produced by the dancers on stage and which he deciphers as a spectator), *El teatro poético en España: Del modernismo a las vanguardias* (Murcia: Universidad de Murcia, 1993), 85–6. For an analysis of this and other *pantomimas* by Gómez de la Serna, see Agustín Muñoz-Alonso López, *Ramón y el teatro (la obra dramática de Ramón Gómez de la Serna)*, Colección Monografías, 12 (Cuenca: Universidad de Castilla-La Mancha, 1993), 119–30. On the link between mime and dance in general, see Thomas Leabhart, *Modern and Post-Modern Mime* (Basingstoke and London: Macmillan, 1989), 8–9, *passim*.

37 'Els ballets russos: Parlant amb en Gual', *La Veu de Catalunya*. I have not been able to ascertain the date of publication, but the article may be consulted in *Prensa, Adrià Gual*, vii, Registre 18 (collection held in the Institut del Teatre in Barcelona).

38 'Divagación a la luz de las candilejas, *La Pluma*, 3 (Aug. 1920), 119. Quoted in Juan Aguilera Sastre and Manuel Aznar Soler, *Cipriano de Rivas Cherif y el teatro español de su época (1891–1967)*, Teoría y Práctica del Teatro, 16 (Madrid: Publicaciones de la Asociación de Directores de Escena de España, 1999), 33. There are also earlier articles by Rivas on the Russian Ballet: C. de Rivas Cherif, 'Los bailes rusos', *España*, 71 (1 June 1916), 10–11; C. de Rivas Cherif, 'Más de los bailes rusos', *España*, 72 (8 June 1916), 10–11. In the first of the articles Rivas argues that the Ballets Russes represent a purification and culmination of Wagner's concept of the synthesis of the arts, just as Debussy and Stravinsky have purified the German composer's music. For Rivas, 'el

baile ruso es, pues, "de la musique avant toute chose"' (the Ballets Russes are, then, 'de la musique avant toute chose') (p. 11). Rivas uses his second article to attack the lack of quality in the Spanish theatre. Staging, he says, is often over-complicated, as it tries to reproduce 'reality': the influence of French theatre, particularly through Díaz de Mendoza, has been especially pernicious in this respect. Rivas does, however, accept that the realist and the non-realist styles are not always easy to separate in the performances of the Ballets Russes.

39   The original edition was republished by Dover Publications of New York in 1967. This section on *Salomé* is a shortened version of my 'Le "Mythe fin-de-siècle" par excellence: Catalan and Spanish versions of Oscar Wilde's *Salomé*', *Romance Studies*, 18/2 (2000), 113–24.

40   Quoted in Katherine Worth, *Oscar Wilde* (London and Basingstoke: Macmillan, 1983), 52.

41   *Comme Salomé (Salomé dans le texte et l'image de 1870 à 1914)* (Université de Toulouse-Le Mirail, 1986), 5. It is most revealing that a recent book on realizations of *Salomé* in European theatre does not mention the Xirgu productions, illustrating how the theatre of the Iberian Peninsula tends to be (unjustly) ignored by outside critics. Salvador Dalí's designs for Peter Brook's production of Strauss's *Salomé* at Covent Garden in 1949 are discussed in the book, which merely highlights how Catalonia's visual artists are much better known internationally than their theatre practitioners. The book in question is William Tydeman and Steven Price, *Wilde, Salomé*, Plays in Production, 4 (Cambridge: CUP, 1996).

42   Worth, *Oscar Wilde*, 69, 73.

43   Delfina P. Rodríguez, *'Salomé': La influencia de Oscar Wilde en las literaturas hispánicas*, Colección Alternativas (Oviedo: Universidad de Oviedo, 1997).

44   It had already been performed in Italian by Lyda Borelli and her touring company at the Teatro de la Comedia on 14 April 1912. Borelli also performed the play in Barcelona in May of the same year.

45   *La Vanguardia* (6 Feb. 1910), 13.

46   See Dru Dougherty and María Francisca Vilches de Frutos, 'Valle-Inclán y el teatro de su época: La recepción en Madrid de *La cabeza del bautista*', and Jesús Rubio Jiménez, 'Una actriz apasionada para un texto apasionante: Mimí Aguglia y Valle-Inclán', both in Leda Schiavo (ed.), *Valle-Inclán hoy: Estudios críticos y bibliográficos* (Alcalá de Henares: Servicio de Publicaciones de la Universidad de Alcalá de Henares, 1993), 61–70 and 71–85 respectively. See also María Fernanda Sánchez-Colomer, *Valle-Inclán, el teatro y la oratoria: cuatro estrenos barceloneses y una conferencia*, Colección Ventolera, 2 (Sant Cugat del Vallès: Cop d'Idees and Taller d'Investigacions Valleinclanianes, 1997), 66–82.

47 Domènec Guansé, 'Toda una vida', in *Margarita Xirgu: Crónica de una pasión*, special number of *Cuadernos El Público*, 36 (Oct. 1988), 29–63 (p. 38).

48 For an excellent study of this area and its cultural activities see Serge Salaün, 'El Paralelo barcelonés (1894–1936)', *ALEC*, 21 (1996), 329–49.

49 Enric Gallén, 'El teatre', in *Història de la literatura catalana*, viii. 379.

50 See Antonina Rodrigo, *Xirgu*, Gent Nostra, 3 (Barcelona: Edicions de Nou Art Thor, 1984), 13.

51 For details, see Raymond Carr, *Spain 1808–1975*, 2nd edn (Oxford: Clarendon Press, 1982), 492–5.

52 See *Almanaque del Diario de Barcelona* (1911), 85.

53 *La Publicidad*, Barcelona (12 Feb. 1910), 5.

54 For details of other contemporary reviews in Barcelona see Antonina Rodrigo, *Margarita Xirgu: Actriz predilecta de García Lorca* (Barcelona: Plaza y Janés, 1980), 68–70.

55 *ABC* (21 May 1914), 18.

56 *El Liberal* (21 May 1914), 3.

57 *El Mundo* (21 May 1914), 1.

58 *El Liberal* (25 May 1914), 3.

59 'Revisió necessària de les grans aportacions de Margarida Xirgu', in *Margarita Xirgu, 1888–1969*, exhibition catalogue (Molins de Rei, Nov.–Dec. 1988; Madrid, Dec. 1988–Jan. 1989), 9–29 (p. 15).

60 *Diario Universal* (21 May 1914), 1.

61 Miquis had been a lot less critical about Lydia Borelli's performance in *Salomé*: see *Diario Universal* (15 April 1912), 2. García de Candamo, on the other hand, was less enthusiastic about the Italian actress: see *El Mundo* (15 April 1912), 1.

62 It is possible that Miquis was put off by her strong Catalan accent.

63 'Rivas Cherif y la Xirgu fueron tal vez los que intentaron con más ahínco presentar al público madrileño las obras renovadoras extranjeras en unas condiciones de modernidad equiparables a las de las representaciones en los países de origen.' (Rivas Cherif and Xirgu were perhaps the ones who tried hardest to present to the Madrid public ground-breaking foreign plays in modern conditions equivalent to those in which they were performed in their countries of origin.) Martín Rodríguez, *El teatro francés en Madrid*, 455.

64 On the reception of Kaiser in Germany, see Peter K. Tyson, *The Reception of Georg Kaiser (1916–45)*, 2 vols, Canadian Studies in German Language and Literature, 32 (New York: Peter Lang, 1984). *Oktobertag* was published in 1928 and premiered in Hamburg in 1928, and translated into Spanish as early as 1929. For details on the reception of this play, ibid., ii. 891–902.

65 *El Sol* (7 May 1931), 3. *Revista de Occidente* had earlier published a

version of *Un día de octubre*, together with two other Kaiser plays: *De la mañana a la medianoche* and one of the two parts of *Gas*.

[66] *Heraldo de Madrid* (7 May 1931), 5.

[67] *Nuevo Mundo* (15 May 1931), n.p.

[68] *La Voz* (7 May 1931), 2.

[69] *El Liberal* (7 May 1931), 2.

[70] *Gas I* was published and premiered in 1918. For details on this play and its reception, see Tyson, *Reception*, ii, 661–82. Curiously, Tyson does not acknowledge the existence of a Spanish translation of *Gas I*, although he does for *Oktobertag*.

[71] This school was one of Rivas Cherif's most important ventures. Founded in 1920, its ethos was socialist. It was responsible for important productions of Spanish and foreign plays. For details on the TEA, see Aguilera Sastre and Aznar Soler, *Cipriano de Rivas Cherif y el teatro español de su época*, 91–109.

[72] Apart from *Un día de octubre* and *Gas*, Olmedilla himself, he tells us, was responsible together with Fernández Rica for the translation of *Voz y cuerda* and *Folletín*.

[73] *Heraldo de Madrid* (4 March 1935), 4.

[74] *El Sol* (3 March 1935). The similarity with García Lorca's views is striking: see, for example, the prologue to *La zapatera prodigiosa* (The Shoemaker's Prodigious Wife).

[75] *El Liberal* (3 March 1935), 8.

[76] On the question of the crisis in the theatre and debates on its possible remedies in Spain during the previous decade, see Dru Dougherty, 'Talía convulsa: La crisis teatral de los años 20', in Robert Lima and Dru Dougherty, *2 ensayos sobre teatro español de los 20* (Murcia: Universidad de Murcia, 1984), 87–155.

[77] *La Voz* (4 March 1935), 5.

[78] E. Estévez-Ortega, 'Máscara exótica: Jorge Kaiser, o el expresionista que pierde la expresión', *ABC* (12 March 1936), 12.

[79] For details see Aguilera Sastre and Aznar Soler, *Cipriano de Rivas Cherif y el teatro español de su época*, 339.

[80] See Enric Gallén, 'El teatre', in *Història de la literatura catalana*, ix. 427.

Chapter 5: Reception of Catalan Theatre in Madrid and Barcelona

[1] Luis Morote, '*Els vells*', in *Teatro y novela (Artículos críticos 1903–1906)* (Madrid: Librería de Fernando Fe, 1906), 105–20 (p. 105).

2   Angel Guimerà, *Tierra baja*, trans. José Echegaray (Madrid: Florencio Fiscowich, 1896), 5.

3   *El Imparcial* (28 Nov. 1896), 3.

4   Eduardo Bustillo, *Campañas teatrales (Crítica dramática)* (Madrid: Est. Tipográfico Sucesores de Rivadeneyra, 1901), 215.

5   *Nuevo Mundo* (10 Dec. 1896), 4.

6   *El Heraldo de Madrid*, (28 Nov. 1896), 4.

7   *El Globo* (28 Nov. 1896), 1–2.

8   Several plays by Guimerà and other Catalan dramatists received their first performance in Castilian rather than in Catalan: 'El Padre Juanico (18.III.1898), que también se estrenó antes en Madrid, confirmaba la valoración que se había producido a propósito de *Tierra baja*. La edición de la traducción se había presentado con una cierta ambigüedad en relación a su autoría. Esta pequeña confusión provocó que a Guimerà se le considerase como un autor español por "propio derecho", ya que había escrito su última obra "en el idioma de la Patria" (*El Globo*, 19 March 1898)' ('Father John' (18 March 1898), which was also premiered in Madrid, confirmed what had been said about *Marta of the Lowlands*. The edition of the translation had been presented with a certain ambiguity as far as its authorship was concerned. This slight confusion caused Guimerà to be considered as a Spanish author 'in his own right', since he had written his latest work 'in the language of the Fatherland', Joan Martori, 'Guimerà en Madrid', *ALEC*, 21 (1996), 313–27 (p. 317).

9   *La Vanguardia* (11 May 1897), 6.

10 *La Renaixensa* (13 May 1897), 408–10 (p. 409).

11 *L'Esquella de la Torratxa* (14 May 1897), 298.

12 *La Vanguardia* (20 Nov. 1897), 6.

13 *La Renaixensa* (20 Nov. 1898), 6766.

14 *L'Esquella de la Torratxa* (25 Nov. 1898), 767–8 (all references from p. 768).

15 On this and other English-language versions of Guimerà plays, see David George, 'Les traduccions de Guimerà a l'anglès', in Enric Gallén (ed.), *Actes del Col.loqui sobre Guimerà i el teatre català al segle XX* (Tarragona: Diputació de Tarragona, 2000), 189–98.

16 *La Veu de Catalunya* (evening edn of 10 Jan. 1907), 2.

17 *La Publicidad* (evening edn of 10 Jan. 1907).

18 For details of productions see Dru Dougherty and María Francisca Vilches de Frutos, *La escena madrileña entre 1918 y 1926: Análisis y documentación* (Madrid: Fundamentos, 1990), 452–3; and María Francisca Vilches de Frutos and Dru Dougherty, *La escena madrileña entre 1926 y 1931: Un lustro de transición* (Madrid: Fundamentos, 1997), 560–1. The play was chosen by Erwin Piscator following a visit

to Barcelona, but the Spanish Civil War prevented the planned production from ever materializing.

[19] *Diario Universal* (12 June 1904), 1.

[20] Albert Balcells, *Catalan Nationalism Past and Present*, trans. Jacqueline Hall (London: Macmillan, 1996), 55.

[21] P. Vila San-Juan, *Memorias de Enrique Borrás* (Barcelona: AHR, 1956), 60.

[22] Pompeu Crehuet (1881–1941) is best known for his Ibsenesque play *La morta* (The Dead Woman, 1904). He was closely identified with the Lliga Regionalista and had various administrative jobs in the Mancomunitat. He was director of the review *De tots colors*, which published texts by D'Annunzio and Hauptmann, two playwrights who influenced his own work.

[23] See his reviews in *El Globo* (27 May 1904), 1 and (12 June), 2 respectively.

[24] The reception of its first performance in Madrid and Barcelona will be considered in Chapter 6.

[25] Vila San-Juan, *Memorias*, 64–5. Admittedly, this was written during the Franco era, but, as was pointed out earlier, Vila San-Juan is generally considered to be a reliable critic.

[26] This liberal newspaper was linked to the radical Liberal politician José Canalejas, who was Prime Minister of Spain from 1910 until his assassination in 1912. For further details on the Spanish press, see José-Carlos Mainer, *La Edad de Plata (1902–1939)*, 3rd edn (Madrid: Cátedra, 1983), 60–7.

[27] A summary of the plot appears in Chapter 6.

[28] *Diario Universal* (27 May 1904), 1.

[29] *El Teatro*, 45 (June 1904), 2–3.

[30] 'El teatro catalán', *El Teatro*, 45 (June 1904), 9–17.

[31] As was observed earlier, it was Díaz de Mendoza who first played the part.

[32] *Diario Universal* (29 May 1904), 2.

[33] *Diario Universal* (30 May 1904), 2.

[34] *El Imparcial* (9 Oct. 1904), 2.

[35] See González Blanco in *El Heraldo de Madrid* (5 Dec. 1904), 1; Arimón in *El Liberal* (5 Dec. 1904), 1; and Miquis in *Diario Universal* (5 Dec. 1904), 1.

[36] See Floridor's review in *ABC* (29 Jan. 1906), 4. According to the author of the most complete biography of Rusiñol, some critics took a different view: 'Al final de la representació hi havia doncs, una part considerable del públic descontenta. Molts dels que havien aplaudit frenèticament les frases efectistes del segon acte van acollir amb escepticisme l'agonia del Místic, llarga i pesada, *"poco teatral"*, en

definitiva. D'altres, sense haver aplaudit l'acte segon, també la van trobar pesada, i alguns fins i tot van acollir amb rialles només mig contingudes el calvari final del protagonista.' (A large part of the audience was unhappy at the end of the performance. Many of those who had wildly applauded the dramatic lines of the second act were sceptical about the Mystic's death throes, which they found long and boring, untheatrical, in a word. Others who had not applauded the second act also found it boring and even received the final suffering of the protagonist with barely contained laughter.) Margarida Casacuberta, *Santiago Rusiñol: Vida, literatura i mite* (Barcelona: Curial and Publicacions de l'Abadia de Montserrat, 1997), 387. In the light of the reviews which I have consulted, I find this somewhat curious, and more so Casacuberta's assertion that Rusiñol lamented the lack of comprehension of his play, as always when one of his plays provoked scandal (p. 388).

37 *El Liberal* (5 Dec. 1904), 2.

38 *La Vanguardia* (8 Dec. 1903), 5.

39 *La Publicidad* (5 Dec. 1903), 4.

40 Jacint Verdaguer (1845–1902) was the leading Catalan poet of the nineteenth century, and acquired enormous and widespread popularity in Catalonia. He was a priest in a rural parish, but spent some years working in Barcelona. He wrote poems based on popular themes, and verse inspired by mysticism. In the 1890s, he indulged in exorcism, and was transferred by the bishop of Vic (centre of conservative Catholicism and Catalanism) to Barcelona for 'health' reasons. He was later certified as mad, but subsequently reached an accord with the bishop, and returned to the preisthood in a parish in Barcelona.

41 The reaction described here suggests the (naïve?) enthusiasm of audiences, who were accustomed to making their feelings known and to interrupting plays at frequent intervals.

42 *El Liberal* (5 Dec. 1903), 1.

43 *La Ilustració Catalana* (13 Dec. 1903), 359.

44 *El Correo Catalán* (5 Dec. 1903).

45 For P. del O., writing in *L'Esquella de la Torratxa*, 'al Iglesias, en lo successiu, tothom el coneixerá per l'autor de *Els vells*' (from now on, everyone will know Iglésies as the author of 'The Old Folk'). *L'Esquella de la Torratxa* (13 Feb. 1903), 98–9 (p. 98).

46 Josep M. Poblet, *Enric Borràs*, Biografies Populars, 6 (Barcelona: Alcides, 1963), 18.

47 *La Vanguardia* (7 Feb. 1903), 6.

48 *Almanaque del Diario de Barcelona* (1904), 99–100.

49 *La Renaixensa* (7 Feb. 1903), 2.

50 *L'Esquella de la Torratxa* (13 Feb. 1903), 98–9.

[51] R. D. Perés, 'Teatro Catalán', *La Lectura*, 1 (1903), 433–9 (p. 436).

[52] Luis Morote, '*Els vells*', 106–7.

[53] *El Liberal* (31 March 1905), 2.

[54] *Diario Universal* (31 March 1905), 1.

[55] The series was postponed a few days due to problems with scenery and indispensable stage props (from 11, 13 and 15 to 17, 19 and 22).

[56] Ana María Arias de Cossío, *Dos siglos de escenografía en Madrid* (Madrid: Mondadori, 1991), 244.

[57] *Diario Universal* (18 April 1912), 1.

[58] *Diario Universal* (20 April 1912), 1.

[59] *Diario Universal* (23 April 1912), 1.

[60] Adrià Gual, *Mitja vida de teatre* (Barcelona: Aedos, 1960), 264.

[61] *El Mundo* (18 April 1912), 1. Disillusioned with his symbolist ideas being mocked in Barcelona, Gual was in Paris from 1901 to 1902, Here, the traditional theatres (Comédie Française and Odéon) made a deep impression on him, as did Lugné-Poë and Antoine.

[62] *El Mundo* (23 April 1912), 1.

[63] *El Heraldo de Madrid* (19 April 1912), 1.

[64] *El Liberal* (18 April 1912), 3.

[65] *El Liberal* (20 April 1912), 3.

[66] *El Liberal* (23 April 1912), 3.

[67] *ABC* (20 April 1912), 7.

[68] *ABC* (23 April 1912), 9.

[69] *Mitja vida de teatre*, 267.

[70] *El Diario de Barcelona* (16 May 1912), 7769.

[71] 'Vividor' in Catalan also means 'long-lasting'.

[72] *El Diario de Barcelona* (19 May 1912), 7914. *Arlequí vividor* was written between 1905 and 1912: see Carles Batlle, Isidre Bravo and Jordi Coca (eds), *Adrià Gual: Mitja vida de modernisme* (Barcelona: Diputació de Barcelona, 1992), 84. It is difficult to prove any plagiarism, as the *commedia dell'arte* was very much in the air, and Benavente himself had used the theme as early as 1892. For an analysis of the incidence of the *commedia dell'arte* in late nineteenth- and early twentieth-century Hispanic literature see David George, *The History of the Commedia dell'arte in Modern Hispanic Literature with Special Attention to the Work of García Lorca* (Lewiston, Queenston, Lampeter: The Edwin Mellen Press, 1995).

[73] *L'Esquella de la Torratxa* (10 May 1912), 312.

[74] *L'Esquella de la Torratxa* (31 May 1912), 363.

[75] This phrase is very much in tune with the vein of acute artistic purism of decadent literature.

[76] *L'Esquella de la Torratxa* (24 May 1912), 346.

[77] *La Vanguardia* (16 May 1912), 13–14.

78 *El Teatre Català* (18 May 1912), 12–13 (p. 13).

79 *El Teatre Català* (25 May 1912), 13

80 *El Teatre Català* (1 June 1912), 12.

81 This is a reference to Ramon Franqueza, owner of the Romea Theatre until his departure following a row with its members in 1911. According to Xavier Fàbregas, 'El 1913, però, s'havia consumat el naufragi de l'empresa del Teatre Català, que feia més de mig segle que funcionava al Romea. Les dificultats de l'empresa i la falta de tacte de l'home que la comanava, Ramon Franqueza, l'abocaren a la bancarrota.' (By 1913, however, the Teatre Català Company, which had functioned for half a century at the Romea, had gone under. The difficulties faced by the company and the lack of tact on the part of its head, Ramon Franqueza, drove it to bankruptcy.) Xavier Fàbregas, *Història del teatre català* (Barcelona: Millà, 1978), 213. Between 1911 and 1917 only plays in Spanish were performed at the Romea.

82 Valuable sources of information are Dougherty and Vilches de Frutos, *La escena madrileña entre 1918 y 1926*; and Vilches de Frutos and Dougherty, *La escena madrileña entre 1926 y 1931*.

Chapter 6: Reception of Spanish Theatre in Barcelona and Madrid

1 In an essay dated 1917, Pérez de Ayala describes it as 'uno de los dos únicos dramas españoles que en nuestros días ha logrado hacerse efectivamente populares. El otro, por de contado, es *Don Juan Tenorio*' (one of only two Spanish plays which are really popular nowadays. The other, of course, is *Don Juan Tenorio*). Ramón Pérez de Ayala, ' "Juan José", de Dicenta', in *Las máscaras*, Libro 3, in *Obras completas*, 4 vols (Madrid: Aguilar, 1966), iii. 455–8 (p. 457).

2 For details of plays which represented working-class life and an analysis of Dicenta's contribution see D. T. Gies, *The Theatre in Nineteenth-Century Spain* (Cambridge: CUP, 1994), 324–30. Gies analyses the reception of *Juan José* in Madrid.

3 Manuel Bueno, *Teatro español contemporáneo* (Madrid: Biblioteca Renacimiento, 1909), 113. See also Federico Urrecha's review of the first night in *Heraldo de Madrid* (edición de la noche, 30 Oct. 1895), 4. For another analysis on the reception of the play in Madrid, see Jesús Rubio Jiménez, *Ideología y teatro en España: 1890–1900* (Zaragoza: Pórtico, 1982), 165–71.

4 Gies, *Theatre*, 329.

5 Unamuno's view is similar: 'No es bueno por tener tesis socialista, sino

que tiene tesis socialista por ser bueno' (It is not good because it presents a socialist thesis, but presents a socialist thesis because it is good). Miguel de Unamuno, 'Juan José', *La Lucha de Clases* (7 Dec. 1895).

6 *La Correspondencia de España* (30 Oct. 1895), 3.

7 *El año teatral, 1895–96* (Madrid: Tip. de El Nacional, 1896), 149–55 (review dated 30 Oct. 1895).

8 It is not entirely clear what 'cuadros' means in this context. A 'cuadro' in the theatrical context is a scene, but it seems to me that this reviewer has in mind the phrase 'cuadro de costumbres', which means 'the description of local customs', in this case those of the Madrid working class.

9 Henry Lyonnet, *Le Théâtre en Espagne* (Paris: Paul Ollendorff, 1897), 112.

10 Ibid., 113.

11 *La Publicidad* (12 June 1896), 3.

12 *La Publicidad* (13 June 1896), 2.

13 *La Vanguardia* (12 June 1896), 3.

14 Reprinted in the *Almanaque del Diario de Barcelona* (1897), 83–4. The Teatre Líric was situated in the Eixample, and operated between 1881 and 1902.

15 Litvak's view is that *Juan José* was rejected by the Líric audiences, but she bases her argument on the reception accorded the play in the *Diario de Barcelona*, which seems not to have been typical of the Barcelona press in general. Lily Litvak de Pérez de la Dehesa, 'Naturalismo y teatro social en Cataluña', *Comparative Literature Studies* (Maryland) (1969), 279–302 (pp. 289–90).

16 *L'Esquella de la Torratxa* (19 June 1896), 386–8 (p. 386).

17 *La Renaixensa* (13 June 1896), 3560–1 (p. 3560).

18 An early recognition from outside Spain of Benavente's role as a modernizer, in tune with new European drama, is Walter Starkie, *Jacinto Benavente* (London: Humphrey Milford, 1924), 19–21.

19 Bueno, *Teatro*, 129–30.

20 *El Mundo* (10 Dec. 1907), 1.

21 *El Heraldo de Madrid* (10 Dec. 1907), 1.

22 *El Liberal* (10 Dec. 1907), 2.

23 ABC (10 Dec. 1907), 2.

24 *La Vanguardia* (19 Jan. 1908), 9.

25 See Chapter 2, note 55.

26 *El Liberal* (Barcelona edition, 20 Jan. 1908), 1.

27 *Almanaque del Diario de Barcelona* (1909), 103.

28 *L'Esquella de la Torratxa* (24 Jan. 1908), 72.

29 This is an ironic variation on a well-known Catalan saying: 'hostes

vingueren que de casa ens tragueren' (guests came and threw us out of our home).

30 *L'Esquella de la Torratxa* (28 March 1924), 179.

31 Benavente's pro-German stance aroused opposition, and, by the 1920s, his plays were considered to be old-fashioned and conservative.

32 *La Veu de Catalunya* (14 Jan. 1923), 11.

33 *Tribuna* (23 Aug. 1923), 2.

34 This is a reference to an ongoing debate: as we saw in Chapter 2, accusations were levelled at Benavente that *La malquerida* was a plagiarized version of *Misteri de dolor*.

35 The quotation is taken from the *Almanaque del Diario de Barcelona* (1905), 125.

36 See *Almanaque del Diario de Barcelona* (1918), 93.

37 Pérez Galdós represents naturalism in his own drama, beginning with his first play, *Realidad*, in 1892. *Marianela*, on the other hand, belongs to the author's early period, when his novels tended to deal with such issues as progress and tradition, religion and scientific progress in a highly polemical manner.

38 *ABC* (19 Oct. 1916), 19.

39 Antonina Rodrigo, 'Margarita Xirgu: La pasión heredada', in the exhibition catalogue *Exposición Margarita Xirgu (1888–1969)*, Molins de Rei, Nov.–Dec. 1988; Madrid, Dec.–Jan. 1988–9, 31–44 (p. 35).

40 *Diario Universal* (19 Oct. 1916), 1.

41 *El Liberal* (19 Oct. 1916), 1–2.

42 *El Mundo* (19 Oct. 1916), 1.

43 For further details on the Madrid premiere of *Marianela* see Antonina Rodrigo, *Margarita Xirgu: Actriz predilecta de García Lorca* (Barcelona: Plaza y Janés, 1980), 123–36.

44 *Almanaque del Diario de Barcelona* (1918), 93.

45 *La Vanguardia* (8 April 1917), 11.

46 *El Liberal* (Barcelona edn, 8 April 1917), 1.

47 This could be a veiled reference to Pérez Galdós's failure to win the Nobel Prize.

48 *El Día Gráfico* (9 April 1917), 3.

49 1917 was a particularly difficult time in Spain, as unrest within the country as a whole and within Catalonia in particular was at a high level. For details, see Raymond Carr, *Spain 1808–1975*, 2nd edn (Oxford: Clarendon Press, 1982), 496–508.

50 For anecdotal details on Pérez Galdós's connections with Barcelona see Mario Verdaguer, 'Don Benito Pérez Galdós en Barcelona', in *Medio siglo de vida íntima barcelonesa* (Barcelona: Barna, 1957), 176–80.

51 The reception of Valle-Inclán's plays in Barcelona has been studied in María Fernanda Sánchez-Colomer, *Valle-Inclán, el teatro y la oratoria:*

Cuatro estrenos barceloneses y una conferencia, Colección Ventolera, 2 (Sant Cugat del Vallès: Cop d'Idees and Taller d'Investigacions Valleinclanianes, 1997). On the reception of *La cabeza del Bautista*, see Dru Dougherty and María Francisca Vilches de Frutos, 'Valle-Inclán y el teatro de su época: La recepción en Madrid de *La cabeza del Bautista*', and Jesús Rubio Jiménez, 'Una actriz apasionada para un texto apasionante: Mimí Aguglia y Valle-Inclán', both in Leda Schiavo (ed.), *Valle-Inclán hoy. Estudios críticos y bibliográficos* (Alcalá de Henares: Servicio de Publicaciones de la Universidad de Alcalá de Henares, 1993), 61–70 and 71–85 respectively. Rubio writes of Aguglia (pp. 84–5): 'Cuando Mimí Aguglia vino por primera vez a España allá por 1907 dejó un recuerdo indeleble por su manera apasionada de interpretar, extremando los recursos del gesto y de la dicción, llevando el realismo a un punto sin retorno por su propio exceso. Fue su campaña una de las más notables en el camino de abandono del realismo mimético decimonónico. No pocos escritores españoles así lo entendieron y se aplicaron a la escritura de dramas que ahondaban en aquella dirección, Valle entre ellos. Al volver ahora, encontró *La cabeza del Bautista* un drama a su medida. Es decir, del exceso de realismo naturalista había nacido una nueva conciencia de la teatralidad. Este y no otro es el meollo de las vanguardias teatrales.' (When Mimí Aguglia first came to Spain around 1907, she left an indelible impression because of her passionate acting style, maximizing the resources of gesture and diction, taking realism to the point of no return due to its own excesses. Her campaign was one of the most notable on the road to the abandonment of nineteenth-century mimetic realism. This is how it was understood by a number of Spanish writers, Valle-Inclán included, who applied themselves to the composition of plays which deepened that process. When she returned, she found 'The Baptist's Head' a play made to measure for her. That is to say, from the excesses of naturalist realism a new awareness of theatricality had been born.) Adrià Gual, of course, reviewed the Barcelona premiere for *El Heraldo de Madrid* (see Chapter 2).

52 For details of the relationship between Valle-Inclán and Xirgu and its relevance to *Divinas palabras* see Manuel Aznar Soler, *Valle-Inclán, Rivas Cherif y la renovación teatral española (1907–1936)*, Publicaciones del Taller d'Investigaciones Valleinclanianes, Colección 'Ventolera' (Barcelona: Cop d'Idees, 1992), 98–120. The most complete study of the reception of *Divinas palabras* is Luis Iglesias Feijóo, 'La recepción crítica de *Divinas palabras*', *ALEC*, 18 (1993), 639–91. See also Luis Iglesias Feijóo, 'Una nueva reseña del estreno de *Divinas palabras*', *ALEC*, 19 (1994), 505–6.

53 Adolfo Marsillach, 'Borrás y unas fotos', in *Teatro de la España del siglo XX*, i. *1900–1939*, special number of *ADE Teatro*, 77 (1999), 237–9 (p. 238).

⁵⁴ *Los estrenos teatrales de Federico García Lorca (1920–1945)* (Madrid: Tabapress, 1992), 101.

⁵⁵ Reproduced in Enrique Díez-Canedo, *Artículos de crítica teatral: El teatro español de 1914 a 1936*, 5 vols (Mexico: Joaquín Mortiz, 1968), v. 141–6 (pp. 145–6).

⁵⁶ Dougherty and Vilches, *Los estrenos teatrales*, 103.

⁵⁷ Reproduced in Enrique Díez-Canedo, *Artículos de crítica teatral*, 145). See also Fernández Almagro's review in *El Sol* (30 Dec. 1934), 8).

⁵⁸ 'La acogida que obtuvo *Yerma* supuso la polarización de dos posturas extremas, desde el entusiasmo más total hasta la más cerrada repulsa.' (The reception of *Yerma* signified the polarization of two extreme positions: total enthusiasm and the most intransigent rejection.) Mario Hernández, 'Cronología y estreno de *Yerma, poema trágico*, de García Lorca', *Revista de Archivos, Bibliotecas y Museos*, 82/2 (1979), 289–315 (p. 299). For the controversy provoked by the production, see also Vilches de Frutos and Dougherty, *Los estrenos teatrales*, 97.

⁵⁹ *Informaciones* (31 Dec. 1934).

⁶⁰ *Los estrenos teatrales*, 103.

⁶¹ *El Popular* (26 Sept. 1935), 1.

⁶² *El Popular* (27 Sept. 1935), 1.

⁶³ *La Vanguardia* (19 Sept. 1935), 1.

⁶⁴ *La Veu de Catalunya* (29 Sept. 1935), 31.

⁶⁵ *L'Esquella de la Torratxa* (27 Sept. 1935), 1514.

⁶⁶ *L'Esquella de la Torratxa* (13 Sept. 1935), 1481.

⁶⁷ Juan Aguilera Sastre and Manuel Aznar Soler, *Cipriano de Rivas Cherif y el teatro español de su época (1891–1967)*, Teoría y Práctica del Teatro, 16 (Madrid: Publicaciones de la Asociación de Directores de Escena de España, 1999), 266, 267.

⁶⁸ On other García Lorca plays in performance, see the two articles by Gwynne Edwards which were cited in Chapter 1: '*Bodas de sangre* in Performance', *ALEC*, 22 (1997), 469–91; and '*Yerma* on Stage', *ALEC*, 24/3 (1999), 433–51.

Bibliography

Aguilera Sastre, Juan, and Manuel Aznar Soler, *Cipriano de Rivas Cherif y el teatro español de su época (1891–1967)*, Teoría y Práctica del Teatro, 16 (Madrid: Publicaciones de la Asociación de Directores de Escena de España, 1999).

Alberti, Rafael, *La arboleda perdida* (Barcelona: Seix Barral, 1975; reprint).

Allegra, Giovanni, *El reino interior*, trans. Vicente Martín Pindado (Madrid: Encuentro, 1986).

Almazán Tomás, V. David, 'La actriz Sada Yacco: El descubrimiento del teatro japonés en España', *ALEC*, 23 (1998), 717–31.

Amorós, Andrés (ed.), *La zarzuela de cerca*, Colección Austral (Madrid: Espasa Calpe, 1987).

Anderson, Andrew A., 'Bewitched, Bothered and Bewildered: Spanish Dramatists and Surrealism, 1924–1936', in C. Brian Morris (ed.), *The Surrealist Adventure in Spain*, Ottawa Hispanic Studies, 6 (Ottawa: Dovehouse, 1991), 240–81.

——, 'Una iniciativa teatral: Ricardo Baeza y su compañía dramática "Atenea" (1919)', in John P. Gabriele (ed.), *De lo particular a lo universal: El teatro español del siglo XX y su contexto* (Frankfurt am Main: Vervuert Verlag, 1994), 29–40.

Arias de Cossío, Ana María, *Dos siglos de escenografía en Madrid* (Madrid: Mondadori, 1991).

Asún, Raquel, 'A la inmensa mayoría: La crítica literaria de Eduardo Gómez de Barquero, *Andrenio*', *Boletín de la Biblioteca de Menéndez y Pelayo*, 56–7 (1980–1), 295–360.

Aznar Soler, Manuel, *Valle-Inclán, Rivas Cherif y la renovación teatral española (1907–1936)*, Publicaciones del Taller d'Investigaciones Valleinclanianes, Colección 'Ventolera' (Barcelona: Cop d'Idees, 1992).

Balcells, Albert, *Catalan Nationalism Past and Present*, trans. Jacqueline Hall (London: Macmillan, 1996).

Batlle, Carles, Isidre Bravo and Jordi Coca (eds), *Adrià Gual: Mitja vida de modernisme* (Barcelona: Diputació de Barcelona, 1992).

Beckers, Ursula, 'La escenografía teatral de Sigfrido Burmann' (unpublished doctoral thesis, University of Madrid, 1992).

Benet, Josep, *L'intent franquista de genocidi contra Catalunya* (Barcelona: Publicacions de l'Abadia de Montserrat, 1995).

Bensoussan, Albert, 'José Yxart 1852–1895: Théâtre et critique à Barcelone', 2 vols (Université de Lille III, Atelier National de Reproduction de Thèses, 1982).

Bohigas Tarragó, P., *Compañías dramáticas extranjeras en Barcelona*, Investigaciones, 2, Nov. 1946 (Barcelona: Diputación Provincial and Instituto del Teatro, 1946).

Bonzi, Lidia, and Loreto Busquets, *Compagnie teatrali italiane in Spagna (1885–1913)* (Rome: Bulzoni, 1991).

Bravo, Isidre, *L'escenografia catalana* (Barcelona: Diputació de Barcelona, 1986).

Brown, G. G., *A Literary History of Spain: The Twentieth Century* (London and New York: Ernest Benn and Barnes & Noble, 1972).

Bueno, Manuel, *Teatro español contemporáneo* (Madrid: Biblioteca Renacimiento, 1909).

Burgos, Carmen de (Colombine), *Confesiones de artistas*, 2 vols (Madrid: V. H. de Sanz Calleja, n.d.).

Bustillo, Eduardo, *Campañas teatrales (Crítica dramática)* (Madrid: Est. Tipográfico Sucesores de Rivadeneyra, 1901).

Caballero Audaz, El (pseud. of José María Carretero Novillo), *Lo que sé por mí (Confesiones del siglo)*, cuarta serie (Madrid: V. H. de Sanz Editores, 1917).

Canals, S., *El año teatral (1895–96)* (Madrid: Establecimiento Tipográfico de el Nacional, 1896).

Carr, Raymond, *Spain 1808–1975*, 2nd edn (Oxford: Clarendon Press, 1982).

Casacuberta, Margarida, *Santiago Rusiñol: Vida, literatura i mite* (Barcelona: Curial and Publicacions de l'Abadia de Montserrat, 1997).

Checa Puerta, Julio Enrique, *Los teatros de Gregorio Martínez Sierra* (Madrid: Fundación Universitaria Española, 1998).

Cobb, Christopher H., *La cultura y el pueblo: España 1930–1939*, Historia/Papel, 451 (Barcelona: Laia, 1980).

Comme Salomé (Salomé dans le texte et l'image de 1870 à 1914) (Université de Toulouse-Le Mirail, 1986).

Condé, Lisa Pauline, 'Galdós and his Leading Ladies', *BHS* (Liverpool), 75 (1998), 79–91.

Conversi, Daniele, *The Basques, the Catalans and Spain: Alternative Routes to Nationalist Mobilisation* (London: Hunt & Co., 1997).

Cuatro siglos de teatro en Madrid (catalogue produced for Madrid as European City of Culture in 1992) (Madrid: Apsel, 1992).

Curet, Francesc, *El arte dramático en el resurgir de Cataluña* (Barcelona: Minerva, [1917?]).

De la Concha, V. G. (ed.), *Época contemporánea (1914–1939)*, which is vol. vii of *Historia y crítica de la literatura española*, ed. F. Rico (Barcelona: Crítica, 1984).

Deleito y Piñuela, José, *Origen y apogeo del género chico* (Madrid: Revista de Occidente, 1949).

Delgado, Maria M., 'Enrique Rambal: The Forgotten Auteur of Spanish Popular Theatre', *Spanish Theatre 1920–1995: Strategies in Protest and Imagination* (3), *Contemporary Theatre Review*, 7/3 (1998), 67–92.

——, *Erasure and Inscription on the Twentieth-Century Spanish Stage: The Popular Theatre of Enrique Rambal*, Papers in Spanish and Latin American Theatre History, 8 (London: Department of Hispanic Studies, Queen Mary and Westfield College, University of London, 2001).

Díez-Canedo, Enrique, *Artículos de crítica teatral: El teatro español de 1914 a 1936*, 5 vols (Mexico: Joaquín Mortiz, 1968).

Dougherty, Dru, 'Espectáculo y pequeño burguesía: El público de Pedro Muñoz Seca', *Hispanística XX*, 15 (1997), 71–8.

—— , ' "Es un asco el teatro": Eduardo Marquina y el estreno de *Mariana Pineda* en Barcelona', in Antonio Monegal and José María Micó (eds), *Federico García Lorca i Catalunya* (Barcelona: Institut Universitari de Cultura, Universitat Pompeu Fabra and Diputació de Barcelona, 1999), 17–31.

——, 'Talía convulsa: La crisis teatral de los años 20', in Robert Lima and Dru Dougherty, *2 ensayos sobre teatro español de los 20*, ed. César Oliva (Murcia: Universidad de Murcia, 1984), 119–24.

——, Theatre and Culture, 1868–1936', in David T. Gies (ed.), *The Cambridge Companion to Modern Spanish Culture* (Cambridge: CUP, 1999), 211–21.

——, 'Una iniciativa de reforma teatral: el grupo "Teatro de Arte" (1908–1911)', in Pedro Peira *et al.* (eds), *Homenaje a Alonso Zamora Vicente*, 5 vols (Madrid: Castalia, 1994), iv. 177–92.

Dougherty, Dru, and María Francisca Vilches de Frutos (eds), *El teatro en España entre la tradición y la vanguardia (1918–1939)* (Madrid: Tabapress, 1992).

——, 'Eugene O'Neill in Madrid, 1918–1936', *The Eugene O'Neill Review*, 17 (1993), 157–64.

——, *La escena madrileña entre 1918 y 1926: Análisis y documentación* (Madrid: Fundamentos, 1990).

——, *Los estrenos teatrales de Federico García Lorca (1920–1945)* (Madrid: Tabapress, 1992).

Edwards, Gwynne, '*Bodas de sangre* in Performance', *ALEC*, 22 (1997), 469–91.

——, '*Yerma* on Stage', *ALEC*, 24 (1999), 433–51.

Espín Templado, María Pilar, *El teatro por horas en Madrid (1870–1910)* (Madrid: Instituto de Estudios Madrileños and Fundación Jacinto e Inocencio Guerrero, 1995).

Estévez-Ortega, E., *Nuevo escenario* (Barcelona: Lux, 1928).

Fàbregas, Xavier, *Història del teatre català* (Barcelona: Millà, 1978).

Fanés, Fèlix, 'The First Image – Dalí and his Critics: 1919 to 1929', in Michael Raeburn (ed.), *Salvador Dalí: The Early Years* (London: South Bank Centre, 1994), 90–6.

Francos Rodríguez, J., *El teatro en España, 1909*, Año II (Madrid: Imprenta de Bernardo Rodríguez, 1910).

Gagen, Derek, '¿El santo o la esfinge? El teatro ante la crisis de 1898', *Rilce*, 15 (1999), 253–66.

Gallén, Enric, *Actes del Col.loqui sobre Guimerà i el teatre català al segle XX* (Tarragona: Diputació de Tarragona, 2000).

——, 'El teatre', in M. de Riquer, A. Comas and J. Molas (eds), *Història de la literatura catalana*, 11 vols (Barcelona: Ariel, 1980–8), viii. 379–449.

——, 'El teatre', in M. de Riquer, A. Comas and J. Molas (eds), *Història de la literatura catalana*, 11 vols (Barcelona: Ariel, 1980–8), ix. 413–62.

——, 'Santiago Rusiñol', in M. de Riquer, A. Comas and J. Molas (eds), *Història de la literatura catalana*, 11 vols (Barcelona: Ariel, 1980–8), viii, 449–80.

—— (ed.), *Romea, 125 anys* (Barcelona: Generalitat de Catalunya, 1989).

García Lorca, Federico, *Obras completas*, 3 vols (Madrid: Aguilar, 1989).

García Plata, Valentín, 'Primeras teorías españolas de la puesta en escena: Adrià Gual', *ALEC*, 21 (1996), 291–312.

George, David, 'A young lad in the arms of an old man: Sergi Belbel Directs Àngel Guimerà's *La filla del mar* (*The Daughter of the Sea*)', in *Spanish Theatre 1920–1995: Strategies in Protest and Imagination* (3), Contemporary Theatre Review, 7/4 (1998), 45–64.

——, 'Le "Mythe fin-de-siècle" par excellence: Catalan and Spanish versions of Oscar Wilde's *Salomé*', *Romance Studies*, 18/2 (2000), 113–24.

——, *The History of the Commedia dell'arte in Modern Hispanic Literature with Special Attention to the Work of García Lorca* (Lewiston, Queenston and Lampeter: The Edwin Mellen Press, 1995).

Gies, D. T., *The Theatre in Nineteenth-Century Spain* (Cambridge: CUP, 1994).

Godoy Marquet, Juan Miguel, '*Comedias y comediantes. Revista quincenal (1909–1912)*: Al servicio de un teatro español de calidad', *ALEC*, 18 (1993), 503–15.

González Blanco, Andrés, *Los dramaturgos españoles contemporáneos*, 1a serie (Valencia: Cervantes, 1917).

Gregersen, Halfdan, *Ibsen and Spain* (Cambridge, MA: Harvard University Press, 1936).

Gual, Adrià, *Mitja vida de teatre* (Barcelona: Aedos, 1960).

Gutiérrez Cuadrado, Juan, 'Crónica de una recepción: Pirandello en Madrid', *Cuadernos Hispanoamericanos*, 33 (1978), 347–86.

Harrison, Joseph, *An Economic History of Modern Spain* (Manchester: MUP, 1978).

Heras, María Àngels, 'Una relectura del modernisme català. Santiago Rusiñol: Desde el dialogisme intercultural a la construcció d'una identitat nacional' (unpublished doctoral thesis, University of Nottingham, 2000).

Hernández, Mario, 'Cronología y estreno de *Yerma, poema trágico*, de García Lorca', *Revista de Archivos, Bibliotecas y Museos*, 82/2 (1979), 289–315.

Holloway, Vance R., 'La crítica teatral en *ABC*, 1918–1936', *American University Studies*, Series 2, *Romance Languages and Literatures*, 181 (New York: Peter Laing, 1991).

Hughes, Robert, *Barcelona* (New York: Vintage Books, 1993).

Ibsen, Henrik, *Los espectros*, trans. Pompeyo Gener (Barcelona: Maucci, 1903).

Iglesias Feijóo, Luis, 'La recepción crítica de *Divinas palabras*', *ALEC*, 18 (1993), 639–91.

——, 'Una nueva reseña del estreno de *Divinas palabras*', *ALEC*, 19 (1994), 505–6.

Iglesias, Prudencio, *De mi museo* (Madrid: Imprenta Ibérica, 1909).

Izquierdo Brichs, Victòria, co-ordinator, *Miró en escena*, exhibition catalogue (Barcelona: Fundació Joan Miró and Ajuntament de Barcelona, 1994).

Kirkpatrick, Susan, 'The "Feminine Element": *Fin-de-siècle* Spain, Modernity, and the Woman Writer', in Joseph Harrison and Alan Hoyle (eds), *Spain's 1898 Crisis: Regenerationism, Modernism, Post-Colonialism* (Manchester: MUP, 2000), 146–55.

Leabhart, Thomas, *Modern and Post-Modern Mime* (Basingstoke and London: Macmillan, 1989).

Litvak, Lily, *Musalibertaria* (Barcelona: Bosch, 1981).

——, *Transformación industrial y literatura en España (1895–1905)* (Madrid: Taurus, 1980).

Litvak de Pérez de la Dehesa, Lily, 'Naturalismo y teatro social en Cataluña', *Comparative Literature Studies* (Maryland) (1969), 279–302.

London, John, 'Twentieth-Century Spanish Stage Design', in *Spanish Theatre 1920–1995: Strategies in Protest and Imagination* (3), *Contemporary Theatre Review* (2), 7/3 (1998), 25–56.

Lyonnet, Henry, *Le Théâtre en Espagne* (Paris: Paul Ollendorff, 1897).

Mainer, José-Carlos, *La Edad de Plata (1902–1939)*, 3rd edn (Madrid: Cátedra, 1983).

Marfany, Joan-Lluís, *La cultura del catalanisme* (Barcelona: Empúries, 1995).

Margarita Xirgu, 1888–1969, exhibition catalogue (Molins de Rei, Nov.–Dec. 1988; Madrid, Dec. 1988–Jan. 1989).

Margarita Xirgu: Crónica de una pasión, special number of *Cuadernos El Público*, 36 (Oct. 1988).

Marrast, Robert, *El teatre durant la Guerra Civil Espanyola*, Monografies de Teatre, 8 (Barcelona: Institut del Teatre and Edicions 62, 1978).

Martín Rodríguez, Mariano, *El teatro francés en Madrid (1918–1936)* (Boulder, CO: Society of Spanish and Spanish-American Studies, 1999).

Martínez Olmedilla, Augusto, *Los teatros de Madrid (Anecdotario de la farándula madrileña)*, 2 vols (Madrid: no publ., 1947).

Martínez Sierra, Gregorio (ed.), *Un teatro de arte en España (1917–1925)* (Madrid: Ediciones de la Esfinge, 1926).

Martínez Sierra, M., *Una mujer por caminos de España* (Madrid: Castalia/Instituto de la Mujer, 1989).

Martínez Sierra, María, *Gregorio y yo* (Mexico: Biografías Gandesa, 1953).

Martori, Joan, 'Guimerà en Madrid', *ALEC*, 21 (1996), 313–27.

——, *La projecció d'Àngel Guimerà a Madrid (1891–1924)*, Textos i Estudis de Cultura Catalana, 46 (Barcelona: Curial Edicions Catalanes and Publicacions de l'Abadia de Montserrat, 1995).

McCarthy, Jim, *Political Theatre during the Spanish Civil War* (Cardiff: University of Wales Press, 1999).

Membrez, Nancy, ' "Llévame al cine, mamá": The Cinematograph in Spain 1896–1920', in Ben Lawton and Anthony Julian Tamburri (eds), *Romance Languages Annual 1989* (West Lafayette, IN: Purdue Research Foundation, 1990), 540–7.

——, 'The "teatro por horas": History, Dynamics and Comprehensive Bibliography of a Madrid Industry, 1867–1922 ('género chico', 'género ínfimo' and Early Cinema)' (unpublished doctoral thesis, University of California at Santa Barbara, 1987).

Morote, Luis, *Teatro y novela (Artículos críticos 1903–1906)* (Madrid: Librería de Fernando Fe, 1906).

Muñoz-Alonso López, Agustín, *Ramón y el teatro (la obra dramática de Ramón Gómez de la Serna)*, Colección Monografías, 12 (Cuenca: Universidad de Castilla-La Mancha, 1993).

Ochoa, Justino, *Santiago Rusiñol: Su vida y su obra* (Madrid: Pueyo, n.d.).

Panadero Martínez, María, 'La pintura de teatro en España (1900–1950)' (unpublished dissertation within the doctorate programme 'Arte del siglo XX', University of Madrid, 1997).

Pérez de Ayala, Ramón, *Obras completas*, 4 vols (Madrid: Aguilar, 1966).

Pérez de la Dehesa, Rafael, 'Maeterlinck en España', *Cuadernos Hispanoamericanos*, 255 (1971), 572–81.

Pérez Galdós, Benito, *The Theatre of Galdós: Realidad*, ed. Lisa Pauline Condé (Lewiston and Lampeter: The Edwin Mellen Press, 1993).

Picasso y el teatro, exhibition catalogue (Barcelona: Museu Picasso, 1996).

Plaza Chillón, José Luis, *Escenografía y artes plásticas: El teatro de*

Federico García Lorca y puesta en escena (Granada: Fundación Caja de Granada, 1998).

Poblet, Josep Ma, *Enric Borràs*, Biografies Populars, 6 (Barcelona: Alcides, 1963).

Rey Faraldos, Gloria, 'Pío Baroja y "El Mirlo Blanco"', *Revista de Literatura*, 47/93 (Jan.–June 1985), 117–27.

Reyero Hermosilla, Carlos, *Gregorio Martínez Sierra y su teatro de arte*, Serie Universitaria, 142 (Madrid: Fundación Juan March, 1980).

Ribbans, Geoffrey, 'Spanish Literature after 1700', in P. E. Russell (ed.), *Spain: A Companion to Spanish Studies* (London: Methuen, 1973), 381–428.

Rodrigo, Antonina, *Margarita Xirgu: Actriz predilecta de García Lorca* (Barcelona: Plaza y Janés, 1980).

——, *Xirgu*, Gent Nostra, 3 (Barcelona: Edicions de Nou Art Thor, 1984).

Rodríguez, Delfina P., *'Salomé': La influencia de Oscar Wilde en las literaturas hispánicas*, Colección Alternativas (Oviedo: Universidad de Oviedo, 1997).

Rubio Jiménez, Jesus, 'Ediciones teatrales modernistas y puesta en escena', *Revista de Literatura*, 53/105 (Jan.–June 1991), 103–50.

——, *El teatro poético en España: Del modernismo a las vanguardias* (Murcia: Universidad de Murcia, 1993).

——, *Ideología y teatro en España: 1890–1900* (Zaragoza: Pórtico, 1982).

——, 'La renovación teatral en el cambio de siglo: 1880–1914', in Miguel Medina (ed.), *Teatro y pensamiento en la regeneración del 98* (Madrid: Resad, 1998), 207–41.

Rudder, Robert S. (ed.), *The Literature of Spain in English Translation* (New York: Frederick Ungar, 1975).

Ruiz Ramón, Francisco, *Historia del teatro español siglo XX*, 6th edn (Madrid: Cátedra, 1984).

Rusiñol, María, *Santiago Rusiñol vist per la seva filla*, 2nd edn (Barcelona: Aedos, 1955).

Rusiñol, Santiago, *Llibertat!/¡Libertad!*, Serie Literatura Dramática, 28 (Madrid and Barcelona: Publicaciones de la Asociación de Directores de España and Institut del Teatre de la Diputació de Barcelona, 2000).

Salaün, Serge, 'El "género chico" o los mecanismos de un pacto cultural', in Equipo de Investigación sobre el Teatro Español (ed.), *El teatro menor en España a partir del siglo XVI* (Madrid: CSIC, 1983), 251–61.

——, 'El Paralelo barcelonés (1894–1936)', *ALEC*, 21 (1996), 329–49.

——, 'Política y moral en el teatro comercial a principios del siglo XX', in María Francisca Vilches de Frutos and Dru Dougherty (eds), *Teatro, sociedad y política en la España del siglo XX*, special monographic number of *Boletín de la Fundación García Lorca*, 19–20 (1996), 27–47.

—— and Claire-Nicole Robin, 'Arts et spectacles: Tradition et renouveau', in Carlos Serrano and Serge Salaün (eds), *1900 en Espagne* (Bordeaux: Presses Universitaires de Bordeaux, 1988), 105–28.

Sánchez, Alejandro (ed.), *Barcelona 1888–1929* (Madrid: Alianza, 1994).

Sánchez Suárez, Alejandro, 'Del regionalismo al nacionalismo', in *La Restauración (1874–1902)*, which is vol. x of Antonio Domínguez Ortiz (ed.), *Historia de España*, 12 vols (Barcelona: Planeta, 1990), 459–97.

Sánchez-Colomer, María Fernanda, *Valle-Inclán, el teatro y la oratoria: Cuatro estrenos barceloneses y una conferencia*, Colección Ventolera, 2 (Sant Cugat del Vallès: Cop d'Idees and Taller d'Investigacions Valleinclanianes, 1997).

Schiavo, Leda, *Valle-Inclán hoy: Estudios críticos y bibliográficos* (Alcalá de Henares: Servicio de Publicaciones de la Universidad de Alcalá de Henares, 1993).

Shubert, Adrian, *A Social History of Modern Spain* (London: Routledge, 1992).

Siguán, Marisa, *La recepción de Ibsen y Hauptmann en el modernismo catalán* (Barcelona: PPV, 1990).

Starkie, Walter, *Jacinto Benavente* (London: Humphrey Milford, 1924).

Teatro de la España del siglo XX, i. *1900–1939*, special number of *ADE Teatro*, 77 (1999).

Tydeman, William, and Steven Price, *Wilde, Salomé*, Plays in Production, 4 (Cambridge: CUP, 1996).

Tyson, Peter K., *The Reception of Georg Kaiser (1916–45)*, 2 vols, Canadian Studies in German Language and Literature, 32 (New York: Peter Lang, 1984).

Ugarte, Michael, *Madrid 1900: The Capital as Cradle of Literature and Culture* (University Park, PA: Pennsylvania State University Press, 1996).

Verdaguer, Mario, *Medio siglo de vida íntima barcelonesa* (Barcelona: Barna, 1957).

Vila San-Juan, P., *Memorias de Enrique Borrás* (Barcelona: AHR, 1956).

Vilches de Frutos, María Francisca and Dru Dougherty, *La escena madrileña entre 1926 y 1931: Un lustro de transición* (Madrid: Fundamentos, 1997).

Worth, Katherine, *Oscar Wilde* (London and Basingstoke: Macmillan, 1983).

Yxart, José, *El arte escénico en España*, 2 vols (Barcelona: Imprenta de 'La Vanguardia', 1894).

Yxart, Josep, *Àngel Guimerà*, ed. Rosa Cabré i Monné, Antologia Catalana, 76 (Barcelona: Edicions 62, 1974).

Zamacois, Eduardo, *Desde mi butaca (Apuntes para una psicología de nuestros actores)*, 2nd edn (Barcelona: Maucci, 1911).

Index